I0878491

THE SCARS WE CARVE

THE SCARS WE CARVE

Bodies and Wounds in Civil War Print Culture

ALLISON M. JOHNSON

LOUISIANA STATE UNIVERSITY PRESS
BATON ROUGE

Published by Louisiana State University Press
Copyright © 2019 by Louisiana State University Press
All rights reserved
Manufactured in the United States of America
First printing

DESIGNER: Michelle A. Neustrom
TYPEFACE: Minion Pro
PRINTER AND BINDER: Sheridan Books, Inc.

LIBRARY OF CONGRESS CATALOGING-IN-PUBLICATION DATA

Names: Johnson, Allison M., 1984– author.
Title: The scars we carve : bodies and wounds in Civil War print culture / Allison M. Johnson.
Description: Baton Rouge : Louisiana State University Press, [2019] | Revision of author's thesis (doctoral)—University of California, Los Angeles, 2013. | Includes bibliographical references and index.
Identifiers: LCCN 2018036951 | ISBN 978-0-8071-7037-3 (cloth : alk. paper) | ISBN 978-0-8071-7143-1 (pdf) | ISBN 978-0-8071-7144-8 (epub)
Subjects: LCSH: United States—History—Civil War, 18611865—Mass media and the war. | United States—History—Civil War, 18611865—Literature and the war. | United States—History—Civil War, 18611865—Social aspects. | Human body—Social aspects—United States—History. | Human body—Symbolic aspects—United States—History. | War and society—United States—History—19th century.
Classification: LCC E468.9 .J64 2019 | DDC 973.7/1—dc23
LC record available at https://lccn.loc.gov/2018036951

The paper in this book meets the guidelines for permanence and durability of the Committee on Production Guidelines for Book Longevity of the Council on Library Resources. ♾

To my parents, Chris and Patti Johnson,
with all my love and gratitude

CONTENTS

ACKNOWLEDGMENTS

I would like to thank a wonderful group of family, friends, and colleagues who have been integral to the writing and completion of this book and deserve much more than a few lines on an acknowledgments page.

The members of my dissertation committee at the University of California, Los Angeles, have remained invaluable resources during this project's journey toward bookhood. Eric Sundquist provided helpful feedback, and Joan Waugh kept me firmly grounded in the Civil War era. I cannot thank Richard Yarborough enough for his astute and incisive editing and advice. He also gave me extensive help with argumentation and style. Michael Colacurcio tirelessly supported my work, my academic career, and me. I am forever grateful to Prof C. for his unwavering advocacy and guidance.

My wonderful colleagues and friends at UCSB and San Jose State University saw me through the final stages of manuscript preparation and kept me sane. Thanks to my friends in Los Angeles and my family in Riverside for unwavering support, tons of fun, and lots of love. Very special thanks to Fuson Wang for reading multiple drafts and always providing helpful feedback (and being the big brother I never knew I wanted). Thanks to my sister Katie for always believing in (and only occasionally throwing lemons at) me.

I dedicated this book to my parents because it would not exist without them. All I am and hope to be is due to them and their love and guidance. To Blake, my husband: thanks for putting up with all the bad puns and being my refuge and my love; I promise I'll dedicate the next one to you.

The Scars We Carve

Introduction

On June 17, 1863, native Virginian Frederika Macky White reported in a small bound notebook that the "dear soldiers" had returned.[1] Absent from their ranks was her only son, Benjamin S. White, twenty-one years old and a member of Stonewall Jackson's famous brigade. "My dear son," she wrote, "was killed on Sunday, May the 3 1863 at the Battle of Chancellorsville." On May 3, 1864, Frederika remembered and recorded in the same notebook the death of her "dear and only son . . . slain in battle." It would take another three years for Benjamin's "precious remains" to return to his mother. A "melancholy pleasure," her son's posthumous homecoming "opened afresh the fountain of [her] grief." By including the arrival of Benjamin's bones in her commonplace book, Frederika recorded the physical as well as the emotional and spiritual legacies of the Civil War. For thirteen years, Frederika added entries on the anniversaries of her son's birth and death, often using the same words and phrases to commemorate his passing. Amidst prayers for strength, Frederika transcribed one of Stonewall Jackson's addresses to his troops, a reflection by the hymn writer Reverend John R. MacDuff, Henry Wadsworth Longfellow's "Not Dead," and other writings she likely found in periodicals and newspapers. Sprinkled throughout White's entries are quotations or full transcripts of poems dealing with death, the afterlife, and soldierly sacrifice.

Frederika's mourning process, one that involved transcribing poems and prose and continually reflecting on and writing about loss and absence, exemplifies the significant role of print culture documenting the war's effects on individuals and their bodies in the national undertaking of recording, understanding, and remembering the conflict. She draws on an extensive corpus of periodical literature in order to situate and contextualize her own loss within a community and country of mourners. However, this larger framework never erases or absorbs her loss and the memory of her fallen son. As his earthly body returns to dust, Frederika's collection of writings grows, physical proof of her son's continuing presence. Though she prays that she will be able to write and mean "Thy will be done," she is unable to fully relinquish her son to heaven or forget that he was (to use her words in almost every entry) "slain in battle." Resisting erasure and forgetting, the remains of soldiers like Benjamin haunt Civil War literature.

However, the textual bodies of white male soldiers like Benjamin are by no means the only symbols of wartime upheaval and destruction. The Civil War sought to answer the question of whether a house divided against itself could stand and whether the social and cultural institutions and mores of the antebellum period could persist in a country riven by extreme violence and upheaval. Disruptive bodies in literature responding to the central questions of the conflict reflect the corporeal consequences of brothers fighting brothers while providing a resounding answer: the nation was shaped and remade by the war and bodies—white and black, male and female, soldier and noncombatant—were crucial to this remaking. Changed human forms in turn argued for or augured transformed or adjusted political and social subjectivities. Located on the pages of popular periodicals and newspapers, disruptive bodies were often radical and subversive. The crucible of war scarred women and black men as well as white soldiers, indicating a breakdown of gendered and racial binaries and further complicating already debated conceptions of a representative American body. As bodies broke and fragmented, so too did strict delineations between public and private, battlefield and home front, male and female, and white and black. The disruptive bodies of amputees, African American soldiers, and women demand recognition as important literary subjects and potent cultural signifiers of citizenship, political agency, and discursive power.

This body of literature reflects the reading materials most readily available to Civil War Americans.[2] I follow Benedict Anderson in approaching Civil War print culture—particularly newspapers and periodicals—as constituting connected communities and / or nations of readers both North and South.[3] In uncovering these texts, I surveyed northern and southern periodicals, focusing particularly on those with the widest circulations—*Harper's Weekly, Frank Leslie's Illustrated News, Southern Punch,* and *The Southern Literary Messenger*—as well as smaller local newspapers. As the main source of information about the conflict, newspapers provided both subject matter and forum for amateur and professional writers. As such, this is not an intellectual history of the ways in which well-known authors responded to upheaval but instead an examination of how Americans, whether northern or southern, authorial or amateur, interacted with and represented the physical effects of war to create a literary record permeated by corporeality, suffering, and human forms that embody reconfigurations of citizenship, personhood, and the nation. I argue for a fundamental shift in the way we define the Civil War canon and propose a critical turn away from scholarly accounts of silence, disembodiment, abstraction, and unstinting patriotism.

Since the 1990s, scholars have moved away from the largely dismissive critiques of Edmund Wilson and Daniel Aaron, who famously labeled the conflict "unwritten."[4] They have also substantially expanded the canon of Civil War literature, looking beyond Aaron's fruitless search for an epic and taking into account amateur writers and nonliterary mediums. Timothy Sweet's seminal study of the relationship between Civil War photography and poetry looked at the political and ideological ramifications of aesthetic representations of the conflict.[5] In her analysis of Civil War iconography, Shirley Samuels interpreted literary, photographic, and visual representations of the conflict in order to explore how Americans responded to "face-to-face encounters with instantiations of the nation."[6] James Dawes grounded his examination of violence's effects on language in a consideration of "force and discourse" during the Civil War.[7]

While earlier critics like Wilson and Aaron mined the wartime writings of canonically established authors, Alice Fahs, and scholars after her, delved into the extensive archive of Civil War popular literature to develop a fuller account of the ways in which Americans responded to and textualized the conflict.[8] Like Fahs, Faith Barrett examined popular literature, focusing particularly on poetry.[9] As part of this ongoing scholarly project of looking closely at popular literature in order to illuminate the important cultural work it performs and its literary merit, this book excavates significant and little-read body-centric literature and art produced by combatants and noncombatants during and shortly after the war. Focusing specifically on print culture—primarily newspapers and periodicals—I argue for a reorientation of the Civil War canon.

In his recent discussion of the evolving canon of Civil War literature, Sweet notes that, in the decades following the conflict's centennial, a number of scholars focused on the body "as a site of meaning production."[10] For the most part, however, such studies argue for the absence of the body or the purposeful elision of individual bodies in literature produced during and after the war. Sweet himself argues that "the wounds of war disappear into a rhetoric of nature and necessity" in Civil War poetry and photography; by naturalizing war deaths, writers and photographers aided the Union cause and the ideologies that bolstered it.[11] Similarly to Sweet, Franny Nudelman finds in wartime literature an insistence on decomposition and rebirth in the interest of maintaining the war effort and covering over the unnatural aspects of mass violence.[12] Nudelman centers her monograph on what she terms the conflict's "greatest abstraction," the process "that enabled the living to rededicate themselves to the project of war in the face of stunning loss and destruction."[13] Nudelman insists on the "absence of the corpse" from Civil War popular culture and identifies "silence" as the predominant response to tragic loss.[14] Lisa A. Long's ontological and poststructuralist approach to the body finds in Civil War literature efforts to heal the wounds of war.[15] She argues that "Civil War writers insist that bodies *don't* matter," contending that writers and medical professionals worked to make unruly bodies "predictable, unalterable, and static."[16] According to Long, writers failed to fully account for corporeal suffering in the interest of "rehabilitating" both the nation and the unwieldy bodies of soldiers and civilians.[17] My focus on moments when rehabilitation and idealization fail and suffering and death remain stubbornly and purposefully concrete complicates scholarly narratives of combatant and noncombatant writers obscuring personal devastation and turmoil and upholding the primacy of the Union or the Lost Cause.[18]

Bodies most certainly appear and matter in Civil War literature and visual culture; more significantly, physical forms embody shifting political, social, racial, and gendered identities and subject positions. As the work of Bruce Burgett, Karen Sánchez-Eppler, Carolyn Sorisio, Joan Burbick, Jennifer Putzi, and Russ Castronovo demonstrates, bodies became increasingly integral to antebellum conceptions of selfhood. Burgett locates the origins of nineteenth-century sentimentalism in "early Enlightenment discourses that focus on the body as both a ground and a site of political debate."[19] The body, he asserts, "becomes the noumenal grounding of existence itself—a point of origin upon which political, ethical, and theological systems are erected."[20] Both Sánchez-Eppler and Sorisio note the importance of the body in antebellum political discourse and conceptions of the nation; Burbick discusses the body's relation to a successful republic, and Putzi underscores the marked body's role in antebellum culture and society.[21] If, as Castronovo contends, the body of a "citizen-subject" undermines "a prevailing narrative of the most cherished political categories in the United States as inanimate and invulnerable to change," then bodies in Civil War print culture animated changing conceptions of citizenship.[22] Indeed, they demanded a seat at the national table by linking citizenship to concrete, somatic materiality. The crucible of war, at the very least figuratively, prepared nonnormative bodies—belonging to what Castronovo terms "depoliticized persons"—for a larger role in the national arena.[23] In newspapers and periodicals, traditionally marginalized bodies—those belonging to women, black men, amputees—became front-page subjects.

Extreme violence and destruction further solidified the centrality of bodies to conceptions of nationhood, identity, and political agency. In the nineteenth-century United States, Castronovo argues, "death produce[d] bodies whose materiality disturb[ed] the impersonality of citizenship, but whose remove from sociopolitical life also idealize[d] the unhistorical and abstract nature of state identity."[24] However, death and wounding in the Civil War created bodies that tied the personal to the political, resisted abstraction, and were firmly grounded in a specific historical moment—a moment in which "state identity" was under threat and in flux. The wound or scar or amputation stump as, to borrow Castronovo's phrase, "both corporeal fact and political metaphor," disallows the sociopolitical remove Castronovo describes—it is death in the midst of life, invested with discursive power because of its corporeal and metaphorical substance. On the pages of Civil War print culture, dead and wounded bodies register and enable new or reconfigured conceptions of citizenship.

A significant portion of wartime literature moves away from what Sánchez-Eppler terms "metaphorical and fleshless political identity."[25] The fragmented and dismembered forms of soldiers, wounded women, and African American soldiers fill the pages of periodicals, powerfully symbolic because of their corporeality. Even the metaphorical bodies of Lady Liberty and her Confederate rivals are fleshy and embodied. Though scholars echo Whitman's famous avowal that the real war would never "get in the books," the effort to produce meaning out of the experience of wounding, amputation, death, and widespread grief—rather than the success or failure of the endeavor—is more relevant to our understanding of the Civil War and its legacy.

These disruptive bodies have significant implications for how we read Civil War literature. On the pages of newspapers and journals, in the left-handed writing of recent amputees, and in the words of little-read and rarely anthologized amateur poets and storytellers, there exists a literary and visual chronicle of the war unaccounted for in scholarly narratives of abstraction, disembodiment, reconciliation, and silence. I present a Civil War that is embodied, individualized, and fundamentally written by closely engaging with print culture, the primary means by which Americans accessed the conflict and contributed to a polyvocal, corporeal, and multimedia record of the war. The ever-increasing digitization of nineteenth-century periodicals and a growing number of searchable archives have shaped and enabled this project. Making use of entities like the Library of Congress's *Chronicling America,* I have been able to observe Civil War print culture in a more holistic and top-down fashion than was previously possible.[26] Within seconds, I could ascertain whether a poem published in South Carolina in May 1862 also appeared north of the Mason-Dixon Line. A simple Google search helped me identify poems I found in archives, tucked away in the scrapbooks of southern women.

Examining popular literature in its immediate context and identifying the cultural work it performs, I follow Paula Bernat Bennet's hermeneutic approach.[27] The complete digitization of periodicals like *Harper's Weekly* meant I could read poems and political cartoons not in isolation but as pieces of a larger discursive production arising out of a particular historical moment. Combining close reading with a focused form of distant reading, I was able to partially recreate the experience of reading periodical literature between 1861 and 1865—page by page instead of disconnected literary artifact by disconnected literary artifact.[28] Such an experience was of course available to scholars reading old newspapers in physical archives. However, searchable databases enable almost instant information about the relative popularity of individual pieces, the geographical distribution of war information and literary content, and the processes by which Americans learned of and responded to the progress of military actions and the major political and cultural issues of the struggle. The result of this approach is a fuller and more nuanced understanding of which bodies mattered during the Civil War and how print culture reckoned with unprecedented upheaval and destruction.

The widespread bloodshed of the War between the States and advances in photography and the distribution of information made it nearly impossible to ignore the devastating nature of mass violence. The war touched most families, as sons and fathers fell in battle or succumbed to disease, and casualty lists in newspapers and on bulletin boards advertised the ubiquity and prevalence of death and injuries. Though it is impossible to know the exact number of casualties, recent estimates count upwards of 752,000 soldier deaths.[29] The combination of improved weaponry and dated tactics led to disastrous results; though rifles replaced muskets, relatively inaccurate single-shot weapons, and fired extremely destructive minié balls, generals continued to order frontal assaults on entrenched defenders.[30] Because the Civil War occurred before major medical discoveries concerning bacteria, sterilization, antisepsis, and antibiotics, thousands of soldiers died from infection and disease.[31] Two-thirds of all deaths were disease-related, and diarrhea, dysentery, typhoid, and pneumonia were rampant in military camps.[32] Newspapers regularly printed lists of killed and wounded soldiers and of military hospital patients and their various ailments.

Millions of Americans subscribed to newspapers in the mid-nineteenth century, and with the war's coming many more turned to this source to receive news of its progress. Newspaper circulations and consumption grew as more and more people relied on journalists' accounts of battles and the bulletin boards provided by newspaper offices to receive updates on the course of the contest.[33] Newspapers informed civilians of the progress of the conflict, detailed the locations and events of skirmishes and battles, listed casualties, and provided literary responses to the war. The importance of print in spreading information and knowledge is the subject of the poem "Printing Press."[34] Published in Marysville, Kansas's *The Big Blue Union* on May 10, 1862, the poem terms the printing press "Mind's railroad" and lauds its "unwearied power" that "sends rays of genius o'er each darkn'd land; / Where memory's record, changing every hour, / Gives place to truth, stamped by the giant hand." Southerners and northerners sent poems and prose pieces to newspapers and magazines, inspiring their compatriots to join the fight, commemorating the fallen, or responding to specific engagements and events. Writers and civilians who lacked the first-hard experience of soldiers shaped the material provided by newspapers and first-person accounts into literary texts. Responding to the effusive outpouring of poetry, some southern periodicals began charging those who wished to be printed.[35] Periodicals reprinted poems from other newspapers, and Americans transcribed verses in commonplace books or cut up newspapers to make scrapbooks. Some poems, like "Stonewall Jackson's Way," reportedly found "on the person" of a dead Confederate soldier, appeared both north and south of the Mason-Dixon Line.[36]

New periodicals appeared in the South in the initial years of the conflict as Confederates attempted to make their own records of memory. Despite initial avowals that the southern people were too busy fighting to write poetry, by the third issue of the *Southern Illustrated News* the editors called for a "National Hymn" for the fledgling confederation and emphasized the necessity of producing a distinct literary culture: "We have eternally separated from the everlasting Yankee nation, and are now engaged in a righteous war for independence. Who will enumerate the horrors of this war—the untold sufferings—the hearthstones that have been made desolate by the loss of some husband, father, son or brother!"[37] Newspapers and periodicals like the *Southern Illustrated News* disseminated factual information about the war and its effects and provided a forum for literary representations of and reflections on the conflict.

Illustrated newspapers like *Harper's Weekly, Frank Leslie's Illustrated Newspaper,* and the *Southern Illustrated News* created a pictorial compendium of the struggle as well. Newspapers could not print photographs, but woodcut reproductions of photographs and sketches by field artists provided the public with images of the war.[38] In April 1861, an article titled "The Only Reliable War Illustrations" appeared on Leslie's front page.[39] Reporting that special artists had been sent to Charleston and Washington, the article declared the paper's illustrations "the only authentic and reliable sketches which have appeared." On the same page, Leslie proclaims, "My corps of Artists is unequalled in the country, and correspondents can depend on their sketches, however rough, being produced in the finest style of art." The editor requests that any "gentleman connected with either Army" send sketches of "important events and striking incidents." On September 20, 1862, fourteen days after it commenced publication, the *Southern Illustrated News* advertised for "two competent wood engravers" and offered "the highest price ever paid in this country."[40] During the three years it was published, the Confederate illustrated weekly printed engravings of noticeably lesser quality than those appearing in northern weeklies. However, the *Southern Illustrated News* continued in its attempts to "present more vividly to the reader the grand and imposing events that are happening around us."[41]

Though the Civil War was not the first war to be photographed, it became the most extensively photographed conflict since the advent of the technology. As a result, Americans increasingly confronted images of wounds and corpses produced by violent deaths. The famous photographer Mathew Brady organized a group of photographers, including Alexander Gardner, Timothy O'Sullivan, James F. Gibson, and George Barnard, and assigned each to different areas; these men and other photographers took an estimated one million pictures between 1860 and 1865.[42] A *New York Times* reviewer attested to the disruptiveness of Brady's exhibition of Antietam photographs in his New York gallery in 1862: "Mr. Brady has done something to bring home to us the terrible reality and earnestness of war. If he has not brought bodies and laid them in our dooryards . . . he has done something very like it."[43] Many purchased cartes de visite featuring battlefield scenes and corpses, remembering and commemorating the dead with the help of photographic documentation of death and destruction.[44] Images of corpses were widely disseminated and changed the way many thought and wrote about the war. Broken, dying, and dead bodies figuratively and literally arrived at Americans' doorsteps and refused to be ignored.

Many antebellum Americans commissioned photographs of dead family members and were thus accustomed to images of peaceful, reposing, and carefully prepared dead bodies; the photographs of Civil War wounded and dead, their corpses dismembered, bloated, and broken, did not fit within the benign tradition of postmortem photography.[45] Civilians could read descriptions of battles and then view their aftereffects in hundreds of photographs disseminated during and after the war. As the corpse became what Nudelman calls a "journalistic subject," the American public became acquainted with the realities of mass violence and its effects on the human body.[46] It should come as no surprise, then, that bodies pervade Civil War print culture.

Bodies served as texts and testaments, insisting on the material, emotional, psychological, and societal scars that resulted from national upheaval and violent discord. In order to demonstrate the centrality of the corporeal to Civil War literature, I focus on the cultural, political, and rhetorical work performed by an interconnected group of disruptive bodies: female personifications of the Union and Confederacy, battle-tested African American soldiers, maimed veterans, and war-torn women. The following chapters indicate the difficulties of representing the "real war" and the bodies at its center. The tendency of both northerners and southerners to personify the Union and the Confederacy as allegorical women had the potential to simultaneously distance actual women from the battlefield and implicate them in the ideological and material stakes of the conflict. Poems lauding the military service of African American soldiers competed with political cartoons lampooning ignorant slaves and ineffectual black recruits. Empty sleeves covered unsightly stumps, and amputee veterans answered by poeticizing their missing and maimed limbs. Despite the prevalence of disembodied allegorical femininity, telegraph lines collapsed the space between the home front and the battlefield by wounding recipients. Each chapter, then, charts disparate but interrelated attempts to fully account for unparalleled destruction and the corporeal, cultural, and social repercussions of war. The bodies at the center of each chapter are contested sites and testing grounds for reconfigured political, social, and cultural identities.

I begin with Columbia, or Lady Liberty, and her southern counterparts in order to indicate the ubiquity of the female body in Civil War literature and visual culture. By moving the allegorical feminine into the political and physical realm of the internecine struggle, Columbia and her sisters documented the significance of the conflict for American women. They also carved out a place for women in the public and political realms, as well as the literary record of the war. As national mother, Columbia watched over all of her sons, regardless of their skin color. The maternal feminine and symbolic black masculinity are integral facets of Civil War material and literary culture.

The bodies of black soldiers, the subject of my second chapter, appeared on the pages of periodicals, sometimes in the company of Columbia. In political cartoons and popular songs, ragged contrabands and uninformed slaves formed the epicenter of the sectional crisis. Writers—both black and white—responded by portraying the transformation of black men's bodies in the crucible of war. Written before the failure of Reconstruction, these works located the justification for African American manhood and citizenship in the dead, wounded, and scarred bodies of black soldiers.

The similarly maimed contestants in the left-handed penmanship contests that form the focus of my third chapter created narratives of service and suffering, negotiating their positions as newly disabled men and providing valuable insight into how Civil War Americans understood physical difference. William Oland Bourne, a philanthropist, hospital volunteer, and newspaper editor, sponsored two penmanship contests in 1865 and 1866 for veterans who had lost their right arms in combat. Contest entries produced by amputees along with periodical poetry and prose focusing on amputation and its ramifications display how veterans imbued their reconfigured bodies with discursive and poetic power, demanding recognition for individual sacrifice and service in the face of potentially silencing narratives of reconciliation, rehabilitation, and national recovery.

The central body of much of Civil War literature, I contend in the final chapter, is female. In the domestic and public spheres, women and their bodies waged war and bore the marks of its violence. The ascendancy of telegraphic communication brought the conflict home as so-called "invisible bullets" created "spirit-wounds," corporeal markers of grief, while also indicating the porous border between the battlefield and the home front. Disrupting the line between public and private, wounded women were counterpoints to the allegorical femininity discussed in the first chapter, thus bringing the process of documenting disruptive bodies in Civil War print culture full circle.

Writing in 1864, the anonymous author of "Some Uses of a Civil War" asserts that "war is a great evil."[47] As evidence, the author submits the marks made by brothers fighting brothers: "These forms, crushed and torn out of all human semblance, are our brothers. . . . The scars we carve with steel or burn with powder across the shuddering land, are scars on the dear face of the Motherland we love." The bodies of American citizens and the geographical and symbolic bodies of the American republic were lastingly scarred and shaped by the violence and destruction of the internecine struggle. In poems and stories, the body and its component parts, marked by violence or imbued with rhetorical power, testify to the "great evil" of war, the issues at stake in the conflict, and the war's lasting influence.

CHAPTER ONE

Columbia's Sisters and Daughters

A month after the bombardment of Fort Sumter and the beginning of hostilities between the Union and the newly formed Confederacy, Columbia, the female personification of the United States, slumbered peacefully amidst the tumult. S.J.A.'s "Not Dead" (1861), printed in *Harper's Weekly*, the leading periodical of the day, begins with an epigraph taken from a "motto on a New York banner"—a flag most likely designed and sewn by local women for a regiment: "The Union is not dead but sleeping."[1] Through the "dark night of wickedness" caused by the rebellion, the people of the North must guard both "our Union and our liberty." S.J.A. calls on "each soldier's arm to grasp the sabre," since only the return of "each star by traitor bands disgraced"—each seceded state—will allow the Union to "joyously" awake from her slumber and "never sleep again." The personified Union's slumber promises hope for future reconciliation and reunion, but also warns of her vulnerability and need for protection. Meanwhile, analogous poems published in southern periodicals and books depicted the Confederacy as a woman or a collection of southern sisters. While Columbia, traditionally interchangeable with the goddess of liberty, personified the northern states and the hope of reunification, a group of southern sisters embodied a new nation separate from the body politic of the Union.

Columbia reigned supreme in the antebellum United States and during the Civil War era. Despite scholarly claims to the contrary, Uncle Sam did not replace Columbia as the most popular American personification until the twentieth century.[2] Uncle Sam and Brother Jonathan, another masculine personification, appeared in Civil War–era political cartoons, a medium made possible by improvements in printing techniques, but they in no way supplanted or surpassed Columbia.[3] A survey of the popular press confirms Columbia's primacy and popularity.[4] Between 1861 and 1865, Uncle Sam appeared twelve times in *Harper's Weekly* and thirteen times in *Frank Leslie's Illustrated Newspaper.* Brother Jonathan graced the pages of the two newspapers sixteen times and seven times, respectively. Due perhaps to editorial preference, and to the smaller number of political cartoons in *Leslie's,* there is a discrepancy between the number of times Columbia appeared in the two publications. While she represented the nation only eight times in four years in *Frank Leslie's Illustrated Newspaper,* she appeared thirty-one times in *Harper's Weekly.*[5]

Patriotic poems, cartoons, and illustrations calling for renewed determination and dedication to the cause of defeating the Confederacy habitually invoked the embattled and all-encompassing Columbia. Columbia's Confederate sisters, personifications of a fledgling nation and its constituent states and cities, waged a rhetorical war for legitimacy and for the ability to epitomize embattled femininity. Symbolic women recruited soldiers for battles only men could fight; however, they also faced the threats of invasion and violence. Consequently, sexuality and nationalism were closely intertwined—to defend the nation-state was to shelter female bodies from rapacious enemies and to retain the purity and structural integrity of national borders and codes of law.

Closely tied to the rhetorical work of allegorical and symbolic femininity is the actual wartime work of American women. As Drew Gilpin Faust notes, the Civil War necessitated the involvement of women and inspired a "discussion of women's appropriate relationship to war—and thus to society in general."[6] Women on both sides worked in hospitals, fought as soldiers, raised money, collected supplies, and knit socks for soldiers; according to Shirley Samuels, "women emerge[d] from the extension of domestic duties—sewing and nursing among them—taking elements of nurture and using them as weapons of war."[7] Social historians have illuminated and examined the experiences and contributions of nonsymbolic women.[8] The process of recording nonsymbolic women's Civil War work began during the conflict and continued afterward in compendiums like *Women of the War: Their Heroism and Self-Sacrifice* (1866) and *Woman's Work in the Civil War: A Record of Heroism, Patriotism and Patience* (1867).[9] However, as Alice Fahs has argued, postwar literature, historiography, and culture focused more on the experiences of soldiers than women; according to Fahs, "the memory of Northern women's war-borne suffering did not prove a lasting legacy of the conflict."[10] As such, recuperative historical work was and remains necessary. What is also necessary, however, is an examination of the ways in which Columbia and her sisters work rhetorically and figuratively to transcend popular narratives of the selfless sacrifice and private "war-borne suffering" of American women—the suffering that Fahs claims only temporarily made northern women part of the national construct.[11] Indeed, they complicate strict gender boundaries and demonstrate that women were not just included in but constitutive of the northern and southern wartime communities.

Even a cursory survey of Civil War print culture reveals that the lived experiences of real women, not just their suffering, were central to the journalistic and literary narrative of the conflict. Side by side with poems and articles detailing the heroic valor of soldiers, verses commemorating nurses at the front and mothers, sisters, and lovers at home asserted the significant contributions of actual women to the Union and Confederate causes. The bodies of women in Civil War print culture, encroaching on the territory of men, touched by violence, and physically involved in the work of war, were very often revolutionary. Leading the vanguard, however, were Columbia and a sisterhood of symbolic female figures. As public-facing rhetorical constructs with both allegorical and symbolic cachet, they established and distinguished the contributions of women. Quite often, Columbia and her sisters were stand-ins for female action in the public arena. Over the course of the conflict, the relationship between and prevalence of allegorical and symbolic female figures shifted; while Columbia and other female personifications called men to arms at the outset, symbolic women and their experiences gained traction as the war intensified. Though passive allegorical figures appeared occasionally, active personifications drew attention to women's real contributions and participation. After Appomattox, Columbia buried her dead and mourned the fallen as an allegorical and all-encompassing representative of the collective and individual grief of actual American women.

Whether removed from the battlefront or in the thick of the action, symbolic female forms in poems and short stories asserted the presence of real women's bodies in the process and progress of war. They also inhabited similar roles and expressed similar emotions to those inhabited and expressed by northern and southern female personifications. This overlap allowed for a reconfiguration of the public and the domestic as clearly delineated spheres. As the war invaded the home front, the symbolic feminine inserted the lives, bodies, and experiences of real American women into public discourse and the literary and visual record of the conflict. Like American women, Columbia and her Confederate counterparts were mothers and sisters, roles indicating the prevalence of the family metaphor in nineteenth-century American conceptions of the nation and its constituent parts. Significantly, both halves of the divided republic deployed the maternal feminine to define the stakes of the contest and justify violence. Though female allegories often have the potential to remove or distance actual women from participation in the public and political realms, the bodies of Columbia and her sisters disrupted this distancing. Alternatingly vulnerable and bellicose, their status as figures did not protect them from the vicissitudes of war. Columbia and her sisters resembled real women but fought rhetorical battles real women could not.

Bodies Politic

Inherently allegorical, female personifications of nations threaten to relegate women's political and social significance to the purely symbolic realm. Barbara Johnson explains the tendency of allegory to perpetuate separate spheres of female and male action and influence, especially since "public art" tends to abstract the female form.[12] The allegorical feminine often justifies violence: men must fight to protect disembodied womanhood as well as the bodies of their wives, mothers, daughters, and sisters. Personifications of the Union or the Confederacy were the focal point of calls to arms and rallying cries, but it was men and not women who were called and rallied. Allegory, as Paul de Man reminds us, creates distance while symbolism presents the possibility of "identity or identification."[13] When female bodies allegorize the nation, women can remain removed from the actual process of nation building and nation protecting. According to Johnson, allegory allows for interpretation "through a predicate of embodiment, location, interest, and readability."[14] Embodied and readable, the female form provided a main *casus belli* for both sides. However, Columbia and her sisters often acted as both symbol and allegory, allowing for identification with real American women and with more abstracted ideals of Union and freedom. As Shirley Samuels notes, the violence of the Civil War caused significant "disturbances in the social structure" and "reorient[ed] women's sphere."[15] Nowhere are these disturbances or the porous boundary between symbol and allegory clearer than on the pages of newspapers and periodicals; illustrations of Columbia and accounts of the sacrifices and service of American women appeared in the same issues or on the same pages.

Historians, literary critics, and art historians have studied female personifications of countries and of the United States in particular, underscoring the intersections of gender and nationhood, but there is no extensive study of Columbia and her sisters in literature and illustrations published during the war. Scholars disagree on the prevalence and purpose of national personifications like Columbia. Mary P. Ryan and Elizabeth Young both recognize the silencing power of allegory and metaphor, Ryan describing the "benign but decorative" role of Lady Liberty in antebellum America and Young indicating the centrality of "voiceless" feminine representations to Civil War conceptions of the body politic.[16] Discussing antebellum political culture, Anne Norton emphasizes the masculinization of the North and feminization of the South and identifies a "metaphoric disparity" between representations of a female Confederacy and a male Union in two collections of Civil War poetry.[17] The larger corpus of Civil War print culture, however, does not reflect that disparity.

A number of scholars have examined the family as a central component in the formation of American nationality and social order.[18] Antebellum Americans relied on familial relationships to understand their social and civic roles as citizens in a democracy. C. Dallett Hemphill measures the growing significance of sibling relationships in the decades leading up to the Civil War in the "increasing use of this relationship as a metaphor for other relations," including church membership, friendship, and political activism.[19] Portraying the "divided family" as a historical occurrence and a controlling metaphor during the Civil War, Amy Murrell Taylor argues that Americans attempted to understand the conflict through the "vocabulary of family," a vocabulary central to the continuing formation of national identity.[20] As mothers and sisters, Columbia and her southern counterparts participated in these constructs and deserve recognition as central components of Civil War conceptions of American identity and the national family.

Columbia and her southern sisters were significant parts of the process Patricia Vettel-Becker describes as the "search for a national identity, a continually contested process that originated with the founding of the republic itself."[21] As the mother of the American people, Columbia is defined primarily by her relationship to her children. During the war, she mourned her fallen sons, a New World *stabat mater dolorosa.*[22] However, Columbia did more than mourn—she demanded action, advocated for soldiers, led the battle charge, let slip the dogs of war, and entered the public realm of politics. Her relationship to the nation was based on her maternity, but her action was not limited to that relationship.

An overview of Columbia's origins and development demonstrates her adaptability and the interconnectedness of race and gender in the formation of an American national identity. As Europeans began to explore the New World, artists imagined a welcoming indigenous woman, often nude and bedecked with feathers. This female and native America appeared in allegorical renditions of the continents, an art form that became popular in the sixteenth century and remained so into the nineteenth.[23] While the conquest and colonization of the Americas silenced millions of actual indigenous women, figurative and iconic native women continued to represent North America in European (and a few American) political cartoons and artistic renderings of the continent.[24] With the advent of revolution, the icon E. McClung Fleming labels "Indian Princess" became the rebellious daughter of Great Britain, and, as Shirley Samuels argues, white female bodies subsumed "racial and sexual violence."[25]

After the Revolution, American artists clothed lily-white rather than tawny female personifications of the new nation-state in star-spangled robes instead of deerskin. As Americans continued to create a centralized identity, the iconic native woman was increasingly supplanted by the white Lady Liberty or Columbia.[26] In her study of Civil War iconography, Shirley Samuels notes this transition and locates in it anxieties about representation and national identity.[27] Though Joshua Taylor argues Columbia did not belong to "geography or a particular race, but to the family of personified virtues," the figure's transition from dark skin to white skin marks the exclusion of the racial other and the primacy of whiteness in the formation of a national symbol.[28] Drawing on iconographic imaginings of the goddess of Liberty, artists and writers combined togas, Phrygian caps, and eagle feathers to bring forth a new Caucasian personification of the nation.[29] It is important to note, however, that Columbia's allegorical status allowed artists and writers to present her as the mother of the American people, regardless of race.

The Lady Liberties, Columbias, and other female personifications that appeared in poems and illustrations participated in and responded to the contest, just like actual American women. While Shirley Samuels insists that political allegory "at once embodies national conflicts and insists that we read *past* or *through* bodies," the close connection between the trials and triumphs of Columbia and her southern sisters and the Civil War experiences of American women interfered with this process. Figuration allowed the allegorical and symbolic feminine to not only inhabit but redefine and expand the wartime roles of American women. Alternatingly belligerent, mournful, angry, indignant, and determined, the Columbias who appeared on the pages of Civil War periodicals blurred the line between the abstracted symbolic feminine and the lived experience of American women. What follows is a roughly chronological survey of Columbia and her sisters' allegorical and symbolic roles, and an examination of those roles in relation to the lived experiences of American women.

Petulant Children and Maternal Love

As the sectional crisis worsened, southern poets, northern poets, and Lincoln himself relied on the familial metaphor and the allegorical feminine to frame the conflict.[30] Significantly, the concept of a house temporarily divided allowed for the possibility of future peaceful reconciliation. While northerners could conceive of Confederate states as estranged sisters who resisted or betrayed the family ties that bound the Union together, southerners could imagine a confederation of autonomous sister states as a new model for nationhood. Removed from the battlefield, female personifications allowed northern poets to engage in nonviolent apostrophes to misbehaving members of the national family. Published in the *Atlantic Monthly* in May 1861, the month following the bombardment of Fort Sumter, "Brother Jonathan's Lament for Sister Caroline" is the elder Oliver Wendell Holmes's rendition of the growing sectional crisis.[31] Employing the conceit of a brother appealing to his delinquent sister, the poem hopes for an eventual reconciliation between siblings. "She has gone," Brother Jonathan begins, "she has left us in passion and pride,— / Our stormy-browed sister, so long at our side." The first state to secede, South Carolina is the defiant sister of Holmes's poem, who "has torn her own star from our firmament's glow, / And turned on her brother the face of a foe!" By May 1861, eleven states had followed South Carolina's lead and seceded from the Union. Commenting on the defiance of the seceding states, Jonathan asserts, "Nature must teach us the strength of the chain / That her petulant children would sever in vain." Imagining South Carolina as a "hasty" and "rash" female ensures that "there are battles with Fate that can never be won." Columbia's children will return to the family, and the firmament will have all its stars once again.

A pair of poems, titled "Two Pictures of the South" and printed in the *Liberator* on July 5, 1861, showcases competing renditions of the maternal feminine.[32] William Gilmore Simms's "Song of the South," originally published as "Oh! The Sweet South" in the *Southern Literary Messenger* on January 1, 1861, appears beside a parody of the poem. Simms, a popular author and editor, writes a paean to "the sunny, sunny South" that establishes the "land of true feeling" as his mother and, at times, his lover. Simms's speaker extols the South's virtues and avers, "She brings me blessings of maternal love." G.E.D.'s parody mimics Simms's poem formally and uses similar and at times identical language. However, the parody denigrates the South, the "Land of slavery, land of wails and wo [*sic*]." Rather than mothering her children, the South "brings . . . tears from the maternal eye" and "sunder[s] kin."

Changing the first line of the second section of Simms's poem from "Oh! love is hers" to "Ah! Hate is hers," G.E.D. focuses on a topic unmentioned in Simms's laudatory poem. G.E.D.'s speaker evokes the captive lives and battered bodies of African American slaves, indicating the reason for his rejection of Dixie: "Oh! by the fate of the unhappy blacks,— / Oh! by the cruel blows, and broken ties,— / And by their groans and lacerated backs,— / By these, and more, that loud for vengeance cries." G.E.D. rejects Simms's personification of the South as mother, lauding instead "the inclement clime / Where Freedom reigns sublime." Read together, the two poems illuminate the rhetorical war raging before the commencement of hostilities. The southern maternal personification, G.E.D. claims, is a mother who brings death rather than life, shadow instead of sunshine. A new birth of freedom, ushered in by swift northern victory, will destroy Simms's South and restore the Union as the only true mother.

Schoolmarm and Seamstress

Prior to the onset of the struggle, Columbia watched with dismay as her children fought and divided into sections. As the mother of both halves of the country, her intact body evinced the relationship common to all Americans and the nation's vulnerability to division and fragmentation. A political cartoon published in the first issue of *Harper's Weekly* for 1860 announces Columbia's role as the enforcer of national cohesion. "Mistress Columbia" appears as a schoolmarm towering over her misbehaving children (fig. 1).[33] Divided into North and South by a line labeled "Mason-Dixon," the classroom is full of misbehaving men. According to the caption, Mistress Columbia has been derelict in her duties and has only recently awoken from a nap. Holding a switch and wagging a finger, Columbia admonishes the men, many of whom seem to be ignoring her lesson regarding the Constitution, a copy of which rests on her lectern. One pupil in the southern section writes "Let us alone" on the wall. The cartoon responds to the growing sectional crisis by embodying in Columbia the country as a whole and the importance of keeping the Union intact, underscoring her symbolic importance to conceptualizations of the nation.

FIG. 1 "Mistress Columbia, Who Has Been Taking a Nap, Suddenly Wakes Up and Calls Her Noisy Scholars to Order." *Harper's Weekly* 4, no. 158 (January 7, 1860): 16. Library of Congress Prints and Photographs Division, LC-USZ62-131564.

Significantly, Columbia is the sole woman in the room; only male students squabble over the future of the nation. Elsewhere in the issue, a two-page engraving showcasing a "great Union meeting at the Academy of Music, New York," presents a completely male audience of "five thousand persons" fervently supporting "the perpetuation of the institutions of our country."[34] However, the symbolic feminine on the last page of the issue evokes American mothers—the women whose children will fight the quickly approaching war—and the investment of women in the outcome of the sectional conflict. Columbia simultaneously suggests the absence of women from the halls of Congress while resembling the politically active women of the abolitionist and temperance movements. As Eleanor Flexner and Ellen Frances Fitzpatrick note, "the influx of women into teaching and their entrance into government offices date from the

Civil War."[35] As a schoolteacher and an active protector of the Constitution, Columbia inhabits roles that increasing numbers of American women would adopt during and after the conflict. In doing so, she blurs the distinction between the domestic and the public in her efforts to bring together a nation divided by the Mason-Dixon Line.

Schoolmarm Columbia resembles household matriarch Columbia, an incarnation of the maternal feminine who appears in a number of illustrations. Envisioned as a seamstress, she attempts to mend a damaged or ripped map of the United States in her efforts to keep the Union whole. The cartoon "Out of a Situation" (1860), published in *Vanity Fair,* portrays Columbia as the lady of the house informing "Biddy Buchanan" that she will not be needed "after next March."[36] Disguised as an Irish maid, President James Buchanan faces a Columbia seated in front of a standing man who resembles Uncle Sam. Columbia stitches together two pieces of a map of the United States, one half labeled "North" and the other "South." As the wife and mother in this American family, Columbia is in charge of the domestic help, and she has deemed Buchanan unfit for office. Buchanan's ancestry and his inefficacy in the face of the sectional crisis make him fair game for the kind of ridicule often heaped on Irish Americans in the nineteenth century. The matronly "Mrs. Columbia," sitting beneath a bust of George Washington, attempts to do what Buchanan could not—hold the nation together. Published prior to the 1860 election, the cartoon outlines the role of the next president: it will be his job to aid Columbia in reuniting the country. Shirley Samuels contends that similar images of Columbia as national housekeeper and gatekeeper "sugges[t] the invisibility of domesticity and housekeeping to conceptions of the republic as a house."[37] However, the cartoon domesticates the political, placing the allegorical feminine in charge of the future of the national house and reducing the ostensibly masculine presidential role to the lowest rungs of the household hierarchy.

Like their allegorical mother, Columbia's daughters took needle and thread in hand while designing and manufacturing battle flags for regiments, often raising money to support their efforts.[38] Mobilizing and expanding armies required supplies; in response, women's needlework moved beyond the realm of the home and engaged the political and social aspects of the war. In 1862, the *Saturday Evening Post* printed the words of the Reverend Robert Colyer, who remarked, "the women of our land have distanced all their sisters on the earth for general steady devotion to the material needs of the soldier."[39] Northern and southern women aided the cause by joining soldiers' aid societies, mending socks, sewing uniforms, and rolling bandages.[40] Women engaged in the production of these "material needs" appear in articles, poems, illustrations, and short stories, simultaneously holding down the home front and supplying men on the battlefield.

On June 29, 1861, the entire front page of *Harper's Weekly* featured a Winslow Homer engraving of young women "making havelocks," a piece of cloth draped over a military cap that protected soldiers' necks.[41] One woman, the only figure facing the reader, wears a kepi hat with finished havelock attached, the cap's brim shading her eyes as she mends a sergeant's jacket. The caption, which reads, "The war—making havelocks for the volunteers," combines with the cap and the draped American flag to indicate the centrality of women's work to the war effort and the concrete contributions of people who share similar features with the allegorical Columbias in other issues of the *Weekly.* Though clad in ruffles and flounces rather than uniforms, the women comprise a different sort of regiment—one as integral to the cause as the uniformed soldiers that appear on the other pages of the issue. The women's handiwork and collective action symbolize rather than allegorize—they are part of the war, not idle bystanders or disembodied guardian angels.

"Maggie Morton's Mittens; or, Working for the Soldiers and What Came of It," a short story published in the *Ladies' Repository* in 1862, describes the efforts of a fictional circle of women, "the Knitting Society" of an unnamed northern town.[42] Asking if the women of the town are "less brave" than the men, the narrator recounts how the women, "with hearts as true as steel to the Union . . . sought needles and scissors, and went vigorously to work over what the little boys pronounced 'the most beautiful Fourth of July flag that had ever been seen.'" Maggie, the titular character, gives the "presentation speech" in a "rich, clear voice," and she and the women continue to labor for the Union cause long after the soldiers depart, knitting mittens and socks. Maggie and her real-life counterparts do meaningful work that is simultaneously symbolic (it inspires and encourages soldiers) and concrete (it keeps soldiers warm). Regimental flags and mittens epitomize this balance between symbolism and material utility—flags elicit camaraderie and collective effort but also orient soldiers on the chaotic battlefield; mittens demonstrate the dedication of the girls the soldiers leave behind but also protect hands.

An article published in *Harper's Weekly* in 1862 provides a real-life counterpart to Maggie Morton and reports on an "interesting event—whose political significance will be readily appreciated."[43] On July 4, 1862, "Mademoiselles Angela Snyder and Lucena Courcelle" of New Orleans presented a flag of "plain blue silk" with thirty-four stars to the Thirteenth Connecticut Regiment. The accompanying engraving shows the "very pretty and loyal young ladies" handing the flag to Colonel H. W. Birge, who thanked the women "for their loyalty, which, through all the trials and temptations to which they had been subjected in the midst of treason, they had preserved pure and bright and warm within their faithful hearts."[44] In their courageous support of the Union, the article avers, the ladies are "of the material that infuses new vigor and fidelity into the hearts of men, and elevates the moral and manly tone of society." In the final sentence of the article, the women seem to merge with the flag they created—both are symbolic material that undergird masculine action. Though the article references "manly society," the engraving, like the illustrations that feature a hands-on Columbia, points to the *political* significance of women's labor, whether symbolic, manual, or both.

Some of Columbia's dedicated daughters had darker skin and joined the cause via communal action and manual effort. Frederick Douglass's *Monthly* reprinted an article describing the collective action of a group of enslaved women "to get a standard for the 1st Regiment of North Carolina Volunteers," a newly formed black regiment.[45] The author of the article laments that the paper cannot print the original handwriting of "Marian, a cook," whose "Sob Scription List" calls on "ladies old and young": "We a potion [*sic*] of us do in tend to go forward and try and Collect money enough to Purchase a decent flag for our Colard Solgers and Jentlemen for it is for [our] good and the good of our Daughters that our husbands and sons do in list to fight our Battles and gain our Libatys therefore there

Remans a work for us to do and Let us rise and do our parte Cheerfully Please giv me Som thing to aid us in this matter." Marian's unedited message appears on the same page as a description of the "gallantry of the negro troops" at the Battle of Milliken's Bend and a paean to "The Black Warrior"; the layout of the page, Marian's call, and the article's alliterative description of the "scanty savings of the slave subscribers" link the patriotic efforts and manual labor of black women to the cause of freedom and the Union's military effort.

South of the Mason-Dixon, the daughters of Virginia send their men to battle with a "fair banner" in the 1861 poem "To a Company of Volunteers Receiving Their Banner at the Hands of the Ladies."[46] Published in the *Southern Literary Messenger* and written by the mononymous Confederate poet Cora, the poem imagines a flag as a material substitute on the battlefield for women who want to fight but cannot. The speaker addresses a "gallant band" of volunteers:

> Soldiers! woman's heart beats high;
> Fain would *she* your glory share,
> March through blood, to victory,
> In a cause so just, so dear.
> But her feeble strength denies,
> Though her heart is brave and true,
> Therefore now her eager eyes,
> Rest upon and follow you.
> Therefore to your charge she gives
> This fair banner. . . .[47]

Though women lack the physical requirements for soldiering (in the context of the poem, at least), their manual labor assures their symbolic presence on the battlefield and encourages men to "win, or die for liberty." "Rather would Virginia weep," the poem intones, "o'er her *sons,* than o'er their *shame.*"[48] The final five stanzas of the poem invoke the maternal feminine, this time in the guise of the Old Dominion, and in doing so collapse the boundary between Virginia's daughters and sons. Once female determination combines with masculine endeavor, "proudly shall *our* mother stand [and] gladly sheathe her conquering blade."[49] As an allegorical construct, Virginia, unlike her daughters, can bear arms, her frame far from "feeble."

Awakening Columbia

Three months after the bombardment of Fort Sumter, a militant Columbia engaged in more aggressive manual labor in the political cartoon "Columbia Awake at Last" (fig. 2), published in *Harper's Weekly*.[50] A less polished version of the image graced envelopes encouraging "all that hate oppression" to "assist putting down Secession."[51] Garbed in the stars and stripes and backed by the spirit of George Washington, Columbia collars a diminutive man representing "secession" and "treason." The man, with an American flag and a palmetto (the state tree of South Carolina) protruding from his hat, has torn a piece of the Constitution from stately Columbia's grasp. A man with a skull-and-crossbones flag stuck in his hat and a man sporting a matching palmetto tree, stand-ins for the seceded southern states, creep away from the intimidating woman. All three men carry knives, instruments clearly intended to injure Columbia and dismantle the Union. Roused by the firing upon Fort Sumter, Columbia is "awake at last" to the threat posed by secession. Though the seceding southern states are armed, Columbia stands firm and appears ready to forcibly bring them back into the Union. The southern states are male but scrawny and shrink from the substantial Columbia. In her imposing physicality and aggression, this Columbia exemplifies Shirley Samuels's notion of "the national monitor" who "regulates," "disposes," and "kills."[52]

Another cartoon, featuring "Bertha (who wants to go to the War with her Brother Jack)," appears directly below the ferocious Columbia (fig. 2).[53] Smaller in size, the vignette resembles the larger cartoon in composition: Jack is on the left and Bertha on the right; Bertha and Columbia are in profile; and Jack has a sheathed sword on his left side. Like Columbia, Bertha is in deadly earnest, rejecting her brother's claim that she will "not be able to bear fatigue." Though the cartoon aims to amuse rather than inspire—Bertha claims that she will make an excellent soldier since she "beat [Jack] walking in the country last Summer; and waltzed Captain

COLUMBIA AWAKE AT LAST.

BERTHA (*who wants to go to the War with her Brother* JACK). "Nonsense, JACK—not able to bear fatigue! Why, I beat you walking in the country last Summer; and waltzed Captain BLOKER and Cousin HARRY until they were really afraid of me."

ADVERTISEMENTS.

OFFICERS OF THE ARMY AND NAVY.—TELESCOPES, OPERA, RACE, and Field, general out-door day and night powerful WAIST-COAT-POCKET double Spy-Glasses, WEIGHING ONLY SIX OUNCES EACH, containing twelve lenses, constructed of German glass, will show distinctly a person, to know them, at one and a half and two miles. Country scenery and ships are clearly seen at eight to ten miles distant. They are powerful and brilliant Telescopes for both eyes. Also powerful Telescopes, possessing such extraordinary power that some, 3½ inches, with an extra astronomical eye-piece, will show distinctly Jupiter's moons, Saturn's rings, and the double stars; and a person can be seen and known two miles and a half distant, and an object from fourteen to sixteen miles. They are in endless variety, of larger and all sizes, with increasing powers.
SEMMONS & CO., Opticians,
669½ Broadway, under La Farge House, New York.

$300,000.
Summer Clothing,
Devlin, Hudson & Co.,
Corner of Warren Street, and corner of Grand Street and Broadway.
The largest and only complete Stock of stylish
SUMMER CLOTHING
to be found in the city.
Having turned our entire force and means into the Retail Department of our business, we are now prepared with an immense stock of all kinds of desirable fabrics in
MEN'S AND BOY'S CLOTHING,
suited to the season, which we offer at exceedingly
LOW PRICES.
DEVLIN, HUDSON & CO.

WARD'S
Perfect Fitting Shirts,
MADE TO MEASURE AT $18 PER DOZEN.
Printed directions for Self-Measurement, list of prices, drawings of different styles of Shirts, sent free everywhere.
S. W. H. WARD, from London,
No. 387 Broadway, N. Y., up Stairs.

FIG. 2 "Columbia Awake At Last."
Harper's Weekly 5, no. 232 (June 8, 1861): 368.
Courtesy HarpWeek and TextBASE, Inc., 1863-06-08.

Bloker and Cousin Harry until they were really afraid of" her—the juxtaposition of the two images aligns the allegorical feminine's ferocity on behalf of the republic with ordinary American women's fervor and desire to serve their country.

The military service of women during the Civil War is well documented,[54] and accounts of female soldiers disguised as men appeared in periodicals.[55] "The Soldier's Sister," a short story published in *Godey's Lady's Book* in 1861, admiringly recounts the exploits of Nellie, a young woman who takes her wounded brother's place on the battlefield, receives a promotion for "gallant conduct," and ends up marrying the commanding office who discovers her secret.[56] The story's narrator is inspired to tell of Nellie's service during the Mexican-American War after she watches Union soldiers head off to battle, noting that "it is a story that in these stirring times may not prove uninteresting." Indeed, it is not uninteresting in that it potentially encourages women to take on nonsymbolic combat roles; it also provides fictional precedent for real-life woman soldiers like Frances Louisa Clayton and Loretta De Caulp, whose stories were published in multiple newspapers.[57] *Vanity Fair* published a fascinating example of cross-dressing and passing, reporting that "a slave woman ha[d] been discovered in one of the Ohio regiments" and promptly discharged.[58] Full of puns and incredulity, the article marvels that "a black woman has passed herself off for a white soldier," wondering, "How do we know that our army, which we have love and esteemed so much, is not largely composed of negro wenches?" Despite its mocking tone, the article documents the military service of a woman of color, one of Columbia's relatively unsung daughters. As DeAnne Blanton and Lauren M. Cook note, "significant numbers"—250 at least, by their count—of women decided "to dress as a man and march off to war," in large part because "cross-dressing female heroines, both fictional and real, were a standard commodity in popular culture."[59] Bertha's claims to soldiering ability are not atypical or purely comic.

Though Bertha seems fated to remain on the sidelines (she sits at a table while her brother appears ready to depart), her dialogue with Jack, in which she questions his manliness and impugns his soldiering ability, indicates an extremely popular trope in Civil War print culture. In poems, short stories, illustrations, and cartoons recalcitrant or hesitant men face off against strong-willed women intent on sending their lovers and husbands off to battle.[60] Ladies refuse to marry noncombatant suitors and, at times, use physical force against recalcitrant or unsuitably hesitant beaux and spouses. In "An Unwelcome Return," a cartoon also published in *Harper's Weekly* in 1861, a "three months' volunteer" attempts to return home after his initial enlistment is over; his wife, labeled "Daughter of Columbia" and armed with a broom, bars him from entering, proclaiming, "Get away! No husband of mine would be here while the country needs his help."[61] Two months earlier, Columbia held secession at arm's length, forcibly removing the dastardly male figure from her presence. Her "daughter" resembles her in stature and features but uses an outstretched broom instead of an arm. Another loyal daughter rejects an elegantly turned-out suitor in "Scene, Fifth Avenue," after learning that he has found a substitute to fight in his place; telling him, "And *I* have found one for YOU!" she keeps him at arm's length in a less belligerent version of Columbia's gesture.[62] The three cartoons indicate the interrelatedness of the allegorical feminine, the symbolic feminine, and actual American women.

Published in the *Ladies' Repository* in 1863, "Jennie Jewitt, the Young Recruiting Officer," applauds the efforts of "a delicate young lady" who "accomplishes more than those who receive salaries for doing the same kind of work in which she engages so heartily and cheerfully."[63] After recruiting all of her male relatives, Jennie resolves to ensure "that no strong young man remains at home" and travels "from house to house, soliciting volunteers" for the Union army. The author, Harriet N. Babb, makes no mention of a chaperone; as an unofficial recruiter, Jennie ventures out of her home and inserts herself into the war effort. Jennie also raises money and recruits other women to help her sew "a beautiful silk banner" for the local regiment. She slowly realizes "what she ha[s] done in urging these men to go to battle, and perhaps to death," but remains firm, even telling a patriotically challenged suitor that his only rival is "my country." Babb ties Jennie's fictional efforts to those of "many other ladies, all over our land, who are giving their best energies to their beloved country," and ends the story with a call for recognition: "'The women are doing their part *nobly* in this struggle,' is the testimony which comes even from lips not overfond of praising 'woman's work.'" The quotation marks that surround "woman's work" undermine the gendered division of labor and recognize the nonsymbolic labor of Columbia's daughters. The prevalence of illustrations, stories, and countless poems about patriotic mothers, wives, and daughters urging sons, husbands, lovers, and brothers to join up reveals the army's most effective recruiters: allegorical, symbolic, and real women.

His Torch Is at Thy Temple Door!

As the war persisted despite initial northern confidence in a short and successful campaign, vulnerable Columbias reflected growing concerns about continued disunion and southern invasion. After the South's initial betrayal of the national mother, ongoing treason threatened to dismember and degrade her body. It is the duty of her northern sons, a number of poems imply, to arm for battle and to sacrifice their bodies so that Columbia remains whole. Similarly, female personifications of Confederate states associated the southern cause with the protection of female chastity and the fight for freedom in the face of tyranny. At once virginal and motherly, Columbia and her southern sisters must rely on male action to remain nationally and sexually intact. This poetic construction ties nationhood to female purity, thus invoking the threatened bodies of real women but also reducing feminine participation in the war to figurehead status.

In two poetic calls to arms, "Our Country's Call" (1861) and "Not Yet" (1861), William Cullen Bryant imagines a helpless Columbia threatened by treasonous foes.[64] "Our Country's Call," the desperate cry of a beleaguered woman, urges the men of the North to "lay down the axe" and pick up a rifle, the pitiable state of the Union necessitating the transformation of farmers into soldiers. "See," Bryant's speaker instructs his readers, "from a thousand coverts—see, / Spring the armed foes that haunt her track; / They rush to smite her down, and we / Must beat the banded traitors back." Preyed on by her enemies, the nation is vulnerable and in need of male protection. In "Not Yet," Bryant rejects the notion of dissolution and disunion, declaring that those loyal to the Union will save her. "Shall we," his speaker asks, "like cravens stand apart, / When those whom thou hast trusted aim / The death-blow at thy generous heart?" Traitorous Confederates, seeking to kill their motherland, impel "hosts [to] rise in harness, shouting, No!" The "sleeping ashes" of the founding fathers also reject the breaking of "gentle ties which long / These sister States were proud to wear." Invoking motherland, founding fathers, and sister states, Bryant urges northern men to once again join together to protect the American family. In doing so, he relies on familial metaphors to illustrate the stakes of the conflict and calls on the power of patriarchal society to protect female and national purity.

The allegorical feminine recruited for the Confederate cause as well; the vulnerability of southern personifications emblematized the legitimate anxieties associated with the Confederacy's status as the invaded as opposed to the invader. Written and published in 1861 and extremely popular throughout the war, James Ryder Randall's "My Maryland" is a rallying cry to the imperiled state's sons and features a bellicose female personification similar to the figure in "Columbia Awake at Last."[65] The poem, which was later set to music, was first published in the *New Orleans Delta* but appeared in many other southern publications.[66] Because the Confederacy is a new nation founded in state sovereignty, it often appears in the guise of one of its constituent parts rather than as a unified whole. While Columbia represents unity and homogeneity, personifications of Virginia and Maryland reflect the primacy of the sovereign state in the face of encroaching federalism, a concept that is central to Confederate wartime rhetoric. A secessionist citizen of Baltimore, Randall employs a familial metaphor to portray his home state as a threatened and embattled mother/sister and encourages her and her sons to rise to the occasion.[67]

In its deployment of the allegorical feminine, Randall's poem warns of the threat of northern tyranny, beginning, "The despot's heel is on thy shore, Maryland! / His torch is at thy temple door, Maryland!" Appealing as a "wand'ring son" to his "Mother-State," Randall's speaker establishes the familial ties that bind him to his homeland. These ties extend to the states of the Confederacy, and the speaker calls on his mother to join her sisters: "Dear Mother! burst the tyrant's chain, Maryland! / Virginia should not call in vain, Maryland! / She meets her sisters on the plain." If Maryland fails to resist "the Vandal," she will be subject to "crucifixion of the soul." Defilement at the hands of Yankee invaders, Randall's poem seems to assert, awaits the southland and southern women if Maryland and her sisters fail to join together.

The threat or implication of sexual violence was common in Confederate publications, and writers warned explicitly of the potential depredations of invaders against southern property and implicitly of the sexual vulnerability of southern women. In 1861, the *Liberator* reprinted selections from Confederate newspapers that showcase vitriol and the vehement belief that Union invasion would specifically target the innocent women and children of the South. The curiously titled *Memphis Avalanche* avers that "the newspaper organs of Lincoln are constantly fulminating the most atrocious threats against women and children of the South. They tell us that these tender objects of our hearts' dearest affections are to be subjected to indiscriminate massacre, and outrage far worse than death."[68] Many women—potentially thousands, by Crystal N. Feimster's estimate—were raped during the Civil War, but statistics are scant and unreliable.[69] As Confederate defeat neared, fears of violation at the hands of conquering Yankees increased.[70] Though black women were much more vulnerable to rape and sexual violence, southern newspapers used the vulnerability of white women as a rallying cry.[71]

Published in at least six newspapers, an appeal to "every property holder in the Confederate States" calls on noncombatant southerners to contribute "money [and] labor" to the winter campaign of 1861. Those "snugly ensconced by blazing fires" must "remember that if through neglect and exposure those brave defenders are stricken down, not only will there be grief in every family, but rapine, confiscation and subjugation at every door."[72] This widespread hyperbole defines the stakes of the fighting by invoking multiple meanings of "rape," a word derived from the Latin word *rapare,* to seize.[73] Federal victory imperils property as well as women's bodies, the appeal implies through carefully chosen adjectives: "Let no sane man think of money-making until every battle field is whitened with the bones of our sensual, brutal and depraved invaders. . . . If, through our neglect and indifference, our armies become disorganized, then will land, slaves, mules, horses, cattle, bonds and stocks become worthless, except to the rapacious Yankee invaders."[74]

As the appeal and Randall's poem make clear, the sanctity of southern land and property was closely tied to the sexual purity of female personifications of Confederate states and their real-life daughters. Though northern invaders threatened the purity and chastity of the motherland, Randall's poem ends optimistically. "She is not dead," Randall's speaker avers, "nor deaf, nor dumb— / Huzza! She spurns the Northern scum! / She breathes—she burns! she'll come! she'll come!" Facing bodily harm and corporeally engaged in the process of disunion, Columbia and Maryland are just as vulnerable to the violence of war and just as active in the contest as male soldiers.

A Stigma Rests upon Her Frame

As national mother, Columbia bears the national shame of the peculiar institution at the center of the escalating conflict, her purity tainted by her relationship to slavery. Male action, poets insisted, would remove the twin taints of treason and slavery, and maintain the physical integrity of American women and the United States. Northern poets created guilty but powerless female personifications of a fundamentally flawed country, while southern poets warned of enslavement at the hands of Yankee invaders. Published two months after Bryant's "Not Yet," T. Hulbert Underwood's poem "Now" (1861) is an answer to Bryant's rhetorical question and an indictment of Columbia's association with slavery.[75] Mirroring Bryant's poem in form and content, "Now" asserts that the republic has already been brought low. "The traitor's arm has laid her low," but her own "statesmen" must also be held accountable for her sorry state. It is they who failed "to 'tear' from Slavery its mask, / And drive it from its cherished lair." Allowing the "dragon" of slavery to grow strong, America's leaders "left a curse to after-time." Underwood twice depicts Columbia as physically marked by the sin of slavery and the war fought to end it: "A stigma rests upon her frame" and "the fire of civil war to-day / Has charred upon the Nation's brow / A brand no tears can wash away." For past sins, Columbia and her people suffer the wrath of God. This wrath is evident in the Potomac's "ensanguined flow" and on the figurative form of Columbia but not on any non-allegorical female bodies, which are absent from the poem.

While the national sin stained Columbia, northern invaders, according to Confederate poets, threatened to enslave southern womanhood. The song "Maryland in Fetters!" (1861), published as a broadside, laments the pitiful condition of the "Mother of wretchedness," implying that defeat will be tantamount to enslavement.[76] The description of the beleaguered state is in stark contrast to the image printed on the broadside (fig. 3). The illustrated Maryland carries a scale, a sword, and an olive branch. At her feet are fasces similar to ones often carried by Columbia. She is most likely a combination of Lady Justice and Columbia, and reflects a commonality between northern and southern representations of the allegorical feminine. However, the title and focus of the poem isolate Maryland, rejecting the notion of an all-encompassing federal feminine personification. Addressing the state, the speaker laments, "The spoiler's foot upon thee, / His ruthless hand is on thee, / With manacles he's bound thee, / Hard is thy fate!" Upheaval and the threat of northern invaders, the song implies, have upset the social and political order—white womanhood wears the shackles of slavery. The song ends with a vehement decree: "Let Lincoln know his place, / Let black men know their face, / And from our injured race / All wrongs be riven." One of these "wrongs" is the degradation and enslavement of Maryland herself. Black men, the poem seems to argue, and not the white female personification of the state, should be shackled. Maryland's freedom is contingent on the perpetuation of the institution of chattel slavery—an institution that shames and stains Maryland's northern personified counterparts.

Published in 1862, Laura Redden Searing's poem "The Legend of Our Victories in '61–'62," published under the pseudonym Howard Glyndon, portrays the Union as a Hester Prynne–like figure, marked by wrongdoing: "Too long this fair young kingdom, / The Empire of the West, / Had borne a blasting stigma / Upon her virgin breast!"[77] Despite Searing's soaring rhetoric labeling the democracy both monarchy and empire, the symbolic importance of the Union's virginity is clear. The Union army's victories remove the stain of sectional strife and keep the Union pure

FIG. 3 "Maryland in Fetters" (1861).
Special Collections & University Archives/Wake Forest University.

by protecting "our women and children." Searing expresses a similar sentiment in "Union Forever" (1864), a poem that addresses the "men of America," calling on them to "press to [their] standard."[78] Searing's speaker apostrophizes Columbia, lamenting her imperiled state: "How art thou fallen, O Daughter of Promise! / From the throne of thy lofty and virgin estate / When thy children are drunk with the blood of thy suffering, / And traitors are ringing the knell of thy fate!" Besmirched by dissension and devirginized by the dissolution of national bonds, the Union must be restored by "a band of the staunch and devoted,— / Men whose integrity never was bought." In both poems, Searing employs the language of sexual purity to call the sons of the Union to action. Like Bryant and Underwood, Searing proposes male action as the cure for the country's woes, leaving actual women out of the equation.

Published in the *New South,* a Unionist paper in Port Royal, South Carolina, Charles A. Barry's poem "Columbia's Invocation!" (1862) also features a stained Columbia, one who "wash[es] out with tears / And hero-blood, her only shame."[79] Northern victory, according to Barry, will cleanse the United States of its sin—chattel slavery, the institution Horace Greeley and Abraham Lincoln discuss one column over from Barry's poem.[80] The beleaguered nation, menaced by "gathering foes," addresses the American flag, asking it to "wave o'er [her] people as they rise / To win [her] back [her] fame again." Barry's speaker calls on "freemen," urging them to "smite to kill" in her defense. "See!" the speaker exclaims, "Freedom bleeds! / She calls you with her stifled breath: / Rebellion to her Temple speeds— / March on, to Victory or Death!" As a personification of the republic and of freedom, Columbia depends on male action for survival. Implicit in Columbia's suffering is the threat to actual women, those who are vulnerable to the encroaching conflict or are asked to relinquish their sons, brothers, and husbands to the cause.

Also implicit, however, is the actual labor of women. An estimated twenty thousand women, around 10 percent of whom were African American, worked in northern hospitals, many of them as laundresses.[81] Though reliable statistics are hard to come by, it is clear that thousands of southern women volunteered or worked at Confederate hospitals.[82] Washerwomen and nurses constantly came into contact with "hero-blood," thus contributing to the cause in a tangible manner. Paeans to female nurses and volunteers regularly appeared in newspapers; though some focused on the tenderness and innately angelic nature of women, others underscored the political and cultural significance of their important labor in hospitals. An article lauding "The Women of the South" claims that a "tribute paid to the women of the South in resolutions which recently passed Congress is not the language of empty compliment, but of sober truth," and describes their service: "All over the land they have been at work, making clothes and preparing provisions for the soldiers, nursing them in hospitals, and in their own houses, seeking to take the place of a mother and a sister to the poor sick and wounded stranger, and, when human help no longer availed, smoothing the brow damp with death, and sending up their prayers with the departing spirit."[83]

The article refers to southern ladies as "the animating spirit of this struggle from the beginning," but its litany of sacrifice and labor reveals that women lend far more than symbolic *esprit* to the struggle. Such rhetoric is typical of what Drew Gilpin Faust terms "the comprehensive narrative of Confederate women and the war," an ideological directive framing the necessary contributions of southern ladies.[84] On April 11, 1862, the Confederate congress passed a resolution recognizing "the patriotic women of the country for voluntary contributions furnished by them to the Army."[85] Also in 1862, a special committee report on the Confederacy's "Medical, Commissary, and Quartermaster's Departments" praised the "women of the country [who], with the tenderness and generosity of their sex . . . have made large pecuniary contributions, taken charge of the hospitals . . . and, as matrons of those institutions, have carried cleanliness and comfort to the gallant soldier far from home and kindred."[86] The committee declares that "simple gratitude demands that public thanks be given, and a public acknowledgment of their faithfulness in the glorious work of effecting our independence." Women's war work led to public thanks and governmental acknowledgment, thus providing a contrast to solely allegorical versions of the feminine "spirit."[87]

Somewhat in the Background

Despite ample evidence of the non-allegorical actions of women, female personifications far removed from the heat of battle proved persistent. Published in *Southern Punch,* a paper modeled on the popular London periodical, the cartoon "Abduction of the Yankee Goddess of Liberty" (1863) portrays a besieged female personification at the mercy of a devilish attacker (fig. 4).[88] However, Lady Liberty suffers not at the hands of Confederate foes but instead in the clutches of the arch-Yankee. Abraham Lincoln, in the guise of "the prince of darkness," absconds with the goddess, taking her to "his infernal regions" in order to silence her "preaching about the Constitution." Claiming that he was "the first to rebel against constituted authority," Lincoln resembles Milton's archfiend Lucifer; the president, not the Confederates, upsets the national balance of power and threatens to destroy liberty. Echoing Shakespeare's power-hungry and murderous Lady Macbeth, Lincoln informs Liberty that "hell is murky."[89] His forked tail, which emerges from behind the goddess's waist, poses a sexual threat while his fiendish plans seek to destroy the core values

FIG. 4 "Abduction of the Yankee Goddess of Liberty."
Southern Punch 1, no. 14 (November 14, 1863): 4.
Courtesy HarpWeek and TextBASE, Inc., 1863-11-14.

of America. Northern tyranny, the cartoon implies, desecrates the very ideals it claims to protect. The southern artist deploys the allegorical feminine (one that closely resembles Columbia but does not bear her name) in order to claim Lady Liberty for the Confederate cause and to align southern success with the protection of helpless femininity.

Columbia confronts the arch-Confederate, a devilish Jefferson Davis, in "Check-Mate!" the cover illustration for the June 3, 1865, issue of *Harper's Weekly* (fig. 5).[90] The illustration mimics Moritz Retzsch's 1837 engraving "The Game of Life or The Chess-Players," in which a young man plays chess with the devil. The accompanying text explains that Davis, "the Spirit of Treason," is "playing with Uncle Sam for his Life." Uncle Sam, "the type of calm, self-possessed manhood," faces the "Prince of Rebellion" with a "countenance expressive of triumph tempered by amiability." Dressed like the Devil in Retzsch's engraving, Davis embodies "all the rapacity of a Tiger and all the cruelty of a Hyena." The description continues: "Between the two players, somewhat in the back-ground, stands a gentle, lovely angel-form, with white and outspread wings—the GODDESS OF LIBERTY, the protecting spirit of Uncle Sam, but not seen by him. She

FIG. 5 "Check-Mate!"
Harper's Weekly 9, no. 440 (June 3, 1865): 337.
Courtesy HarpWeek and TextBASE, Inc., 1865-06-03.

looks in rapture down upon the victorious termination of the struggle. But now let us look again at the game itself."

A silent and invisible presence, Liberty is removed from the actual contest—a separation made even more evident by the rhetorical return to the "game itself." Grant is the king on Uncle Sam's side and "the Queen is COLUMBIA, a lofty, majestic figure, unfurling her vindicated flag." Her position on the board "supports the more active officers." Even though Columbia is part of the game, she is not an active officer, and it is Uncle Sam (the representative of the government) that moves her around the board. Removed from the actual process and progress of war, Columbia and Liberty point to the allegorical significance of femininity while excluding actual women from the national "game"—the political moves that led to the Civil War and the conflict that resulted.

However, the same issue of *Harper's Weekly* reports on the trial of "the conspirators" responsible for Lincoln's assassination. A two-page illustration of the courtroom features three female figures, one barely visible sitting at the edge of the dock, and two in the foreground sitting next to each other with their backs turned to the sketch artist.[91] The former is Mary Surratt, later executed for her part in the plot, and the other two women are most likely witnesses for the prosecution: Mrs. Mary Hudspeth, who intercepted letters addressed to conspirators while riding in a train car, and Mrs. Martha Murray, "mistress of the Heredon Hotel."[92] The article recounting the trial also mentions another female witness, Miss Norah Fitzpatrick, and describes Surratt's interactions with Mrs. Slader, "a blockade runner, or bearer of dispatchers." Clearly, these women and others like them were active participants in the "game."

Despite the lingering presence of the helpless and removed allegorical feminine, Columbia acted as the sponsor of Union combatants during and after the war. In doing so, she testified to the steadfast devotion of American women to the cause and to the well-being of soldiers, and also performed a public and political role. Two certificates, one published in 1861 and the other in 1863, closely associate Columbia with the defenders of the Union. *In Defence of the Union and the Constitution* (1861) certifies that the recipient of the award fought "in support of the Government to suppress the rebellion of 1861" (fig. 6).[93] *The Union Defenders Certif-*

FIG. 6 *In Defence of the Union and the Constitution* (1861).
Library of Congress Prints and Photographs Division, LC-DIG-pga-03676.

icate (1863) acknowledges the recipient's role in defending the "government, the Union, and the Constitution."[94] Both certificates prominently feature Columbia, portraying her as the embodiment of the Union the soldiers fought to save and the patron saint of the men who waged war in her name. The 1863 certificate displays Columbia in the forefront of the image, raising the American flag and pointing to a battlefield. The only female figure, she looks over her shoulder, urging the viewer to recognize and celebrate her defenders. The 1861 certificate, however, combines allegorical femininity, symbolic masculinity, symbolic womanhood, and the wartime suffering and sacrifice of northern women. At the center of the image, Columbia holds two laurel wreaths, her arms outstretched. She extends her star-spangled robe to shelter a woman crouching with her children, ostensibly rewarding the soldier by looking after his family. In drawing two laurel wreaths instead of one, the artist perhaps allows for a double recognition—one wreath for the soldier, one wreath for his wife. Both Columbias stand on the ground rather than floating above it. Through figuration, Columbia and her sisters insert the immaterial and, more importantly, material contributions of women into the commemoration of the "defence" of the Union.

Her Self-Enwoven Fetters Shake

Women made many material contributions to the abolitionist movement and remained active in the public arena during the conflict and after emancipation. Reformers and activists like Susan B. Anthony and Elizabeth Cady Stanton sponsored petitions for an emancipation amendment and worked closely with hundreds of thousands of northern white women, many entering the public realm for the first time, to abolish slavery.[95] Free black women formed anti-slavery organizations and auxiliaries to the American Anti-Slavery Society, the preeminent abolitionist group.[96] Northern poets and artists manifested the relationship between the work of real women and the end of slavery by deploying the allegorical feminine, Columbia, who, as northern victory became more and more aligned with abolition, broke the fetters of bondage and acted as an agent of emancipation.

Poets describing Columbia as shackled and fettered echo abolitionist poems describing the horrors of slavery and thus connect the body of the Union to the bodies of enslaved people. William Lloyd Garrison's song for the Anti-Slavery Celebration at Framingham, Massachusetts, "Our National Visitation" (1862), describes Columbia's punishment for "her manifold transgressions."[97] God's wrath leaves the nation "scourged and torn," her "glory" departed. Garrison argues that Columbia herself "has forged the galling fetter." Columbia divests herself of her chains in the poem "National Ode: Suggested by the President's Proclamation of January 1, 1863" (1863).[98] Responding to the Emancipation Proclamation, the poem urges Columbia to "awake, / Her self-enwoven fetters shake, / And vivify the pulses of the land!" The "slimy coils" of slavery encircle Columbia's white limbs only; significantly, the poem references the "black, blank faces" of the slaves only once. The song and poem rely on the white female body for its rhetorical power rather than depicting "scourged and torn" slave bodies. In this way, both blur the boundary between black and white (since a white body can be fettered) while reinforcing the racial hierarchy.

Despite Columbia's symbolic complicity in the rise and spread of slavery, she also appears as the champion of the freedmen and the arbiter of justice. Two poems published after the Emancipation Proclamation, "The Promise Must Be Kept" (1864) and "November 8, 1864" (1864), envision Columbia as a defender of freedom and advocate for the total abolishment of slavery. Published in the *New York Tribune* and the *Liberator*, the former is an answer to opponents of the Emancipation Proclamation seeking to revoke the promise of freedom. The freedom-wielding nation rejects cries to "degrade the proclamation": "See on her sacred shore Columbia stand, / While broken chains lie 'round her on the strand, / And hear her cry to every down-trod land: / 'BEHOLD A NEW CREATION!'"[99] The motherland seemingly gives birth to freedom for the slaves, a poetic conceit that ostensibly limits femininity to what Julia Kristeva calls "the Maternal."[100] However, Columbia destroys the chains that bind her, a labor that moves beyond the restricted role of maternity and into the political and societal realm. "November 8, 1864" (1864), a poetic celebration of the reelection of Abraham Lincoln, imagines an even more powerful Columbia.[101] The speaker describes a vision inspired by the election: "I see bold Freedom with a giant's stroke / Hurl to the earth the bondman's heavy yoke; / I see her strike from off his horny hands / The galling chains and fetters where he stands." Columbia, personified in this iteration as Freedom, is the agent of emancipation who breaks the chains of the bondman, one of her many children.

Kneel, Motherland!

Columbia, as the country's matriarch, enacted publicly the private grief of thousands of mourning mothers, wives, daughters, sisters, and lovers. After demoralizing and costly Union losses, Columbia vehemently advocated for her defenders and her fallen children. In doing so, she did more than commemorate Union soldiers—she publically demanded answers, protesting the violent deaths of her sons as well as publically expressing the grief and frustration of bereaved women. In two political cartoons, a belligerent and infuriated Columbia confronts Lincoln regarding the deaths of her soldier sons. Published in *Harper's Weekly* in 1863, "Columbia to Lincoln" features an intimidating and accusatory Columbia pointing her finger at the president.[102] "Where are my 15,000 sons, murdered at Fredericksburg?" she demands, and rejects the joke offered by the notoriously wise-cracking president. During the battle of Fredericksburg, disastrous frontal attacks against entrenched Confederates led to devastating Union casualties. Columbia's indignation reflects public sentiment about the battle and female engagement with the course of the war and the political and military decisions made by men. In the 1864 cartoon "Columbia Demands Her Children!" Columbia, again pointing an accusing finger, rejects the president's call for 500,000 volunteers, demanding that Lincoln "give [her] back [her] 500,000 sons (fig. 7).[103] In both cartoons, Columbia protects the interests of her sons, rejecting the avoidable slaughter at Fredericksburg and Lincoln's call for more men. As protester and public advocate for Union soldiers, Columbia enters the national arena.

Before southern surrender, Columbia's grief often served as a rallying cry for continued dedication to the Union cause. Poets and illustrators deployed her tears to justify continued bloodshed. "The Soldier's Grave" (1862), a poem published in a Unionist paper in Kansas, imagines a more intimate scene in which Columbia mourns a solitary soldier's death.[104] Addressing the soldier, the poem's speaker informs the young man that his country mourns specifically for him: "Rest, soldier, rest! thy country comes, /With tender love and true, / Freely to deck thine honored head— / Her banner o'er its turf to spread, / And on thy lonely grave to shed / Fond

FIG. 7 "Columbia Demands Her Children" (1864).
Library of Congress Prints and Photographs Division, LC-DIG-ppmsca-15768.

memory's pearly dew." As chief mourner, Columbia grieves for each soldier who died to protect her, just as actual women grieved the loss of their family members and husbands. Hoping to encourage other young men to follow the fallen soldier's example, the speaker requests that the soldier throw his "mantle from the sky" so a "rising race" of American men will come to the country's defense "and in Jehovah's armor strong, / Her life, her Union save!"

Two of Thomas Nast's engravings, both published in *Harper's Weekly,* further illustrate the political cachet of allegorical feminine grief. "Honor the Brave" (1863) features a mourning Columbia who, with head bowed, places a laurel wreath on a flag-draped coffin (fig. 8).[105] The border surrounding Columbia depicts soldiers and sailors "on land" and "at sea" who fight to protect her. Beneath the main title are the words "The Union must and shall be preserved." The illustration establishes both the importance of saving the Union and the severe cost of doing so. Columbia simultaneously honors the children who have sacrificed their lives to defend

FIG. 8 "Honor the Brave."
Harper's Weekly 7, no. 356 (October 24, 1863): 680–81.
Courtesy HarpWeek and TextBASE, Inc., 1863-10-24.

her and calls on her sons to continue the fight. "Compromise with the South" (1864), published two months before the presidential election, deploys Columbia's grief to portray the dire results of voting Democratic.[106] Columbia kneels weeping in front of a grave "in memory of the Union heroes who fell in a useless war." A Union veteran with an amputated leg bows his head as he shakes the hand of a Confederate soldier who stands with his boot upon the grave. To his rear, a family of slaves are chained together. The message of the illustration is clear: a Democratic victory will lead to the betrayal of every Union soldier who died or was wounded to protect the Union, the degradation of Columbia, and the continued enslavement of African Americans. Columbia's mourning at a prototypical grave calls on northerners to reject compromise with Copperheads and Peace Democrats, and to continue fighting until total victory is achieved.

Columbia's role in the process of commemoration became increasingly prominent after Union victory. She acted as chief mourner of her fallen sons, including Abraham Lincoln. The mother of the country made mourning, a usually private and domestic undertaking, public, indicating the increasingly civic and communal aspects of grief. Mourner and bearer of memory, Columbia carried out the duties of American women in the aftermath of northern victory, southern defeat, and the abolition of slavery. As noncombatants, women were responsible for remembering and commemorating their dead husbands, sons, and brothers. Doing just that, women draped themselves in black, claimed the bodies of loved ones, and decorated graves, becoming what, in its Confederate manifestation, Drew Gilpin Faust labels a "uniformed sorority of grief."[107]

Though Nast's Columbia kneels in front of an imagined grave, *Harper's Weekly* also published engravings of newly established cemeteries; based on photographs, a number of the engravings feature women. In one full-page spread, Clara Barton raises the American flag over the recently planted headstones of fourteen thousand soldiers who died in Andersonville Prison.[108] Barton "first suggested the possibility of accomplishing this noble work," which consisted of organizing, attempting to identify, and burying the corpses of "soldiers starved and poisoned and brutally murdered." In another engraving of a Confederate cemetery at Franklin, Tennessee, a woman walks side by side with a man; another, dressed all in black, walks alone.[109] After the war, Columbia's daughters wandered among the graves, decorated headstones, and commemorated the fallen.[110]

The illustration "Abraham Lincoln's Coffin" (1865), also published in *Harper's Weekly,* portrays another kneeling Columbia laying a laurel wreath on top of the president's resting place and covering her face with her hand (fig. 9).[111] To the left and right of Columbia, divided from her by a white border, a soldier and a sailor, defenders of the Union, bow their heads in grief, covering their faces in a gesture that matches Columbia's as feminine and masculine mourning combine to embody the collective grief of the nation. "A Dirge—April 15, 1865," a poem published in the *Liberator* a month after the cessation of hostilities, also foregrounds Columbia's central role in the process of mourning Lincoln.[112] The poem begins with a description of the people's response to the President's death: "There's wailing from a million hearts—there's gloom on every hearth; / The shouts of victory are dumb—hushed is the sound of mirth." In the midst of this widespread outpouring, "the Nation, in black robes of woe,

FIG. 9 "Abraham Lincoln's Coffin."
Harper's Weekly 9, no. 435 (April 29, 1865): 267–68.
Courtesy HarpWeek and TextBASE, Inc., 1865-04-29.

sits watching by her Dead!" Watching along with Columbia is "that dusky race, whose chains of slavery / He broke." Lincoln, the savior of the Union and the emancipator of the slaves, undergoes an apotheosis. Watched over by Columbia, his body takes on symbolic significance and, along with Columbia, demands that the reunified country deal fairly with the freedmen. Columbia, as the national mother, will continue to mourn the fallen president and to encourage the reunited states to worship him and "follow where LINCOLN's footsteps led."

Similarly, a symbolic feminine sisterhood in Thomas Nast's illustration "Our Arms Victorious" (1865) announces Lincoln's place in the American pantheon (fig. 10).[113] In the center of the illustration are five toga-wearing figures gathered around a bust of Lincoln upon a pedestal. Justice holds her scales and sword while Victory places a laurel wreath upon Columbia's head and gazes adoringly at a toga-wearing and laurel-wreathed Lincoln. Sheathing her sword, Columbia rests her foot upon a cowering male

FIG. 10 "Our Arms Victorious."
Harper's Weekly 9, no. 443 (June 24, 1865): 392–93.
Courtesy HarpWeek and TextBASE, Inc., 1865-06-24.

personification of the defeated South, draped in a robe labeled "C.S.A." Perched next to Columbia is a freedman, a broken shackle at his feet. The illustration ties the allegorical feminine to martial, judicial, and political aspects of the Civil War and the process of emancipation and reunification. Though allegory predominates in Nast's illustration, vignettes of soldiers returning home and men and women celebrating victory frame the central symbolic image. One vignette portrays the battlefield dead, invoking a "victory dearly won." American women, the illustration implies, will enthrone the fallen president and the war dead in public and private shrines of memory.

An allegorical portrayal of this victory, the illustration *The End of the Rebellion in the United States, 1865* (1866), gathers together three closely connected and often interchangeable female personifications, Justice, Liberty, and Columbia (fig. 11).[114] Columbia and Liberty stand upon an altar while Justice, sword in hand and backed by the newly inaugurated Andrew Johnson, strides towards recalcitrant Confederates. General Ulysses S. Grant leads a vanguard of Union soldiers to meet the surrendering Robert E. Lee and his beleaguered troops. In the forefront of the illustration are an African American soldier and a freed slave. The latter kneels in front of the altar, gazing up at his maternal benefactors. Columbia, her eyes on the black soldier, gestures to the freed slave, seemingly displaying to the soldier the results of his wartime actions. The only women in the image, Columbia, Liberty, and Justice represent the ideals protected by the soldiers of the Union and the martyred President Lincoln. The three white female figures form the focal point of the illustration, one devoid of any black women, and northern and southern men appeal to their majesty. While Columbia and Liberty wear loose-fitting white robes, Justice dresses like a contemporary woman, her feet on the ground instead of an altar as she leads the charge to bring former rebels to justice. In this way, Justice aligns allegorical femininity with actual (white) female agency and alludes to the political and social activism of northern women. The blending of the allegorical and the real, the symbolic feminine and the nonsymbolic feminine, underscores the centrality of female personifications to artistic and poetical depictions of the Civil War while indicating shifting conceptions of female political and social agency.[115]

FIG. 11 *The End of the Rebellion in the United States, 1865* (1866). Library of Congress Prints and Photographs Division, LC-DIG-pga-03676.

Columbia Victrix

As news of Lee's surrender at Appomattox traveled along telegraph lines, northern papers filled with effusive verse celebrating the preservation of the Union and the triumph of freedom. Unsurprisingly, a number of poets chose to invoke a victorious Columbia. She was not unscathed—she, like the United States, had suffered through the vicissitudes of war and had scars to show for it. In her monumental, intact, and all-encompassing physicality, Columbia represented the perseverance of federal power; she had broken all shackles and was free of the stain of slavery. Nevertheless, her healing process was incomplete, as was the nation's. In her whiteness, Columbia also hinted at the reconciliationist imperatives that would eventually result in the betrayal of the freedmen and the whitewashing of Civil War history. As the mother of white *and* black Americans, however, Columbia's survival and resurgence aligned with emancipation and the promise of freedom for all.

W. J. Linton's poem "Columbia Victrix" has at its center a triumphant Columbia typical of many poems celebrating the end of the struggle.[116]

"God bless Columbia," the second stanza begins, "Free from the stain, / Rid of the curse of old, / Saved by her pain!" Columbia has been cleansed in the crucible of war, and Union triumph has ensured the excision of slavery from the national body. Columbia's "pain" stands in for the corporeal and emotional costs of defeating the South and freeing the slaves. "After the battle-storm," the speaker predicts, "Peace [will] heal her scars." Having passed through a trial by fire, Linton implies, the country will rise stronger than before. Bayard Taylor expresses similar sentiments in his poem "Comments."[117] Having divested herself of any association with slavery ("the Evil, on its falling throne"), Columbia is "Free, and for Freedom now she stands a giant / To shield her own." Refusing to be cowed by her enemies, Columbia "stands erect, majestic on her mountains— / SHE WILL NOT DIE."

Similarly, Augusta Cooper Kimball's "Shout" and Mrs. E. A. Kidder's "Peace Jubilee" deploy Columbia to exultantly cheer the reconciliation of North and South and the coming of freedom. In "Shout!" Kimball describes "a nation renewed! / That moults the old garment that bound her, / That rises with evil eschewed."[118] "With purpose of Justice imbued," Columbia rids herself of the curse of slavery. "Shout," Kimball's speaker urges, "that a creature of God, / Long known as our national ban, / And reckoned a thing, as a beast, / Is counted and titled a man!" Formerly enslaved, the black man has proved his manhood by facing the enemy "with a courage as high and serene / As any of Liberty's sons!" The freedmen are now part of the national family, a family that is no longer divided by sectional strife. Americans must also shout, the speaker intones, "for the States coming back!" Rather than spurning former traitors, northerners must "draw them so near, it will seem / One heart only throbs in the Union!" In "The Peace Jubilee," Kidder makes clear why this happy reconciliation is possible.[119] Once again, Columbia is the agent of victory, freedom, and reconciliation. "Fair Columbia," Kidder's speaker proclaims, "resplendent with beauty, / From the fiery baptism comes forth; / She hath cancelled, by doing her duty, / The sins of the South and the North." Having survived the war and promulgated freedom, Columbia allows for the reconciliation of two formerly belligerent entities. In her fairness and in her Christ-like capacity to absolve sins, Columbia has the potentially problematic capacity to remove all traces of slavery, the root cause of the struggle.

A cartoon published in *Harper's Weekly* in May 1865 features a less victorious and monumental Columbia. Dainty and adolescent, the Columbia in "The Return Home" is no longer the fierce and bellicose figure of the war years. An unimposing Columbia addresses a Union soldier on his way home.[120] "Tell me, Soldier," Columbia says, "did you not pass a Wayward Sister of mine on the road?" A female figure carrying luggage heads toward the pair, walking on a path marked "to the U.S." "I did," replies the soldier. "I fetched her a good part of the way myself, but she says she didn't require my services any more now; and here she comes over the hill." The soldier has done his duty, and it is now up to Columbia to bring her errant sister back into the family fold. Columbia's cultural work was far from over, even though Uncle Sam would eclipse her in popularity in the twentieth century. Nevertheless, her importance to American culture is forever enshrined in the nation's capital.

Liberty Enlightening the World

"The Statue of Freedom" (1864), a poem by Mrs. P. R. Woodbury published in the *Liberator,* celebrates the addition of the eponymous personification atop the Capitol building.[121] Designed by Thomas Crawford in 1855, the statue was installed on December 2, 1863.[122] Philip Reid, an enslaved man working at a foundry in Washington, D.C., oversaw the casting of the bronze statue.[123] An excerpt from the *New York Tribune* precedes the poem and ties Freedom, who combines characteristics of Columbia and Lady Liberty, to the course of the struggle and emancipation: "During more than two years of our struggle, while the national cause has seemed weak, she has patiently waited and watched below; now that victory crowns our advances, and the bond are being freed, she comes forward, her hand outstretched as if in guaranty of National Unity and Personal Freedom." During the Civil War, while American women "waited and watched" and came forward to serve the cause, figures like Freedom, Lady Liberty, and Columbia performed significant cultural and political work.

When Edouard de Laboulaye, the president of France's Anti-Slavery Society, proposed a monument honoring the United States and Union victory in 1865, he imagined a statue similar to the one atop the Capitol building. Ten years later, he and the sculptor Frédéric Auguste Bartholdi designed a powerful and monumental woman dressed in classical robes trampling a broken chain.[124] *La Liberté éclairant le monde,* more commonly known as the Statue of Liberty, holds high her torch and, like the Statue of Freedom, illustrates the ongoing importance of the allegorical feminine to American identity. Lady Liberty's ancestry includes Columbia, her sisters, and the American women, both figurative and actual, who fought the Civil War.

CHAPTER TWO

The Bones of the Black Man

"A Man Knows a Man," a cartoon published in *Harper's Weekly* ten days after Lincoln's assassination, features a black soldier dressed in a federal uniform shaking a white veteran's hand (see fig. 12).[1] Both men fought for the Union and for the fallen president, losing legs in the process. One soldier (it is unclear which) says to the other, "Give me your hand, Comrade! We have each lost a LEG for the good cause; but, thank GOD, we never lost HEART." The men, of similar stature and height, are on an equal footing. The composition of the illustration and the accompanying dialogue present readers with a framework for understanding the military contributions of the United States Colored Troops (U.S.C.T.) and indicate one of the central rhetorical debates of the Civil War: how would African American military service influence the status of black men in the postbellum United States? The cartoon implicitly endorses one possible answer—because the black soldier lost a leg, he has gained his place in the brotherhood of American men.

Four months later, *Harper's Weekly* published two full-page engravings by Thomas Nast, the popular cartoonist and advocate for black equality (fig. 13).[2] In "Pardon," the first engraving, a disgruntled Columbia gazes disgustedly down on Robert E. Lee and other entreating former Confederates. In the caption that accompanies the image, Columbia poses the first part of an important question in postwar politics and society: "Shall I trust these men"? Next to the southern general kneels Jefferson Davis, holding out a paper that reads "Pardon." In the second engraving, entitled "Franchise," Columbia stands with her hand on the shoulder of a black

FIG. 12 "A Man Knows a Man."
Harper's Weekly 9, no. 434 (April 22, 1865): 256. Library of Congress Prints and Photographs Division, LC-DIG-ds-09703.

veteran. The soldier's missing leg embodies his commitment to the Union cause. Standing on a raised platform, Columbia and the soldier look out on an invisible audience; significantly, it is Columbia who entreats in this image, her left hand gesturing towards the corporeal proof of black manhood, dedication, and bravery. The caption completes Columbia's question: "and not this man?" The answer, in Nast's formulation, is abundantly clear. The country, Nast asserts, has only two choices: pardon the traitor-

FIG. 13 "Pardon and Franchise."
Harper's Weekly 9, no. 449 (August 5, 1865): 488–89. Library of Congress Prints and Photographs Division, LC-DIG-ds-07129.

ous rebels who sought to destroy the Union *or* enfranchise the black men who fought and sacrificed their bodies to save it. Despite scholarly claims to the contrary, black martial masculinity was not an ephemeral trace of wartime necessity that vanished after Reconstruction. Illustrations like these heralded the arrival of a reconfigured black masculinity, based in the trauma of the Civil War, that would persist into the twentieth century.

The cartoon and engravings exhibit a transactional and transformative process by which the bodily sacrifice of black soldiers is a down payment on lasting freedom and enfranchisement. The military service and physical suffering of black men helped keep the Union intact; therefore, the reconstituted nation owes black soldiers and their brethren recognition and reward in the form of full citizenship. Between 1861 and 1865, Americans both black and white, unaware of the coming failure of Reconstruction and the empty promises of freedom, located the justification for African American manhood and citizenship in the bodies and blood of black soldiers. Poems, articles, newspaper illustrations, and soldiers' letters equate the enlistment and contributions of 179,000 African American soldiers with manhood, citizenship, and racial redemption.[3]

Instrumental in the formation of the U.S.C.T., Frederick Douglass recognized the transformative potential of black military involvement: "Once let the black man get upon his person the brass letters, U.S.; let him get an eagle on his button, and musket on his shoulder and bullets in his pocket, and there is no power on earth which can deny that he has earned the right to citizenship."[4] In Douglass's opinion, blue uniforms and bullets would enact what the Thirteenth, Fourteenth, and Fifteenth amendments eventually made law: black bodies in blue will usher in political agency and citizenship. The "person" of the black soldier is tangible proof of upward mobility and racial uplift; Douglass's confidence and belief in the efficacy of arming black men centers on a symbolic transformation of the black male body.

Rather than anachronistically applying the hard lessons of Reconstruction and the nadir period, and in order to deepen our critical understanding of the black male body's cultural significance on the rhetorical battleground of wartime print culture, I seek to recover the rhetoric of the wartime moment. As Christopher Hager has recently noted, "black regiments witnessed the convergence of linked projects, political and literary: to secure a place in the legal and the discursive United States."[5] The pages of newspapers and periodicals were the testing ground for reconfigured notions of black masculinity, just as the battlefield was. Indeed, the transformation of black men from objects to subjects, from slaves to soldiers, is one of the central tropes of Civil War popular literature.[6] Alice Fahs and Jennifer James both discuss this trope, but they focus instead on the ways in which wartime writers and artists circumscribe and limit the revolutionary potential of arming men who were formerly enslaved. Fahs contends that popular literature deployed a "number of strategies," including "imagined white control of black actions, ridicule, or, most often, death," to deny "blacks full membership in the nation."[7] Reading wounds as stand-ins for psychological trauma, James insists that black writers after the Civil War very rarely invoked wounded black bodies in the interest of avoiding the stigma of disability.[8] During the conflict, however, wounds on black soldiers' bodies became metaphors of proven ability, heroic sacrifice, and readiness for citizenship.

In delineating these strategies, Fahs and James have the benefit of hindsight, and read the failure of Reconstruction and the coming of Jim Crow onto sincere and substantial imaginings of a country in which the military service of black men results in recognition and "full membership." Though Fahs acknowledges the prevalence of "evocation[s] of the achievement of black manhood through soldiering" in popular literature, she consistently qualifies the rhetorical power of symbolic black service and suffering, insisting instead on a glut of negative imagery that counteracted less substantial positive imagery related to black soldiers.[9] Attending to the symbolic power of black soldiers' bodies in Civil War print culture provides an important counterpoint to the strategies Fahs describes. Limiting our focus to these strategies does a disservice to the revolutionary and widespread trope of the transformation that occurred once black men, following Douglass's advice, got upon their persons "the brass letters, U.S."

Central to Fahs's and James's arguments is the idea that the deaths of black soldiers preclude or diminish the potential for continued black male agency and participation in the postbellum republic. Fahs explains that "heroic death became a dramatic and also convenient way of celebrating black manhood without a sustained imagining of mixed-race society."[10] James similarly claims that the involvement of black men in the Union army "could only be accepted if the black male body were effectively removed from both national time and national space, allowing the white male body to retain its more deserving existence."[11] Carole Emberton focuses on the ways in which some aspects of black military service reproduced or resembled the conditions of involuntary servitude, arguing that "black soldiers' deaths on Civil War battlefields represented the bitter irony of man-making in the age of emancipation" and failed to secure political and social equality for African Americans.[12] Black soldiers did receive less pay than their white counterparts until the summer of 1864, fought in segregated units, and were barred from most leadership positions.[13] However, all Civil War soldiers, regardless of their race, faced "forced enlistments, corporal punishments, and violent death."[14] Emberton also claims that black abolitionists assumed that "military service represented a linear, unproblematic path to national citizenship" despite the "racialized framework through which many white Americans . . . viewed the citizen-soldier ideal."[15] The texts in this chapter avoid such assumptions; instead, they evidence that African American *and* white writers and artists proclaimed black military service a suggestive mile marker on the path.

Apart from popular literature from the perspective of "white Americans," perspectives and opinions were espoused by editors of, writers for, and contributors to African American periodicals—the segment of Civil War print culture most invested in the U.S.C.T.—as well as the soldiers themselves. A fuller examination of black soldiers in literary and visual culture reveals that bodily transformation and, at times, death were necessary components of entering into a narrative of military service previously restricted to white bodies. The symbolic death of a white soldier doesn't limit the influence of combat to the soldier himself—he dies to save the Union and, depending on the politics of the writer or artist, to end slavery. A black soldier dies to save the Union and free his people. Though Fahs and Emberton claim his death cuts off the possibility or mitigates the threat of black manhood, it instead qualifies as a heroic death that secures emancipation; in other words, the soldier's sphere of influence is not limited to himself and does not end with his death. Indeed, his symbolic death is integral to reconceiving the place of African Americans in the United States. Just as Christ's death was a prerequisite for universal salvation, so too were the deaths of black soldiers essential to the salvation of the Union and the abolition of slavery.

As the images discussed above make clear, not all black soldiers in popular literature died. Those who survived were visible proof of the transformative influences of the conflict. Elaine Scarry's claim that the wounds of a Confederate soldier and a Union soldier fail to "indicate the different political beliefs of the two sides," which assumes that both soldiers are white, overlooks black soldiers' bodies as inherently political sites of discursive production.[16] The black male body was broken and bled by the war, but this breaking and bleeding was significantly and symbolically different from the mangled and scarred black bodies of slaves in abolitionist literature. Jennifer Putzi argues that, since "American audiences were trained by abolitionist rhetoric to respond to scars with sympathy rather than respect or admiration," the Civil War failed to produce "a progressive redefinition of black manhood."[17] However, the physical repercussions of military service are different from the effects of slavery, both in application and in symbolic significance; the political and social repercussions of black men serving as soldiers for the Union, Douglass and others argue, would make slaves into men. While abolitionist publications relied on sympathy-inducing descriptions of scarred backs, literature and art depicting African American soldiers provided bullet wounds and amputated limbs as proof of a country served and citizenship earned.

Bodily transformations of black soldiers in popular print culture evince Frederick Douglass's reconfiguration of black male embodiment and agency. Derisive send-ups of black soldiers necessitated this reconfiguring rhetoric. There were three interrelated aspects of the transition from slave to soldier to citizen in wartime print culture: illustrations of the visual transformation of slaves into soldiers; writers' invocations of the symbolic and political significance of the somatic aspects of black military service, especially bones and blood; and black and white soldiers' printed responses to and opinions about African American military service. Together, all three illuminate the centrality of the U.S.C.T. to the political and cultural stakes of the Civil War. In order to recover an important counter-narrative to what scholars have described as the tendency of postbellum literature and culture to ignore or purposefully omit the contributions of black soldiers in the interest of reconciliation, I will trace the publication history of a poem that carried the reconfiguration of black manhood, born in the crucible of war, and the legacy of African American Civil War soldiers into the twentieth century.[18]

By focusing specifically on bodies, writers and artists reconfigured the traditional abolitionist formulation of salvation via white souls in black bodies described by Karen Sánchez-Eppler, who argues that sentimental fiction grounded emancipation in "the obliteration of blackness," and Shirley Samuels, who notes that both abolitionist and proslavery texts called for "white interiors."[19] If, in antebellum literature, the only hope for true freedom for African Americans was salvation through a white soul in a black body, then poets and artists during the war provide another option—

black bodies in blue uniforms. This new form of salvation had political results in this life rather than spiritual ones in the next. Black soldiers earned citizenship, franchise, and manhood through participation in the conflict that would determine the fate of their people. This is not to say that the discourse of the deracialized soul disappeared because of black men's service during the Civil War, but rather to excavate powerful competing discourses—ones that did not require black men to transcend their black bodies in order to achieve equity with white men. Political and social equality, instead of salvation, were the rewards of a baptism in blood.

The Dark Artillery

There is no doubt that ridicule and derision of African American soldiers were widespread in popular periodicals and wartime ephemera.[20] While abolitionist and Republican-leaning papers ran articles describing the process of arming contrabands and lauding the heroism of the black soldiers, southern periodicals and some northern antiwar and anti-Republican newspapers ridiculed and critiqued the military's so-called exploitation of black labor and the eventual enlisting of black men. Prior to the formation of the U.S.C.T. in 1863, northern politicians and military leaders confronted a substantial contingent of black men and women enthusiastically seeking to support the Union cause. Free black men in the North eagerly volunteered as soldiers at the outset of the contest but were initially turned away; others signed on as laborers, wagon drivers, and cooks.[21] Black women joined hospital staffs as laundresses and nurses.[22] Even after the Union army formed colored regiments, black soldiers received less pay than white soldiers until 1864.[23] Accusations of exploitation were not completely unfounded. However, comic portrayals of black soldiers primarily attempted to neutralize the threat of armed black men governmentally sanctioned to commit violence against white men.

Two images published in the North in 1861 exemplify a popular view of the Union army's early employment of runaway slaves as wrong-headed and ludicrous exploitation little better than enslavement. An envelope published in Philadelphia features a slight Union soldier perching on the shoulders of a large black man and looking through a spyglass.[24] Titled

"Taking an Observation from a Dark Point," the illustration portrays one possible use for former slaves in the Union army—a position not far removed from their previous condition as chattel. Beneath the image are the words of the "Negro": "Dis child is a real Union niggar, and no mistake." Taking the place of a horse, the black man is proud of his new career in the military and his affiliation with the Union cause. The illustration mocks his pride and ridicules the notion that former slaves could function as anything more than mindless props. A political cartoon published in *Frank Leslie's Illustrated News* similarly reduces black bodies to the level of inanimate objects with an ostensibly comic suggestion for making "the contrabands useful" (fig. 14).[25] Grinning contrabands with cannons strapped to their backs happily serve in the "dark artillery," blissfully ignorant of their highly dangerous position. Unlike the white soldiers, the new recruits are barefoot and wear ragged makeshift uniforms instead of Union blue; the army, the cartoon implies, has as little respect or regard for the well-being of black men as southern plantation owners.

FIG. 14 "Dark Artillery; or, How to Make the Contrabands Useful."
Frank Leslie's Illustrated News 12, no. 309 (October 26, 1861): 368.
Library of Congress Prints and Photographs Division, LC-USZ62-98516.

Despite the absurdity of the images, both (perhaps unintentionally) communicate the vigorous enthusiasm of former slaves for the Union cause; neither illustration questions their dedication or willingness to help defeat the Confederacy. A cartoon published in the *Southern Illustrated News,* however, portrays a former slave as unfit for service and uninterested in the contest. Labeled "An Illustration of the New Yankee Doctrine About the Darkey," the cartoon portrays a "corporal" from a Massachusetts regiment stereotypically named Cuffee "advancing rapidly to the rear during an engagement." Responding to a white officer who attempts to stop his retreat, Cuffee says, "No, sah! can't go back dar—dis chile too *'motional* for dat sorter thing."[26] Both subject to unmanly emotions and fleeing from the battlefield, Cuffee is inherently unsuited to the soldiering life. The wide-eyed and "'motional" Cuffee lacks the courage to fight and, like the former slave on the envelope, is a "chile" instead of a man. You can take the slave from the plantation, the cartoon implies, but you can't take the plantation from the slave. Initially employed as laborers, black soldiers had to prove that their bodies were good for more than digging trenches and burying white soldiers.[27]

The Person of the Poor Fugitive

In each of the above images, white soldiers control black soldiers, attempting to mold unruly, childlike former slaves into serviceable objects or cannon fodder; if the enlistment of black men is to be successful, the images imply, white men must exert force. Texts and illustrations depicting the process by which slaves became soldiers and thus men rejected this premise and provided alternative and empowering versions of African American military service. Moving from cotton fields to battlefields, black men underwent a significant physical transformation that had symbolic and political ramifications. As Union blue covered scarred backs and slaves became soldiers, the popular press disseminated a reconfigured version of black manhood. Two former slaves became soldiers on the pages of *Harper's Weekly,* their federal uniforms marking them as men. *Harper's Weekly* presented to its substantial readership the process by which slaves became men and in doing so advocated a revised way of reading black bodies as powerful and redemptive instead of subjugated and objectified.

Of the two soldiers, "Gordon" is by far the most famous; the image of his scarred back was widely distributed during the war as proof of the brutality of the peculiar institution, and a number of scholars have examined the implications of this distribution.[28] On July 4, 1863, the paper published "three portraits, from photographs by McPherson and Oliver, of the negro GORDON, who escaped from his master in Mississippi, and came into our lines at Baton Rouge" (fig. 15).[29] The provenance of the photographs and the identity of "Gordon" are uncertain and difficult to verify; the meaning and message of the triptych have also proved difficult to pin down, if the scholarly debate regarding the image is any indication. The first portrait depicts Gordon "as he entered our lines," dressed in ragged clothes and barefoot but facing forward with the confidence of a man who was a scout for Union troops, was beaten by Confederates and

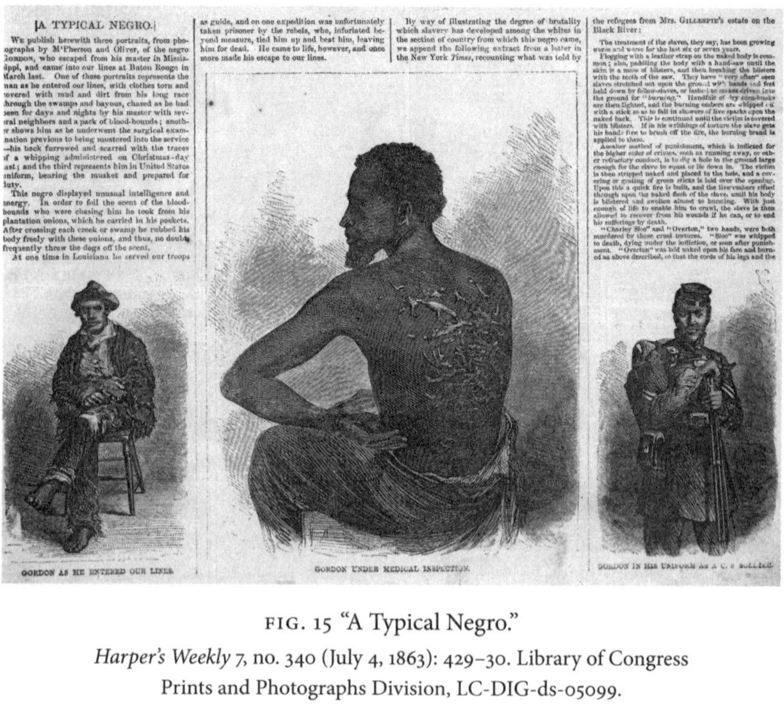

[A TYPICAL NEGRO.]

We publish herewith three portraits, from photographs by M'Pherson and Oliver, of the negro Gordon, who escaped from his master in Mississippi, and came into our lines at Baton Rouge in March last. One of these portraits represents the man as he entered our lines, with clothes torn and covered with mud and dirt from his long race through the swamps and bayous, chased as he had been for days and nights by his master with several neighbors and a pack of blood-hounds; another shows him as he underwent the surgical examination previous to being mustered into the service—his back furrowed and scarred with the traces of a whipping administered on Christmas-day last; and the third represents him in United States uniform, bearing the musket and prepared for duty.

This negro displayed unusual intelligence and energy. In order to foil the scent of the blood-hounds who were chasing him he took from his plantation onions, which he carried in his pockets. After crossing each creek or swamp he rubbed his body freely with these onions, and thus, no doubt, frequently threw the dogs off the scent.

At one time in Louisiana he served our troops as guide, and on one expedition was unfortunately taken prisoner by the rebels, who, infuriated beyond measure, tied him up and beat him, leaving him for dead. He came to life, however, and once more made his escape to our lines.

By way of illustrating the degree of brutality which slavery has developed among the whites in the section of country from which this negro came, we append the following extract from a letter in the New York *Times*, recounting what was told by the refugees from Mrs. Gillespie's estate on the Black River:

The treatment of the slaves, they say, has been growing worse and worse for the last six or seven years.

Flogging with a leather strap on the naked body is common; also, paddling the body with a hand-saw until the skin is a mass of blisters, and then breaking the blisters with the teeth of the saw. They have "very often" seen slaves stretched out upon the ground with hands and feet held down by fellow-slaves, or lashed to stakes driven into the ground for "*burning*." Handfuls of dry corn-husks are then lighted, and the burning embers are whipped off with a stick so as to fall in showers of live sparks upon the naked back. This is continued until the victim is covered with blisters. If in his writhings of torture the slave gets his hands free to brush off the fire, the burning brand is applied to them.

Another method of punishment, which is inflicted for the higher order of crimes, such as running away, or other refractory conduct, is to dig a hole in the ground large enough for the slave to squat or lie down in. The victim is then stripped naked and placed in the hole, and a covering or grating of green sticks is laid over the opening. Upon this a quick fire is built, and the live embers sifted through upon the naked flesh of the slave, until his body is blistered and swollen almost to bursting. With just enough of life to enable him to crawl, the slave is then allowed to recover from his wounds if he can, or to end his sufferings by death.

"Charley Sloo" and "Overton," two hands, were both murdered by these cruel tortures. "Sloo" was whipped to death, dying under the infliction, or soon after punishment. "Overton" was laid naked upon his face and burned as above described, so that the cords of his legs and the

GORDON AS HE ENTERED OUR LINES.

GORDON UNDER MEDICAL INSPECTION.

GORDON IN HIS UNIFORM AS A U. S. SOLDIER.

FIG. 15 "A Typical Negro."

Harper's Weekly 7, no. 340 (July 4, 1863): 429–30. Library of Congress Prints and Photographs Division, LC-DIG-ds-05099.

left for dead, and "came to life." The central and largest portrait shows "Gordon under medical inspection," his back bared to his waist. His face turned to the side and his gaze averted, Gordon resembles antebellum illustrations of specimens of slavery's brutality. The copy accompanying the image notes that Gordon's back is "furrowed and scarred with the traces of a whipping administered on Christmas-day last." If, as David Silkenat contends, the engravings depict different men and the article is a "partially invented narrative," then the rhetorical work of the triptych supersedes journalistic objectivity.[30]

Gordon's suffering corresponds with Christ's birthday, despite previously published accounts placing the whipping in October, and his story appears on the anniversary of the republic's birth.[31] Though the article labels his condition "typical" in keeping with the widespread brutality of the peculiar institution, Gordon's "unusual intelligence and energy" and his miraculous resurrection and journey call into question the article's title and the underlying assumption that slaves are scarred backs and nothing more. The third image further undercuts the assumptions inherent in the title, as Gordon dons a uniform and is "bearing a musket and prepared for duty"; he faces the viewer with the same steady gaze he displayed in the first image, proud of his status as a "U.S. soldier."

The layout and size of the images, with Gordon's scarred back the focal point, have led some scholars to read the illustrations as limiting Gordon's ability, mobility, and identity. Marcus Woods reads Gordon as "a patient of the North" who must be "sanitized," Jennifer James contends that the images underline the necessity of rehabilitating inherently disabled black bodies, and Carole Emberton claims that the triptych "offered reassurances" to white readers "that black men would make obedient soldiers whose violence could be controlled and channeled to appropriate ends."[32] Alice Fahs and Jennifer Putzi both argue that the centrality of Gordon's back closes off the possibility of the transformation ostensibly promised by the engravings.[33] However, the editors of *Harper's Weekly* may have purposefully enlarged the central image in order to clarify a complex web of scars. More importantly, the layout, in setting each illustration in chronological order, foregrounds Gordon's difficult journey and his eventual transformation. By the time Gordon posed for a photographer, his back was disfigured but healed; clearly, his scars did not prevent him from passing the medical inspection. His is not a physical transformation from infirmity to able-bodiedness, but a rhetorically constructed process by which a slave becomes a fighting man. Gordon's back may initially draw the eye, but the layout culminates with Gordon in uniform. Covered by Union blue, Gordon's back will be subjected to a new type of violence. This violence transforms slaves into men and scars into signs of citizenship. The triptych and the uniform do not obscure Gordon's blackness or erase his past as a slave, nor do the scars on his back forever mark him as a slave and not a man; instead, the scars emphasize the necessity of defeating "the whites in the section of country from which this negro came," and Gordon's transformation proclaims the crucial role black men will play in that defeat.[34]

Published in *Harper's Weekly* one year later, two illustrations—"The Escaped Slave" and "The Escaped Slave in the Union Army"—visualize another man's progress from slave to soldier as a linear progression; it is absolutely necessary to read these images alongside the triptych featuring Gordon (figs. 16 and 17).[35] Unlike the images of Gordon, the two portraits of the unnamed "escaped slave" are equal in size, and the orientation of the images is top-down rather than left to right. In the top image, the man sits in ragged clothes that resemble Gordon's; in the bottom image, the former slave sports a jauntily tipped hat, a federal uniform, and a confident grin. In both engravings, the slave-turned-soldier faces the viewer and demands recognition. The accompanying article, entitled "The Escaped Slave and the Union Soldier," would at first glance seem to advertise a story involving a white Union soldier and an escaped slave; however, as the illustrations and the article make clear, the titular figures are one and the same. Like Gordon, the man, "who fled from Montgomery, Alabama, to Chattanooga, for the express purpose of enlisting in the army of the Union," represents more than just his own transformation from slave to soldier. "Can we not," the article accompanying the images asks, "have faith in that heroism which has been so gloriously illustrated at Wagner and Olustee and Petersburg, and which, in the face of the Fort Pillow massacre, yet offers itself afresh in the person of a poor fugitive, who, from the heart of the enemy's country, gives himself, at the risk of death

FIG. 16 “The Escaped Slave.”
Harper’s Weekly 8, no. 392 (July 2, 1864): 428. Image courtesy of the House Divided Project at Dickinson College.

FIG. 17 “The Escaped Slave in the Union Army.”
Harper’s Weekly 8, no. 392 (July 2, 1864): 428. Image courtesy of the House Divided Project at Dickinson College.

or of a torture worse than death, to a cause simply because it is inevitably associated with the problem of his freedom?"

The "person" of the fugitive is transformed when "endowed for the first time with his birth-right of freedom, and allowed the privilege dearer to him than any other—that of fighting for the nation which is hereafter pledged to protect him and his." As Fahs notes, the text "represent[s] an imaginative shift from aligning African Americans primarily with slavery to aligning blacks primarily with black manhood and membership in the nation."[36] More so than the article accompanying the image, the visual "person," or physical form, of the unnamed fugitive slave embodies hope and "faith" for a fundamental transformation in American society and culture: the welcoming of a fugitive race into the national family and the transformation of slaves into citizens and men.

Though the nation's pledge would prove empty, the two images exemplify a transformation or conversion central to depictions of black soldiers during the Civil War. "Oppressed with . . . weariness" in the first engraving, "this same negro" is "crowned with freedom and honor" in the second. Both Gordon and the unnamed "escaped slave" present a new version of African American manhood: the black soldier who dedicates his body to his country, to freedom, and to the redemption of his race. Making visible the metamorphosis of slaves into men and citizens, the illustrations encourage a predominantly white audience to transform—to learn how to trace in the scarred backs and uniformed bodies of former slaves the path by which slaves become countrymen and citizens. Images likes the ones published in *Harper's Weekly* and prose and verse describing the heroic service of black soldiers and the bodily and political ramifications of that service enact a new form of training for white audiences, one that counteracts the antebellum training Jennifer Putzi describes.[37] This training continues in poetic tributes to the heroism and sacrifice of black soldiers.

Must They Die as Slaves?

Hundreds of poems designate the battlefield as the testing ground for black masculinity, franchise, and citizenship. Central to many of these poems are the bodies of black soldiers, dressed in Union blue and marked by war. These poems place African American soldiers' bodies at the forefront of wartime debates over black citizenship and manhood. Significantly, the soldiers retain their blackness; poems addressing primarily white audiences outline a revised hermeneutics of race—one that does not require deracialization or the removal of all traces of bondage. As such, a significant subset of Civil War literature insists not just on the symbolic power of bones and blood but also on the revolutionary potential of blue uniforms on black skin.

A letter accompanying a poem published in the *Liberator* on February 5, 1864, asks the editor, William Lloyd Garrison, to "give publicity" to the "spontaneous gushing of a black girl's soul, who has felt the influence of slavery and the blighting breath of prejudice too long to keep silent."[38] The product of this gushing, "The Black Heroes," poses a question ubiquitous in contemporary debates about enlisting black soldiers. Inspired by the famous charge of the Massachusetts Fifty-Fourth Regiment at Fort Wagner, the young poet asks, "O, must they calmly die at last, / Those heroes black and brave, / With prejudice still clinging fast— / O, must they die as slaves?" Numerous poems answered with a resounding "no." Looking to the future, the poem ends with a final question: "And must such noble deeds / Our fetters stronger bind, / Or shall they to fair Freedom lead, / And make us *all* mankind?"[39] The rhetorical questions call on the primarily white and northern audience of Garrison's "far-famed paper" to answer with words and deeds that will ensure the legacy and political efficacy of black military service.

Laura Redden Searing also addresses a white audience in her poem "Butler's Black Brigade."[40] The "black brigade" earns not whiteness but manhood and citizenship. By continually referring to the soldiers' "dusky skin" and blackness, the poem proffers a revised understanding of black manhood that does not require transcendence of embodied blackness. Searing systematically brings up and then dismisses doubts about the suitability of "branded men" for soldiering, vehemently accusing and indicting a doubting "you" of reading black skin as evidence of "pale" blood and inferiority. "You," she proclaims, "have crushed them long / They've forgotten the way to turn! / They have brains, and yet they remember not; / And hearts, but they never burn!" Slavery, and not innate racial inferiority, is responsible for the purported weaknesses of black men.

Possessed of the same organs and faculties as white men, black men retain their humanity despite centuries of bondage. This humanity was betrayed, the speaker implies, "last July." Searing's footnote identifies the event as the New York draft riots in July 1863.[41] "They had done no wrong," the speaker asserts, "but their skins were black, / 'T was fitting that they should die!" With biting irony, Searing rejects the victimization of black men, women, and children during the riots as proof of the inability of black men to be soldiers. The men who reportedly "cowered" in July "stand to-day / As stanchly as fairer men." Courage, she implies, is not exclusive to men with white skin. Righteously indignant, the speaker apostrophizes: "Oh, ye will not take in a kindly clasp, / The hand that is darker than yours! / . . . Oh, shame for your senseless and narrow creed! / And shame for your savage hate!" Searing's angry rhetoric urges a rejection of a bigoted creed that marks black minds and bodies; a new creed and a new form of reading blackness (not removing it) is required.

The final stanza of Searing's poem centers on the titular general, identifying Benjamin Butler as the herald of black equality. Butler, "the grim old man," the speaker asserts, "will tell you another tale." Both famous and infamous for his occupation of New Orleans and his decree that slaves were contraband of war, Butler was the first Union general to enlist African American soldiers—despite his initial doubts regarding their potential as soldiers.[42] Butler's "tale" warns of retribution for Fort Pillow, the "St. Bartholomew" of black Americans. On April 12, 1864, 1,800 Confederate cavalry under the leadership of Nathan Bedford Forrest, who would later found the Ku Klux Klan, launched a final assault on Fort Pillow. Of the 600 federal troops garrisoning the fort, 280 were killed. Newspapers reported on the barbarity of the Confederate troops who targeted white officers of black regiments and killed surrendering Union soldiers.[43] Equating murdered black soldiers with massacred French Huguenots, Searing asserts the humanity of the black race and the historical significance of African American participation in the war. "Perhaps," the speaker concludes, "when they hallow this common cause / With their thousands of nameless graves, / Your selfish hearts will proclaim at last, / They are men, and they are not slaves!" Though dead, the soldiers live on in memory; their sacrifice immortalizes them and influences the present and the future of their race in the United States. By arguing that the "nameless graves" must be recognized by white Americans, Searing centers the redemption of a race in the bodies of its soldiers.

By Their Blood, That Land Was Bought

Searing contends that black soldiers "hallow this common cause" of saving the Union and freeing the slaves. Their blood, invoked in poems and articles about the U.S.C.T., rhetorically sanctifies a new birth of freedom. Countless poems published during the war describe blood-soaked battlefields, rivers dyed red, and lifeblood seeping from wounded soldiers. A common trope in Civil War literature, blood connects soldiers through a shared humanity: Union or Confederate, black or white, all combatants bleed. The transformative power of shedding blood was immortalized by Shakespeare's Henry V: "For he to-day that sheds his blood with me / Shall be my brother; be he ne'er so vile, / This day shall gentle his condition."[44] Shedding blood for a common cause, Hal claims, makes men equal with kings and transforms strangers into brothers. Shedding blood for the Union and freedom, a number of texts argue, makes slaves into men and men into citizens. While the rhetoric of white souls in black bodies necessitates a transcendence of skin color, red blood flowing from the veins of black soldiers and white soldiers alike allows for an embodied rejection of racial inferiority. Blood and bones synecdochically represent the contributions of black men and their earned membership in the brotherhood of man.

Addressing a meeting of "colored citizens" in Boston in 1863, a man identified as "Judge Russell" echoes the promises of St. Crispin's Day in urging his audience to form a regiment. Russell insists on the symbolic, political, and cultural significance of shedding blood: "[T]he day that dawns upon a great battle-field in which your blood is mingled with that of other regiments, fighting side by side with you, that same day will see every prejudice against your race washed out and obliterated."[45] Though reality would fall far short of Russell's soaring vision, a significant corpus of texts imagines an almost millennial reconfiguration of American society resulting from black blood mingling with white on the "great battlefield." In death, slaves turned soldiers are free. Their blood "gentle[s] [the] condition" of their people, promising freedom for those who live on.

This reconfiguration, however, does not require the erasure of blackness. While black soldiers and white soldiers alike bleed, the rhetorical significance of their bleeding differs. Indeed, black soldier bodies bleeding evoke what Scarry terms "different political beliefs."[46] Poems about black regiments and black soldiers ground calls for recognition and respect in the blood *and* dark-skinned bodies of its soldiers. "The Heroic Black" is one such poem. Published in the *Liberator* in March 1864, it immortalizes "a colored soldier in Tennessee."[47] According to an explanatory epigraph, the "mortally wounded" soldier "told his officer that he could not live, but would die fighting for the flag of liberty; and continued to discharge his rifle until he fell dead on the field of glory." Written in ballad stanzas and set to the tune of "Auld Lang Syne," the poem self-consciously inserts the heroic figure of an anonymous black soldier into the history of the war and the heroic tradition of patriotic sacrifice. Like many poems about dying white soldiers, "The Heroic Black" stages an apotheosis of the "brave and loyal heart."

The first stanza describes the soldier's plight, beginning with the battle's effect on his body. "The ball ha[s] crush'd a vital part," but the brave young man continues to fight "till his life-blood cease[s] to flow." The second stanza perpetuates the poem's focus on the soldier's form, noting that "his skin was of the ebon hue," but also asserting "his heart was nobly brave." The blackness of the soldier's skin is not incompatible with his trueness to "country, flag, and freedom." Though the poem uses language common to many elegies written about heroic white soldiers, the soldier is not whitewashed in death—he is both "ebon" and "brave" and is predominantly defined by his refusal to "live a slave." The fifth and final stanza underscores the symbolic power of the soldier's corpse: "Though low in earth the martyr lies, / Still rings his battle-cry— / From hill to hill the echo flies—'Fight on for liberty!'" A martyr for freedom, the dying, dead, and buried body of the black soldier is a rallying site for the continued "righteous cause." Marked by the violence of war and not by the cruelty of slavery, the soldier's body is powerful in life *and* death.

Similarly written in ballad stanzas and published in the *Colored American* in December of 1865, Sarah E. Shuften's "Ethiopia's Dead" celebrates and memorializes the black soldiers "who have fallen in the great struggle for liberty and independence."[48] Shuften, the wife of the editor of *Colored American,* the first African American newspaper in Georgia, illustrates the ubiquity of black bodies and their symbolic significance in the recently ended conflict.[49] Shuften mimics hundreds of poems eulogizing white soldiers and, in doing so, insists on the rightful place of black soldiers in the literary history of war's destruction. The first three stanzas describe the corporeal cost of the fighting: "brave Ethiopia's dead" remain "on hills, in vallies [*sic*]" and "on every field of strife, made red / With gorey [*sic*] victory." Though "their bones bleach on the Southr'n hill," the soldiers retain their blackness and their affiliation with Ethiopia, a personification of African heritage. Despite this association, the soldiers are loyal sons of Columbia and saviors of the Union: "The land is holy where they fought, / And holy where they fell; / For by their blood, that land was bought / That land they loved so well." Shuften makes liberal use of anastrophe, an etymological "turning back" to the black bodies of "Ethiopia's dead," one that precludes any symbolic bleaching of their souls.

Not only do black soldiers redeem their race, but they are also the "saviors of the land" of their birth and bondage, their blood freeing them and cleansing the nation's sin. Shifting from the landscape of death to the geography of history, Shuften's speaker proclaims the global and historical significance of "that valiant band": "From east to west, from hill to vale, / Then be their names adored— / Europe, with all thy millions, hail! / The Peace bought by their sword." The people of Europe, "Asia, and Africa" will no longer be called on to pity the plight of the powerless slave; rather, they shall "celebrate in varied tongues / Our *free* and happy land." Globally and locally, Shuften promises, black soldiers usher in a new day in which "man shall meet in every face, / *A brother and a friend.*"

One of Ethiopia's sons, Thomas B. Wester, orderly sergeant for Company I, Forty-Third United States Colored Infantry, employs a similar synecdoche by which black corporeal sacrifice, measured in bones and blood, secures equality. In a letter written in December 1864 and printed in the *Christian Recorder,* a Philadelphia-based African American newspaper, Wester ridicules Confederate attempts to enlist slaves.[50] In spite of rebel lies, Wester notes, "Some of them are now in our army, fighting side-by-side with the white men." Wester bases his demand for equal rights on the physical proof of military service: "The bones of the black man are at the present time whitening the battle-fields, while their blood simultaneously with the white man's oozes into the soil of his former home." The bones of black and white soldiers are equally white and equally dedicated to the Union cause. Because black men have offered up their bodies to the United States, Wester "hope[s] that the day is not far distant when we shall see the colored man enjoying the same rights and privileges as those of the white man of this country."

Wester's insistence on the whiteness of black soldiers' bones at first seems like an invocation of deracialization; however, Wester hopes for a future in which the "*colored* man" is equal to the white man and bases this hope on the deaths and wounds of men whose brothers will participate fully in the society created by the war. Men who bleed together, implies Wester, should vote together. William H. Watson, a free black man who served as a sergeant in Company K, Twenty-Fifth U.S.C.T., also predicts a new dawn of equality purchased by the deaths of black soldiers.[51] Encountering slaves for the first time, Watson reports in his letter to the *Christian Recorder* that "they have frequently shown [him] the deep marks of the cruel whip upon their backs." Watson listens as "the old mothers . . . tell how they have been treated" and grounds his resolve to not "go home until every slave in the South is set free" in the backs *and* voices of black men and women. "There is a day coming," he promises, "when there will be no such thing known as lashing the colored man till the blood runs down his back in streams."

This blood, Watson implies, will be washed away by the blood of black and white soldiers. "Come with me, ye victims of prejudice," he intones, "where the grave of the white and the black soldier lie side by side, and tell me which is the colored man and which is the white, and which of the two you would rather be? Would you base your answer upon color?" Watson's invocation of two indistinguishable graves resembles Scarry's claim about wounded Confederate and Union soldiers. However, for Watson, graves covered over with grass and not whitewashed bodies evince the common brotherhood of black and white men. Death, as ever, is the great equalizer; death on behalf of the Union, both Wester and Watson argue, should be the greatest equalizer in American history.

Side by Side

Like Wester and Watson, members of the U.S.C.T. regularly contributed to African American periodicals, thus adding their voices to debates about the aptitude and ability of black men, and asserting their perspectives on the rhetorical implications of their service.[52] In his study of epistolary culture in black regiments, Christopher Hager argues that "black soldiers' acts of writing did more than the personal and practical work of epistolary communication; they also did the conceptual and political work of shaping African American civic identity."[53] As Jim Cullen notes, the writings of black soldiers reveal "the widely shared sense that the Civil War did indeed mark a watershed for black manhood."[54] Published in the *Christian Recorder* on April 15, 1865, the day the great emancipator passed into eternity, a letter written by William Waters, Company K, Twenty-Sixth United States Colored Troops, speaks to the high stakes of African American participation in the Union army. Referencing a ubiquitous query of the early years of the war, Waters writes, "We have often heard it said, that the negro would not fight,—would not stand fire,—was only intended to stand behind the white man's chair."[55] "I deny the assertion," Waters affirms, adding, "Has not the negro proved to be a true soldier? Has he not done the task assigned him? Who won the battles of Port Hudson, Miliken's Bend, and Olustee? Was it not the negro? Yes, my fellow countrymen, the negro will fight. It has been proved. I defy either whites or blacks, to deny it." Waters's rhetorical questions inexorably lead to one answer: the "negro" will fight, and soldiers like Waters will claim their rights as "countrymen." The list of battles, including Fort Wagner, Port Hudson, Miliken's Bend, and Olustee, became a litany repeated in many celebrations of the United States Colored Troops.

White soldiers fought in the same battles, and many of them recognized that a war for the Union was a war against slavery; moreover, the experience of fighting alongside the U.C.S.T. often proved conducive to shifting opinions about emancipation and black franchise and citizenship.[56] A letter written by "A Colored Private" of the renowned Fifty-Fourth Massachusetts Regiment attests to a spectrum of white soldiers' opinions on the issues of emancipation and equality. Addressing William

Lloyd Garrison, the famous abolitionist and editor of the *Liberator,* the enlisted man writes,

> I thought you might be pleased to know that your principles were strongly represented in the department that loaded the 100-pounder gun that threw the first three shells at Charleston city, S.C. No. 1 is a strong abolitionist and has worked well among the soldiers. . . . No. 2 is now in favor of emancipation, though he don't think the negro is his equal. No. 3 was an old emancipationist years ago, always took your paper. And the gunner is a Republican. The other members seem to go with the strongest party, but believe in extirpating slavery from the land at the present time.[57]

In the crucible of war, as white men and black men fight and die together, strongly held convictions and prejudices waver. Writers depicting this fighting and dying hope for similar results; the onus is on readers to recognize that black men have redeemed their race and earned the blessings of liberty.

In 1867, William Wells Brown, the African American author of *Clotel; or, The President's Daughter,* published a chronicle of the military service of black men in previous American military actions and, most significantly, the recent conflict. In order to preserve the social and political shifts that occurred on the battlefield, Brown's *The Negro in the American Rebellion: His Heroism and His Fidelity* provides an exhaustive account of the arming of black men and the battles in which black soldiers participated. Brown's account ends with a resolution written at the end of the war by the white officers of the Sixth Regiment U.S.C.T.:

> 1. *Resolved,* That, in our intercourse with them during the past two years, they have shown themselves to be brave, reliable, and efficient as soldiers; patient to endure, and prompt to execute.
> 2. That, being satisfied with their conduct in the high position of soldiers of the United States, we see no reason why they should not be fully recognized as equals, honorable and responsible citizens of the same.[58]

For these officers, the calculus of the war is clear: military service should secure manhood and citizenship for black men.

The changing views of another white soldier, Captain Charles A. Edmonds of Company H, Seventeenth Regiment Michigan Volunteers, reflect both recognition of black people's entitlement to citizenship and resistance to their full participation in American political structures. In a poem written for a left-handed penmanship contest held by William Oland Bourne, Edmonds narrates his personal experiences with black soldiers and his views on the significance of black military service.[59] After sending an initial version to the contest judges in September 1865, Edmonds sent a second version in December, noting, "I think it would be a good plan to destroy my first specimen."[60] Though Edmonds claims the first version is faulty because of mistakes, the most significant difference between the two poems is his discussion of African American suffrage.

Using the racist language of the time, Edmonds describes "Nigger Sambo's" transition from slave to freeman to soldier. Edmonds concludes with a diagnosis of the current political problem:

> Now the question "What of Sambo?"
> Echoes to us; from our Statesmen:
> Some are saying "Let us make him / Equal to the Whites in voting."
> Some say, "No, our country never / Was intended for the Nigger:"
> Still they clamor for the Rebels,
> And they say they are entitled
> To their rights within the Union,
> For it is the "Constitution."

In answering this question, Edmonds draws on his experience as a soldier:

> I have been a Union Solider;
> Fighting, side by side with Sambo;
> We have fought the "*Rebs*" together;
> I for Country, he, for freedom;
> Fighting to maintain the Union
> Rebels fighting to destroy it.

Now, the Rebels they are conquered,
And, the time of "Reconstruction"
Has arrived, when we must settle
What the *status* of the Rebel
What the status of poor Sambo.
I'm in favor, now of giving
Hemp to all the leading Rebels,
Freedom and the *right* of *Voting*,

To the true "American citizens of African descent," who have nobly dared, so freely bled to aid the Union cause, and to secure the *blessings* of *liberty* to themselves and to posterity forever.

In September 1865, Edmonds breaks the sometimes halting meter of his verse to assert his belief that African Americans, having bled for their country, are entitled to the rights of citizenship. Having lost his right arm in the conflict, Edmonds bases his argument on the corporeal cost of war and the importance of rewarding loyalty and punishing treason.

Two months later, Edmonds focuses on the rights of the "Rebs" and removes all traces of black suffrage and rights. "I'm in favor, now of giving," Edmonds concludes, "Freedom and the right of voting, / In the South, to all the loyal / Who can read the Constitution / And can write as good as I can!!" In its second iteration, Edmonds's poem implicitly excludes former slaves from the vote, foreshadowing the literacy tests purposely intended to keep African Americans from voting. It is unclear why Edmonds changed his tune so rapidly and dramatically. Perhaps, as he became more removed from his experiences "fighting, side by side," with black soldiers, Edmonds became less concerned with the fate of African Americans and more concerned with the reconciliation of North and South. Whatever the cause, Edmonds's changing opinions indicate the forces in American politics and culture that would enable the failure of Reconstruction and a narrative of sectional reconciliation predicated on mutual whiteness at the expense of black Americans.

* * *

Das Schwarze Regiment

Even as the Thirteenth, Fourteenth, and Fifteenth amendments failed to secure basic rights for African Americans and the nation moved toward the nadir of race relations, the bodily sacrifice and exemplary service of black soldiers during the Civil War retained some of their symbolic and rhetorical power. According to John A. Casey Jr., "black men who had served in the northern army rapidly faded from public consciousness" in the 1880s and 1890s, due in large part to efforts by African American writers to distance black men from violence.[61] However, the publication history and lasting popularity of George Henry Boker's "The Second Louisiana" reveal a significant counter-narrative to the alleged whitewashing tendencies of postwar literature and culture. Regularly reprinted, the poem became a kind of shorthand for reminding readers of the U.S.C.T.'s contributions and the precedent those contributions set for future considerations of black manhood, citizenship, and military capacity. Though the afterlives of "The Second Louisiana" involve continuing discrimination against African American men in the military, they also disclose the consistent recirculation of the heroic and deserving black soldier body.

On June 27, 1863, *Frank Leslie's Illustrated News* printed on its first page an account of the Second Louisiana United States Colored Troop's actions at the battle of Port Hudson. The siege of Port Hudson in late May 1863 included a frontal attack by the first black regiments to engage in a military assault.[62] Though unsuccessful, this assault, according to the article, proved the dedication and bravery of black soldiers. The article begins with "the question of whether negro soldiers will fight if properly led" and provides an answer by quoting General Nathaniel Banks's description of the regiments' performance: "They answered every expectation. Their conduct was heroic. No troops could be more determined or more daring." Banks notes that the regiments "suffer[ed] very heavy losses" and provides his endorsement for the continued use of black troops: "Whatever doubt may have existed heretofore as to the efficiency of organizations of this character, the history of this day proves conclusively to those who were in condition to observe the conduct of these regiments, that the Government will find in this class of troops effective supporters and defenders. The severe test to which they were subjected and the determined manner with which they encountered the enemy leave upon my mind no doubt of their ultimate success."[63]

Banks's affirmation of black soldiers based on their dedication and heroism is somewhat tempered by his insistence that "they require only good officers, commands of limited numbers, and careful discipline to make them excellent soldiers." Black men can fight, but they must be painstakingly shaped and disciplined; this caveat represents for some scholars a major limiting factor for the symbolic efficacy of African American military service, though white soldiers also required training and discipline.[64] Banks, and the military as a whole, barred black officers from the ranks of commissioned officers, believing that the only "good" officers were white officers.[65]

Nevertheless, Banks's report appears in the publication that only two years prior printed *Dark Artillery; or, How to Make the Contrabands Useful* (see fig. 14 above); an illustration of the assault, also published in the June 27 issue of *Frank Leslie's Illustrated News,* stands in stark contrast to the earlier image (fig. 18).[66] Battlefield heroics, complete with waving flags, hand-to-hand combat, and a gallant attack on the entrenched "rebel works," have replaced stereotypically grinning and ineffectual contraband cannon fodder. The "special artist" renders the assault from the perspective of the rearguard, a vantage point that positions the viewer as part the regiment's forward movement. A poem lauding the Louisiana Second continues the illustration's rhetorical work.

George Henry Boker's "The Second Louisiana," published beneath General Banks's report, portrays the assault on Port Hudson as not only the first trying of black men as soldiers but also the test of the black race's claims to freedom.[67] A Philadelphian poet and dramatist who served as secretary and later president of the Philadelphia Union League, Boker eulogizes the black regiment, aligning African American troops with the cause of freedom and manhood.[68] Central to his paean to the black regiment is the transformation of the slave body into the soldier body. As Daniel Hack notes, Boker repurposes the meter of Tennyson's "Charge of the Light Brigade," thus inserting the black regiment into the literary pantheon of heroic sacrifice.[69] Indeed, the poem was also published under

FIG. 18 "Assault of the Second Louisiana (Colored Regiment) on the Rebel Works at Port Hudson, May 27."
Frank Leslie's Illustrated News 16, no. 404 (June 27, 1863): 216–17.
Library of Congress Prints and Photographs Division, LC-USZ62-133081.

the title "Charge of the Black Brigade."[70] Written in dactylic dimeter that mimics the rhythmic beating of drums, the poem was disseminated in broadside form in English and German. Translated as *Das Zweite Louisiana Regiment,* the German version celebrates "das schwarze regiment" (the black regiment) and exemplifies one major role of poems documenting the service of black troops.[71] The dissemination, which continued into the twentieth century, of Boker's poem involved the circulation, to black and white audiences, of a new version of black manhood, one that insisted on freedom and citizenship on the basis of blood spilled and lives and bodies dedicated to the Union.

Boker's poem begins with a tableau of soldiers "dark as the clouds of even, / Ranked in the western heaven." Like a "dread mass" of storm clouds, the soldiers await "the breath that lifts . . . / Tempest and falling brand / Over a ruined land." Likening the soldiers to a storm of vengeance overtaking the South, Boker emphasizes the momentousness of the assault and inserts dark-skinned soldiers into the epic narrative of the war. Facing the oncoming storm, the soldiers are "so still and orderly, / Arm to arm, knee to knee." At the end of the first stanza, Tennyson's "Into the valley of death / Rode the six hundred" becomes "Waiting the great event / Stands the black regiment." Each subsequent stanza ends with a variation on the refrain, the last three words always "the black regiment."

Though the soldiers carry the same "bright bayonet[s]" as white soldiers, Boker reiterates their blackness; soldiering, the poem suggests, does not extirpate racial difference, but instead removes the stigma of servitude and powerlessness from black male bodies. The second stanza contains an ostensibly problematic vision: "down the long dusky line / Teeth gleam and eyeballs shine." Though the description resembles stereotypical images of harmless slaves with wide eyes and white teeth, the poem soon transfers its focus to the "bright bayonet . . . [that] flashe[s] with a purpose grand"; it is this purpose that transforms slaves into men.

Marked by their "dusky" skin, the black soldiers wait for the drum to tell them "their time [has] come" and "what work [is] meant / For the black regiment." At the beginning of the third stanza, the flag-sergeant defines this "work":

> Though wounds or death betide,
> Let the whole nation see
> If we are fit to be
> Free in this land; or bound
> Down, like the whining hound—
> Bound with red stripes of pain
> In our old chains again!

The marks of war are far preferable to the marks of servitude; the black soldiers expose their bodies to wounds and death so that the bodies of their people will no longer be subjected to enslavement. The fourth and fifth stanzas, set apart by their length (sixteen and eighteen lines, respectively, as opposed to the ten lines of the other stanzas), describe the charge and its results and underscore the symbolic significance of the assault. "The bondmen" driving "their lords like chaff" harvest the deaths of their former masters as "down they tear man and horse." Triumphant in the fourth stanza, the soldiers fall heroically in the fifth, "glad to breathe one free breath, / Though on the lips of death." Beginning with, "'Freedom!' their battle-cry," the fifth stanza aligns the black regiment with the cause of saving the Union, famously celebrated in the song "The Battle Cry of Freedom."

However, the speaker also explains that "they meant the word, / Not as with us is heard." As a white man addressing white readers, the speaker explains that, for black soldiers, freedom is not "a mere party-shout." "On the gory sod, / Rolled in triumphant blood," the black soldiers embody the cause of freedom; as they "fall" they experience a "burst to liberty." In this formulation, the bodies of black soldiers take on greater symbolic meaning than the bodies of white soldiers. While white soldiers fight for the Union, black soldiers fight for the Union and their freedom.

As the poem ends, so too does the transformation of the black soldiers. "Hundreds on hundreds fell," the speaker intones, "But they are resting well; / Scourges and shackles strong / Never shall do them wrong." In death, the black regiment is free; the bodies resting beneath the ground have purchased liberty and the end of slavery. Though members of the black regiment fall and achieve liberty in death, Boker does not foreclose the possibility of liberty in life. Instead, his poem imagines glory for the black regiment that extends beyond death and has bearing on the ongoing lives of African Americans in a world shaped by war. In life, the black regiment should be "hail[ed] as comrades tried." *Das Zweite Louisiana Regiment* advises its audience, which most likely included the large number of Germans and German Americans in Union blue, to "Räpft mit ihm Seit' bei Seit'!" "Fight with them, side by side," the English version concludes, "Never, in fields or tents, / Scorn the black regiments!" As "the black regiment" becomes "the black regiments," Boker makes the heroism of the Second Louisiana emblematic of the U.S.C.T.'s potential and, perhaps more importantly, urges continued coexistence and cooperation; white and black men who fight "Seit' bei Seit'" will one day live "side by side."

Boker's forward-looking language is in keeping with the longevity of the poem's popularity in spite of reconciliationist imperatives and the advent of Jim Crow. The poem even appears to have outlived Boker's popularity; in 1901, the *Chicago Daily Tribune,* primarily discussing his dramatic work, noted that "his writings now are hard to find."[72] Nevertheless, "The Second Louisiana" appeared under different titles in various publications during and after the war, and accounts of African American military achievements consistently deployed the final lines.[73] An 1864 broadside celebrating emancipation in Maryland incorporates the lines "never in field of tent scorn a black regiment"; the words float below "GOD SAVE THE REPUBLIC" and above a battle scene (fig. 19).[74] The poem appears in full on the verso page as "The Black Regiment," a title adopted by most future publications, alongside Bible verses, Andrew Johnson's "speech to the colored people of Nashville," and antislavery statements from John Quincy Adams and Robert Jefferson Breckinridge.[75] As "The Second Louisiana" became "The Black Regiment," and as the nation moved toward and then into the twentieth century, Boker's laudatory verses emerged as the quintessential literary testament to black heroism.

When Henry P. Cheatham, a former slave and member of the House of Representatives from North Carolina, addressed an audience in Raleigh on the thirty-fifth anniversary of the Emancipation Proclamation, January 1, 1898, he invoked the rhetorical power of Boker's poem and the legacy of black military service in order to contextualize the contemporary situation of African Americans and prepare for future struggles.[76] "When war swept across the face of the nation," Cheatham intoned, "the poor, patient and humble slave, on the sea and on the land, fought to uphold the flag of the Union and 189,000 black soldiers in more than 214 active engagements won our freedom on the field of battle." Without introduction or attribution, Cheatham recited the last ten lines of "The Second Louisiana"; presumably, many people in the audience were familiar with the oft-reprinted and alluded-to lines.

This lack of citation continued in subsequent publications, indicating the poem's persistent popularity. In 1900, the *Colored American* reported that Sergeant W. H. Carney, formerly of the Fifty-Fourth Massachusetts, had finally received a Medal of Honor for his acts of "personal valor" during the assault on Fort Wagner, South Carolina, the most celebrated military action involving the U.S.C.T. (and the climax of the 1989 film *Glory*).[77] Carney and sixteen "living and dead heroes," the article continues, were honored at the "Negro exhibit at the Paris Exposition"; as a result of lobbying on Carney's behalf, the secretary of war rectified the War Department's initial "oversight." The *Colored American* reports that "at all subsequent encampments, re-unions and other official functions, the bronze star with its broad striped ribbon will be conspicuous on the broad chest of the brave hero." The alliterative chain of phrases highlights

FIG. 19 *In Commemoration of Emancipation in Maryland, November 1, 1864* (detail).
Philadelphia: Ringwalt & Brown, ca. 1864. Gilder Lehrman Collection, GLC05701.

Carney's continued physicality—his "broad chest," bearing the "bronze star," carries the legacy of the heroic actions of the U.S.C.T. into a new century. After recounting the daring deeds of Carney and another member of the Fifty-Fourth, the article concludes with the (slightly modified) last three lines of "The Second Louisiana": "Hail them as heroes tried, / Never in field or tent, / Scorn the Black Regiment." Thirty-seven years after Carney "seized the colors and dashed forward into the face of the storm," Boker's poem retains its rhetorical power, as do the tried and true bodies of "the long, dusky line."

In later years and disparate engagements, "The Second Louisiana" appeared as proof positive of black military heroism; the lines called for recognition of past service and justification for fair treatment of contemporary black soldiers. In 1906, an editorial from the *New York Sun*, reprinted in the *Washington Post* and *Sedalia Weekly Conservator*, a Missourian African American publication, responded to President Theodore Roosevelt's racially motivated decision to dishonorably discharge 167 black soldiers from the Twenty-Fifth U.S. Infantry allegedly involved in the so-called "Brownsville Raid" on August 13, 1906.[78] The regiment, recently returned from the Philippines, was garrisoned in Brownsville, Texas, which proved to be a hostile environment. An alleged attack of a white woman led to an enforced curfew. At midnight on August 13, a bartender was shot and a police officer maimed; white locals blamed black soldiers. The soldiers insisted on their innocence and were accused of conspiracy.[79] The editorial calls for recognition of "another Negro regiment," the Twenty-Fourth U.S. Infantry, whose "display of a higher order of valor" during and after the battle of San Juan Hill (July 1, 1898), contributed to Roosevelt's success.[80] "At a time when a battalion of Negro troops may be sacrificed by a scratch of the pen for the sin of not turning informers," the editorial avers, "it is a duty to resurrect from forgotten records such a story as that of the heroic 24th Infantry." Black soldiers "have distinguished themselves on every field, from Port Hudson to Santiago, justifying the invocation of George H. Baker [*sic*]: 'Hail them as comrades tried; / Fight with them side by side; / Never, in field or tent, / Scorn the black regiment.'" The timeline and legacy are clear: though Boker initially celebrated the Second Louisiana's actions at Port Hudson, his lines came to stand in for a litany of battles and hundreds of individual regiments.

Their cultural and rhetorical cachet even remained intact at the end of World War I. The *New York Herald* printed "The Black Regiment" in recognition of the return of the 369th Infantry Regiment, more popularly known as the "Harlem Hellfighters."[81] The *Kansas City Sun* reprinted the poem from the *Boston Post,* noting that "General Pershing's high praise of the gallantry of colored soldiers now wearing the United States uniform in France recalls the heroic devotion of colored regiments in the Civil War."[82] The *Crisis,* the mouthpiece of the NAACP, noting the publication of "George Henry Boker's 'Black Regiment'" in the *Herald,* also reprinted a segment of the poem, and linked the impressive record of the 369th, which fought with the French Army, to the heroism of the black regiments across multiple conflicts: "No matter where they fought—they fought, and as colored troops of the United States have always fought, 'nobly.' Fort Wagner and Kettle Hill and northern Mexico knew the record of their gallantry. And now Europe knows it."[83]

The Harlem Hellfighters returned home to a country that made them second-class citizens; neither their service nor the service of their nineteenth-century counterparts secured immediate equality for black people. Nevertheless, the consistent deployment of Boker's poem—even in the midst of lynch law, segregation, and disenfranchisement—ensured the survival of a significant counter-narrative. Civil War–era print culture disseminated a reconfigured version of black manhood; today, it is an archive that illuminates the persistent rhetorical significance of black military service and the centrality of black soldiers' bodies to the literature of and the political debates surrounding the conflict. As the pages of African American periodicals in particular make clear, many black men fervently hoped that their time in the Union army—wearing "the brass letters, U.S."—would secure their freedom and citizenship.[84] Like the amputee veterans discussed in the next chapter, they used the written word to reimagine their postwar lives and based their claims to recognition and respect on bodily sacrifice.

CHAPTER THREE

The Left-Armed Corps

In 1864, recuperating Union soldier F. L. Mahan scrawled his name, regiment, and hometown in large, sloppy letters on the page of a reminiscence book (fig. 20). Beneath his entry, another, steadier hand wrote, "The above was written with the left hand. Mr. Mahan lost his right arm in the battle of Resaca, Ga. 15th May, 1864, under Genl Hooker—W.O.B."[1] A year later, "W.O.B." (William Oland Bourne), most likely inspired by his interactions with one-armed veterans like Mahan, held the first of two left-handed penmanship contests. Bourne, a hospital volunteer and newspaper editor, called on men who lost their right arms while fighting for the Union to submit "specimens" of their best left-handed "business" writing in the form of personal statements.[2] Quite a few of the contestants sent verse as well, using the flexible yet structured genre to poetically present their reconfigured bodies and newfound social positions to the public and to posterity.[3] Bourne hoped to publish a "memorial volume, containing the sketches, tales, poems, and war narratives of the Left-Armed Corps," proclaiming that the manuscript would be "one of the best literary contributions to the history of the war, as well as the memorial of an entirely new feature in literature—the united production of several hundred left-armed veterans of the battle-field."[4] Though the volume was never published, Bourne was right—the writings of the self-proclaimed "Left-Arm" veterans deserve canonical status and enable "entirely new" ways of understanding how Americans responded to and interpreted the Civil War.

Asked to record their memories of the conflict, hundreds of soldiers sent in "specimens" of their best penmanship. Because of its scientific

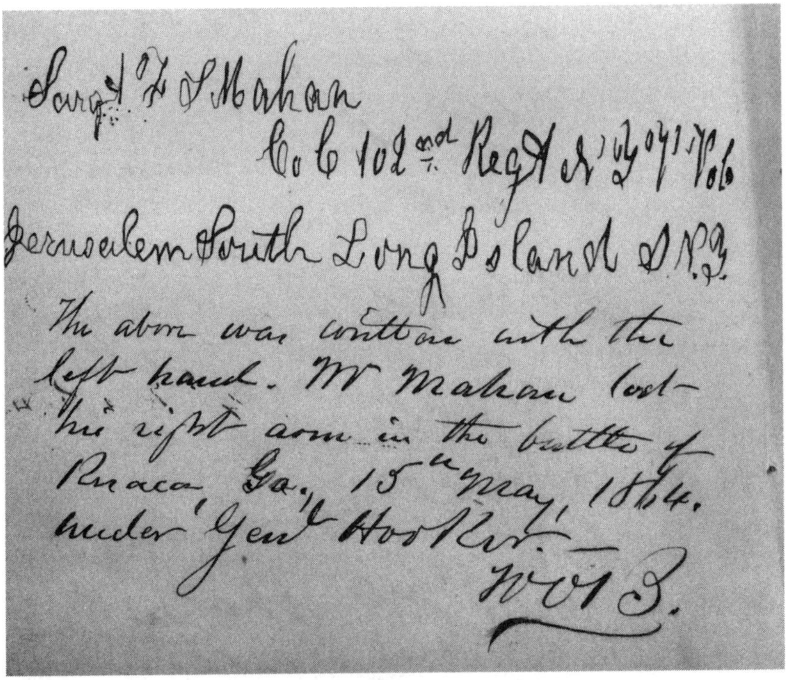

Sergt. F. S. Mahan
Co. C 102nd Regt. N. Y. V. Vols
Jerusalem South Long Island S.N.Y.

The above was written with the left hand. Mr Mahan lost his right arm in the battle of Resaca, Ga., 15th May, 1864. under Genl Hooker. —
W.O.B.

FIG. 20 Civil War reminiscences by soldiers and sailors in Central Park Hospital, New York City.
William Oland Bourne Papers, Manuscript Division, Library of Congress.

connotations, the word "specimen" indicates the inextricable relationship of the veterans' penmanship to their physical experiences of the war; derived from the Latin *specere*, to look at, "specimen" also marks the slanted handwriting as evidence to be examined.[5] The scrutinizing stare of the contest judges and the public, documented in the lists of contest winners and in broadside and newspaper descriptions and advertisements, attempted to make the fragmented bodies of amputees "useful" and framed the penmanship specimens as proof that left-armed men could successfully reintegrate into American society and the increasingly industrial workforce.[6] Though Bourne's contests attempted to normalize the amputees by reinscribing them as economically viable citizens, they also provided an opportunity for amputees to construct their own identities by narrativizing their experiences as soldiers and maimed men. As Frances M. Clarke notes, many contestants "embraced the only chance they might ever have to explain the nature of their service and the meaning of their injuries in a public setting."[7] In his study of the contest, Brian Matthew Jordan argues that "these men sought to make sense of the war indelibly inscribed on their bodies" by creating narratives.[8] Navigating competing imperatives of self-expression, national recovery, and silence, many of them presented their newly abled left arms as proof of their resilience as well as the difficulties of adjustment. Many of the amputees mourned their loss but also recognized the significance of their sacrifice—they saved the Union and freed the slaves and they were proud of it; however, their faith in the cause was small comfort for personal pain or the difficulty they had putting themselves back together in a society that labeled them crippled and incomplete.

Bourne, referring to the "collection of Left-Hand Papers" produced by the contests, deemed it "the first and only collection of this kind"; I follow his lead in declaring the writings "worthy of preservation as one of the peculiar illustrations of our great conflict."[9] Moreover, these sinister manuscripts and wounded writers demand a fundamental revision of how we think about Civil War literature and the assumptions we make about Civil War writers. Some scholars have been too quick to follow Whitman's prophecy that "the real war will never get in the books."[10] Daniel Aaron holds that "America's cultural guardians" kept "the territory of the common soldier" out of books; Timothy Sweet finds in the poet's avowal the foundation of Whitman's reliance on typification, while Franny Nudelman and James Dawes describe strategies of abstraction and purposeful silence in the face of mimetic difficulties.[11] If the predominant critical consensus is to be believed, most literary accounts of the war elided mass suffering with unstinting patriotism and willful forgetting in the interest of reconciliation and reunification; this is true too of scholarly considerations of Bourne's contests. According to Clarke, entrants strove to "fashion themselves as exemplary sufferers" in order to "incorporat[e] bodily loss into a sense of civic and masculine identity," while Benjamin Cooper claims that the contest worked to "undo the trauma of the past."[12] However, a rhetorical approach to the contest entries and close attention to the ways in which the veterans engaged literary tropes to represent their bodies reveals a counterpoint to critical accounts of patriotic forgetting.

Though Whitman recognized the difficulties of textualizing the "interior history" of the war and of documenting its effects, he provided a possible solution by focusing primarily on the somatic aspects of soldiering: "the actual soldier of 1862–'65, North and South, with all his ways, his incredible dauntlessness, habits, practices, tastes, language, his fierce friendship, his appetite, rankness, his superb strength and animality, lawless gait, and a hundred unnamed lights and shades of camp, I say, will never be written—perhaps must not and should not be."[13] Whitman failed to heed his own warning ("perhaps must not and should not be"), making his pronouncement only *after* he had given readers more than "a few stray glimpses into that life, and into those lurid interiors."[14] I propose that Whitman's prediction, given his close focus on bodies, referred primarily to the *corporeal* war—the "animality" and "rankness" of physical forms inextricably tied to the souls of the soldiers he loved. Well aware of the difficulties of representation, Whitman implied that those who lived through the conflict should still *try* to account for the "minutiae of deeds and passions" for posterity, and that the body is a good place to start. After all, Whitman collected his observations in "lurid and blood-smutched little notebooks."[15] Out of the scribblings, he claims, "arise active and breathing forms," reminders of the broken, wounded, and dying human bodies Whitman included so often in his poetry.[16]

Despite his mimetic misgivings, Whitman proclaimed that "the hospital part of the drama from '61 to '65, deserves indeed to be recorded."[17] Bourne's veterans were uniquely qualified to do so. The "actual soldier[s]" of the Left-Armed Corps submitted their bodies to public scrutiny, relying on their ability to textualize their lived experiences. Though their stories never "g[o]t in the books" in the format Bourne initially envisioned, they persist to this day as testaments to the (to repurpose Russ Castronovo's term) "recalcitrant materialities" of individual soldiers' lives.[18] Despite Edmund Wilson's pronouncement to the contrary, not all gore is patriotic; the proof lies in a vast archive of periodical literature and first-person accounts of soldiering, wounding, and amputation.[19] These left-handed papers suggest that pride and grief are not mutually exclusive and that heroic sacrifices are not always made willingly. Amputated limbs cannot be reconciled, reunited, or normalized—they haunt Bourne's collection, stark revenants of the most destructive war ever fought on American soil.

Left-armed veterans single-handedly wrote the "real war" by submitting accounts of its violence and utter destructiveness and were able to do so because of the persistence and adaptability of the historically denigrated left arm. Though empty sleeves dominated the pages of newspapers and popular periodicals, members of the Left-Armed Corps poeticized their maimed right arms and their remaining appendages. The result is a literary record that emphasizes pain and corporeal degradation while simultaneously reimagining embodied masculinity and able-bodiedness. Three interconnected literary subjects and often contradictory cultural signifiers are central to this record: the empty sleeve, the amputated right arm, and the adaptive left arm.

The "empty sleeve" is both category and cultural signifier; often, it speaks of loss on behalf of a group of mostly silent veterans. In its synecdochical relationship to the preserved Union and its incorporeality, a limp piece of cloth sanitizes the story of disfigurement. As such, a disembodied empty sleeve is fitter for mass consumption than a shattered right arm or weak left limb. Empty sleeves blur the boundary between object and subject; they are close to the body but not of the body, mute but extremely fluent and communicative, indicative of absence but present all the same. As Brian Matthew Jordan asserts, "unlike the endless rows of mute, white headstones, [empty sleeves] could speak and be heard."[20] They speak on behalf of silenced soldiers, calling for pity instead of requiring a direct confrontation with the lasting effects of violence.[21] Amputated right arms, however, tell a longer story. While sleeves are mass-produced and similar in appearance, wounds and amputation stumps are unique to the individual. The rules of Bourne's contests required that amputees identify the battles in which they lost their arms, and many of them went beyond simple identification to describe in graphic detail their wounds and amputations.

It should come as no surprise that a number of contestants chose to tell their stories of loss through verse. Even a desultory survey of Civil War print culture shows that, for amateur and professional authors alike, poetry constituted the primary means of responding to the bloodshed. By making their ragged stumps into poetic subjects, veterans engaged in this widespread literary response; more interestingly, they employed, to use Bourne's language, a "peculiar" form of apostrophe in which the etymologically required "turn away" is purposefully incomplete as still-healing and painful stumps exist simultaneously with absent and intact former limbs.[22] The mangled right arm or stump that embodies concerns about masculinity, economic viability, and potency also serves as an unsanitized and irreducible counterpart to the empty sleeve.

Amputation stumps and clumsy left hands are much more prevalent in the contest entries than artificial limbs. Rather than advocating proficiency and a return to wholeness through the use of prosthetic right arms, the contest focused instead on the capacity of the neglected and maligned left arm. Central to the poetic project of re-membering fragmented bodies was the ability of the left arm to replace the right, an eventuality promised by Bourne's contests but complicated by individual accounts and visible evidence (in the form of surprisingly elegant or understandably sloppy left-handwriting specimens) of the difficulties of adaptation and recovery. The left arm, then, signifies both the hope for and the potential failure of rehabilitation, and offers insight into nineteenth-century discourses of bodily difference. Instead of letting their sleeves speak for them, the Left-Armed Corps purposefully participated in a collective act of testifying to both national trauma and individual experience.[23] In the face of representational difficulties and physical hindrances, amputees refused to become objects of pity and invested their left arms and missing or maimed right arms with significant symbolic power.[24]

Empty Sleeves that Speak

In poetry and prose, writers in the popular press focused on the empty sleeves of silent veterans. One month before the 1868 presidential election, William Oland Bourne's newspaper, the *Soldier's Friend,* printed an article titled "Empty Sleeves" that acts as an interpretive guide for postwar readers.[25] "In our streets," the article begins,

> in our offices, on our farms, everywhere we meet "empty sleeves"; sleeves the wind blows against broken ribs, whips about crippled bodies; sleeves whose emptiness tells of arms blown off in battle; of

> arms lost in strife for the life of a nation; of arms shattered with flag in hand. Empty sleeves that speak more eloquently than tongue or type of patriotism, of courage, of faith in the right, of hope in Justice; empty sleeves that tell of honor upheld, of a nation saved, of homes defended, of valor, of daring.

"Empty sleeves" becomes a category that subsumes other, more specific corporeal configurations: men with empty pant legs, soldiers retaining limbs but crippled for life, and veterans bearing scars. As poetic objects, the sleeves tell what the amputees cannot. In this way, the dominant discourse of empty sleeves created a subversive opportunity to turn pitiful absence into the speaking presence of right stumps and functional left hands.

According to the *Medical and Surgical History of the War of the Rebellion,* the Union army reported 16,147 amputations involving parts or all of the arm and 13,833 amputations of any part of the legs.[26] Empty sleeves were slightly more common than empty pant legs and, as the *Soldier's Friend* article makes evident, more symbolically significant.[27] They "speak," "proclaim," and "tell," "rebuk[ing] those who did their utmost to make Slavery national and Freedom sectional." The "wearers" of empty sleeves are "living reminders of Libby, of Andersonville, and those other hells in which Union soldiers who fought for the old flag of Liberty against the rebel flag of Slavery were tortured." In this construction, objectified veterans become "wearers" and "reminders" instead of reliable subjects who can tell their own stories, while sleeves are uniform repositories of patriotic memory.

David Barker's poem "The Empty Sleeve" and the illustrations it inspired reveal the cultural cachet of the titular item and the process by which it elides amputees' individual stories and voices. The poem, which appeared in *Frank Leslie's Illustrated News* in 1863 and features a generic and tellingly silent "one-arm man," insists on the significant communicative power of a veteran's empty sleeve.[28] However, it simultaneously obscures the amputee's identity and undermines the sleeve's ability to act as an objective correlative aligned with the emotional experience of war. Barker's speaker begins with a simple request of the "gazing throng" that ostensibly gazes at a "one-arm man" standing in the "moon's pale light."

The speaker, newly enlightened, tells the crowd, "Till this very hour I could ne'er believe / What a tell-tale thing is an empty sleeve, / What a weird, queer thing is an empty sleeve." Slightly modified versions of these lines repeat at the end of each stanza, creating a refrain that registers the transformative effects of the war (a sleeve is now "a tell-tale thing") but also disassociates "a weird, queer thing" from the lived and embodied experience of the "one-arm man." Structurally, the poem foregrounds absence by manipulating traditional heroic couplets. The first two seven-line stanzas of trochaic pentameter end with a rhyming triplet; there is no eighth line to complete the series of rhyming couplets, just as the "one-arm man" at the center of the poem is incomplete. His incompleteness draws the eyes of onlookers who attempt to interpret the marked body of the silent soldier. Despite the speaker's denial of intention, the poem unequivocally links the empty sleeve with Union victory and delimits the symbolic significance of the empty sleeve.

Though Barker claims that his is a "tale devoid of an aim or plan," his insistence on what the sleeve "tells" and lack of emphasis on the interiority and individuality of the veteran lionize the fabric and silence the one-armed man. Tellingly, the speaker (and writer) of the poem is an observer who, unlike the members of the Left-Armed Corps, speaks outside the experience of wounding and amputation. The sleeve, not the veteran, "tells in a silent tone to all" a generic story of a soldier departing the domestic space to answer the "country's call." The family scene gives way to what else the sleeve "tells":

> It tells of a battle-field of gore,
> Of the sabre's clash, of the cannon's roar;
> Of the deadly charge, of the bugle's note,
> Of a gurgling sound in a foeman's throat;
> Of the whizzing grape, of the fiery shell,
> Of a scene which mimics the scenes of hell.

The empty sleeve invokes both the dystopic hellscape of the battlefield and the survival and return home of the "one-arm man," promising eventual victory and reintegration. In the final stanza, the poem rhetorically moves away from the horror of grape and shell, underscoring the sleeve's patriotic importance: "Though it points to a myriad wounds and scars, / Yet it tells that a flag with stripes and stars / In God's own chosen time will take / Each place of the rag with the rattlesnake; / And it points to a time when the flag shall wave / O'er a land where breathes no cowering slave." Calling on the "throng" to "heave / One proud huzza for the empty sleeve, / For the one-arm man and the empty sleeve," Barker's poem illustrates the ability of the empty sleeve to absorb the stark reality of war's destruction in the interest of collective recovery. "One proud huzza" drowns out and replaces the sounds of battle and the identity of the "one-arm man."

The small illustration accompanying "The Empty Sleeve" in *Frank Leslie's Illustrated News* displays a smaller "gazing throng" comprised of two children in conversation with an older veteran who bears an empty sleeve on his left side and carries a walking stick in his right hand. Sitting on the side of the road, his uniform frayed, the one-armed man confronts the curious children and seems to speak to them. The illustrated soldier differs from his silent poetic counterpart. J. C. Buttre's engraving of the same name, however, features a silent one-armed veteran sitting with a cherubic child in his lap (fig. 21).[29] The child examines the veteran's empty right sleeve and attempts to look into it while the veteran stares stonily into the distance with downcast eyes. When William Oland Bourne's *Soldier's Friend* reprinted Barker's poem in 1867, text preceding it reminded the readers of "the charming steel engraving by J. C. Buttre, from the original drawing by Miss A. R. Sawyer."[30] "The author of the following poem," the copy reads, "has given a beautiful tribute to 'The Empty Sleeve,' worthy of its place at the side of the portrait." The *Soldier's Friend* implies that the engraving inspired the poem; however, a description of the image and how it "will send a thrill through many loyal and loving hearts, and . . . find a place in many homes" in the *Ladies' Repository* clarifies that the engraving was first printed in 1866.[31] Editorial confusion aside, the poem and the illustrations work in tandem to circumscribe the signifying power of amputees' bodies and commoditize a sanitized and suitable-for-children version of bodily loss. The description of Buttre's engraving in the *Ladies' Repository* surmises that the soldier is "thinking of the solemn Past when he contended for the Right on the battle-fields

FIG. 21 John C. Buttre, *The Empty Sleeve* (Boston: N. Y. & B. B. Russell & Co., 1866). DeGolyer Library, Southern Methodist University, Central University Libraries, Civil War: Photographs, Manuscripts, and Imprints.

of Freedom" while the child asks why the sleeve is empty. The veteran "thinks" but remains silent, an empty sleeve covering over the stump of his arm—a right lost "for the Right."

A postcard printed in the 1870s resembles the earlier engraving; this time, however, an actual armless veteran, Henry H. Meacham, author of *The Empty Sleeve: Or the Life and Hardships of Henry H. Meacham in the Union Army,* holds a child in his lap (fig. 22).[32] As in the engraving, the curly haired child examines the empty right sleeve while the veteran looks into the distance instead of at the child, his sleeve, or the camera; unlike the engraved soldier, however, Meacham appears stoic rather than forlorn, the edges of his mouth turned up and his brow unfurrowed. Via the subtitle of his autobiography, Meacham personalizes the categorizing label applied to his portrait and his postwar body, thus blurring the line

G. P. Critcherson, *The Empty Sleeve* (ca. 1870).
DeGolyer Library, Southern Methodist University, Central University Libraries, Civil War: Photographs, Manuscripts, and Imprints.

between subject and object. In all three images, inquisitive children encounter remnants of violence and attempt to understand them; they rely in part (as in the illustration accompanying the poem in *Frank Leslie's*) or completely on the communicative power of the empty sleeve rather than the veteran himself. Childish innocence confronts the stark evidence of war, looking for an arm that will never return. It is the empty sleeve and not the mangled stump or the veteran himself who must explain the loss to the child.

Buttre's engraving in turn inspired "The Empty Sleeve," a song published in 1866 that similarly celebrates the Union's victory by identifying what the sleeve "tells."[33] An explanatory note accompanying the song describes the engraving, noting that "the little fellow" on the soldier's lap "with natural curiosity and childish inquiry takes 'the empty sleeve' and looks wonderingly for the lost arm." While the child looks for the arm, the song focuses on the sleeve; the child, the song promises, will soon learn to invest the sleeve with meaning instead of focusing on the arm. The veteran's account of his experience is secondary to a piece of fabric—the sleeve speaks for itself. When his father and the empty sleeve are gone, the son "shall tell how bravely fought / His sire on Freedom's side." The song teaches the generations who did not fight how to maintain the rhetorical power of the empty sleeve and remember and pass on the meaning of the war.

Written to be sung in harmony, the song encourages the dissemination of this meaning; those who sing the chorus will, like the child, learn that "that empty sleeve, it is a badge / Of bravery and honor; / It whispers of the dear old flag, / And tells who sav'd our banner." Lest the absent appendage be forgotten, the chorus continues: "Three hearty cheers for those who lost / An arm in Freedom's fray, / And bear about an empty sleeve, / But a patriot's heart today." Significantly, the crowd sings while "those who lost / An arm" remain silent. The sleeve communicates absence and presence, the loss of an appendage but the winning of a war. "The strife for freedom is gone by; The war-cry sounds no more," the song begins, "But the heroes come with empty sleeves / From out the battle's roar." As the sounds of battle fade away, a silent host of survivors marches home, their empty sleeves fluently "whisper[ing]" and "tell[ing]" observers that the returning veterans have lost their arms, but retained their patriotic hearts.

Together, the poem, song, and associated images illuminate the cultural cachet of empty sleeves; "queer" and "tell-tale," empty sleeves cover over pain in the interest of sanitizing the evidence of violence and reintegrating ragged stumps (and the experiences of the veterans who bear them) into a collective narrative of recovery. Colleen Glenney Boggs contends that empty sleeves necessitate the "proliferating limbs" of others to supplant it; literary attempts to provide substitutes for missing limbs perpetuate the violence of war and transfer disability to the general

Honor to the Brave!

TO THE LEFT-ARMED CORPS OF THE UNION.

Five Hundred Dollars in Premiums for Penmanship!

Office of The Soldier's Friend,
No. 12 Centre Street, N. Y.

The editor of "**THE SOLDIER'S FRIEND**," in compliance with urgent requests from members of the Left-Armed Corps, hereby announces that he will distribute a **SECOND** series of prizes, amounting to **FIVE HUNDRED DOLLARS** in premiums for the ten best specimens of **LEFT-HAND PENMANSHIP**, by soldiers and sailors of the Union who lost their **RIGHT ARMS** by disability or amputation in the late war for the Union.

There will be ten equal prizes of **FIFTY DOLLARS** each, the award of the prizes to be made by distinguished officers of the Army and Navy, who will furnish Autograph Letters to the successful competitors.

Each premium will bear the name of the officer making the award, and will be known as follows:

THE GRANT PREMIUM,
THE FARRAGUT PREMIUM,
THE SHERMAN PREMIUM,
THE SHERIDAN PREMIUM,
THE HOWARD PREMIUM,
THE MEADE PREMIUM,
THE HANCOCK PREMIUM,
THE HOOKER PREMIUM,
THE GEARY PREMIUM,
THE LOGAN PREMIUM.

The manuscripts will be sent to the Editor of "**THE SOLDIER'S FRIEND**," to be registered, numbered, and prepared for inspection, and when so prepared the awards will be made.

DIRECTIONS.

☞ *Writers are requested to pay particular attention to the following Directions:*

The writers must furnish a sketch of their military history, from the date of their enlistment to their discharge, including company, regiment, rank, a list of battles, date and place where wounded, etc.

Original essays, poems, tales, incidents and anecdotes of the war may be added, and are earnestly desired.

The paper must be wide-ruled white letter paper, and ☞ ***to be of the same size as this Circular,*** and leaving an inch margin at the top, bottom, and sides.

The sheets must not be gummed or fastened together, but correctly numbered at the top.

Write on only one side of the paper.

Write in black ink. Pencil writing will not be admitted on the catalogue.

There must be *at least* two pages, but writers are *not limited* in the length of their contributions.

No one is entitled to compete who can use his right arm, or who had learned to write with his *left hand* PREVIOUS *to the date of his wound.* Those *only* are entitled who have learned to write **SINCE** the date of their disability in the service.

A proper affidavit must be made to the facts, to prevent imposition and injustice.

Photographs are requested in every case where it is practicable to furnish one.

Writers are SPECIALLY CAUTIONED against sending manuscripts or correspondence to the Headquarters of any of the officers who are to award the prizes, as it will not serve their purposes in the least, and will only make unnecessary expense and delay. *All manuscripts must be sent to the office of The Soldier's Friend, to be registered and classified.*

☞ None of those who drew prizes on the first competition will be entitled to compete for the present prizes. But they are invited to contribute new specimens to the collection.

Manuscripts should be sent wrapped around a wooden roller, or in a pasteboard or card cylinder, to preserve them in the best order. They should be rolled *lengthwise*, and not across the page.

The lists will remain open to competition till the *first day of JULY next.*

The manuscripts are to be collected in permanent form for preservation, and to remain in the possession of the editor of THE SOLDIER'S FRIEND for publication.

Circulars will be sent on application.

Address

WM. OLAND BOURNE,
Editor of The Soldier's Friend,
No. 12 Centre Street, N. Y.

FIG. 23 Handbill advertising Bourne's contest.
William Oland Bourne Papers, Manuscript Division, Library of Congress.

"civilian population."[34] However, looking at the ways in which disabled contest entrants constructed their subjectivity and politicized their bodies by elegizing their absent right arms and investing their remaining left arms with discursive power excavates a form of substitution that is self-contained, incomplete and, quite often, imperfect. The empty sleeve represents a potentially silencing cultural construct that members of the Left-Armed Corps confronted and answered by narrating their experiences and poeticizing their missing limbs and their left arms—writing with their remaining hands of what lies beneath the empty sleeve.

A United Production

On July 29, 1865, the *New York Times* ran an article titled "Left-Handed Penmanship" that announced a contest intended to furnish "fresh pleasure or benefit for the soldiers." William Oland Bourne, the article informs the reader,

> now offers premiums amounting to five hundred dollars for the four best specimens of penmanship by "left-armed soldiers of the Union." Any man who has lost his right arm in the service may compete. He may write an original or selected article upon a patriotic theme, and he must write not less than two nor more than seven pages. . . . The writer must also give his name in full; his regiment, company, and rank; the list of battles in which he was engaged; the place where he lost his arm, and his post-office address.[35]

The committee in charge of reading the submissions and awarding prizes included William Cullen Bryant, poet and president of the Sanitary Commission, and Theodore Roosevelt Sr. One hundred thirteen veterans sent submissions to the second competition, and ten received fifty-dollar premiums and autographed letters from celebrated Union officers such as Ulysses S. Grant, David Farragut, and Philip Sheridan.[36] Broadsides and invitations, some bearing slogans like "Disabled, But Not Disheartened!" and "The Left Arm Corps again in the Field!" (figs. 23 and 24) advertised the contest and announced the "Grand Exhibition of Left-Hand Penman-

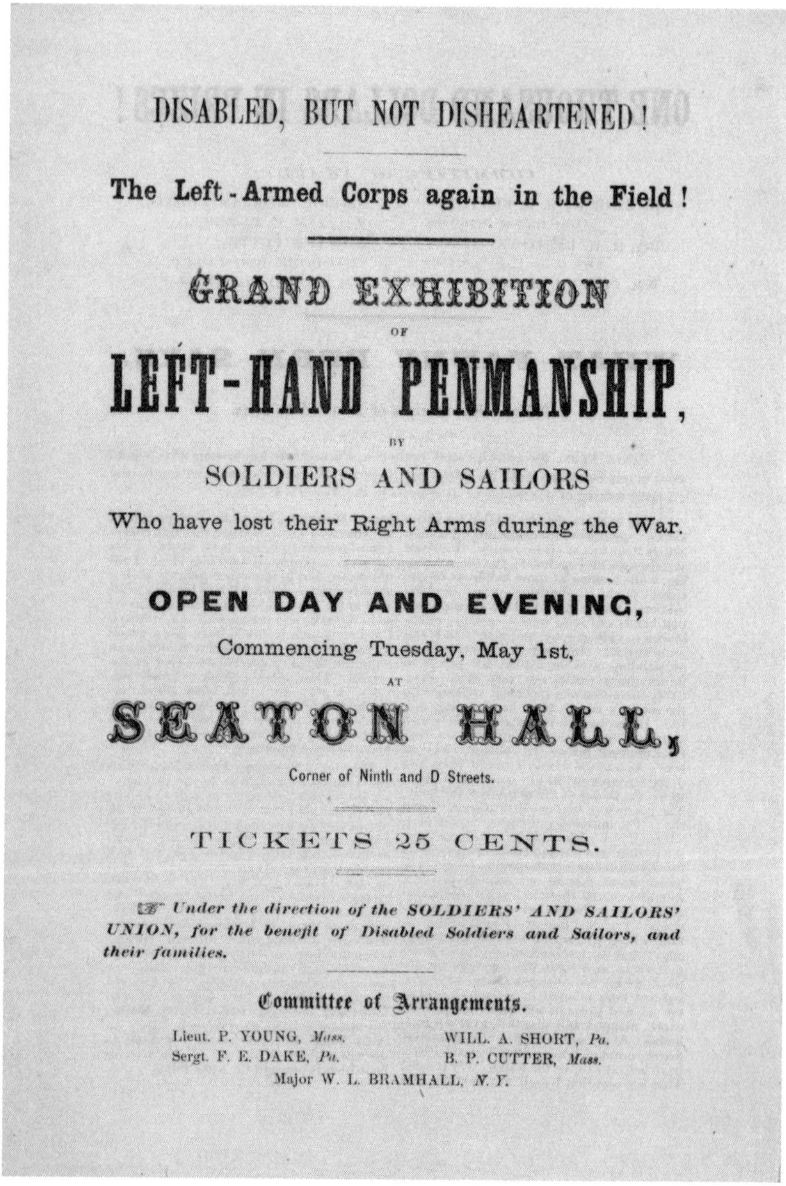

DISABLED, BUT NOT DISHEARTENED!

The Left-Armed Corps again in the Field!

GRAND EXHIBITION

OF

LEFT-HAND PENMANSHIP,

BY

SOLDIERS AND SAILORS

Who have lost their Right Arms during the War.

OPEN DAY AND EVENING,

Commencing Tuesday, May 1st,

AT

SEATON HALL,

Corner of Ninth and D Streets.

TICKETS 25 CENTS.

☞ *Under the direction of the SOLDIERS' AND SAILORS' UNION, for the benefit of Disabled Soldiers and Sailors, and their families.*

Committee of Arrangements.

Lieut. P. YOUNG, *Mass.*	WILL. A. SHORT, *Pa.*
Sergt. F. E. DAKE, *Pa.*	B. P. CUTTER, *Mass.*

Major W. L. BRAMHALL, *N. Y.*

FIG. 24 Handbill advertising exhibition of left-handed penmanship. William Oland Bourne Papers, Manuscript Division, Library of Congress.

ship, by Soldiers and Sailors Who Have Lost their Right Arms during the War," an event organized by the Soldiers' and Sailors' Union and held at Seaton Hall on May 1, 1866.[37]

Directions for the second competition instructed entrants to submit signed affidavits affirming their disability and encouraged the submission of photographs.[38] That contestants were required to send affidavits confirming their former right-handedness and the wounding, disfigurement, or amputation of the right arm or hand during or because of military service indicates the contest organizers' desire to differentiate the veterans from malingerers, men who had lost their limbs prior to the war, or the group Martha Stoddard Holmes terms "begging adult male impostor[s]."[39] While some contestants sent three-quarter views of their shoulders and faces, others enclosed photographs that emphasized their left arms and empty sleeves. George Bucknam, who lost his right arm and several fingers of his left hand while serving in the Third Massachusetts Battery, sent two photographs of himself, both of which show him seated at a desk with pen in hand (fig. 25).[40] An empty sleeve rests on his knee, and his two-fingered left hand grasps a pen that hovers over paper. Alfred D. Whitehouse, a member of the Eighth New York Militia who submitted specimens to both contests and won a prize for ornamental penmanship, also sent a photograph of himself with pinkened cheeks and empty sleeve (fig. 26).[41] The photograph, which Whitehouse attached to the meticulously decorated cover page of his submission, foregrounds his left arm; indeed, the words "Left Arm Corps" wrap around the bottom of the portrait.

Given the cultural milieu of the latter half of the nineteenth century, it is important to note that Bucknam and Whitehouse's portraits are significantly different from photographs of freak-show performers and medical oddities that became increasingly popular in the same period.[42] Medical photographs were usually devoid of information identifying the person attached to the body. Though photographs of amputees "helped maintain the cultural distinction between the 'tragically' disabled and the congenitally 'deformed,'" they tended to present pathology instead of personhood.[43] Contestants like Bucknam and Whitehouse submitted photographs they commissioned and decided how to present their reconfigured bodies and lives to the public.

FIG. 25 Photograph of George Bucknam.
William Oland Bourne Papers, Manuscript Division, Library of Congress.

Bourne's organizing and advertising efforts worked to frame the handwriting of veterans like Whitehouse and Bucknam within an overarching literary narrative of reintegration and re-membering.[44] According to the reward committee's report, the "leading purpose" of the competition was "placing before the disabled men of the country incentives to a worthy ambition to become self-reliant, and to fit themselves for positions of honor and usefulness."[45] Bourne, a non-disabled man, had seen the results of amputation but had not endured the surgeon's saw. He hoped that contest entries—a collection of fragments—would augur not just the eventual reunification and reconstruction of the fragmented nation but also the successful reintegration of amputees into an increasingly capitalistic American society. In her analysis of the competition, Clarke argues that Bourne "saw his competitions as a way of lauding inspirational suffering and promoting self-sufficiency."[46] Erin O'Connor's formulation of pros-

FIG. 26 Alfred D. Whitehouse's first entry.
William Oland Bourne Papers, Manuscript Division, Library of Congress.

thesis as a vehicle for "social recuperation" and remasculinization mirrors the ostensible goals of the penmanship competition; in Bourne's framing of the contest, left-handed penmanship becomes a type of prosthesis by which amputees recoup their roles as financial providers and enter the rapidly expanding world of business as stenographers and secretaries.[47]

The testimonies of the veterans, however, complicate the optimistic aspirations of the contest and call into question assertions that artificial limbs can fully replace amputated ones. Some contestants commented on the difficulties of finding comfortable artificial limbs and adapting to left-handedness.[48] One veteran sent two photographs of himself; one prominently displays his stump, and the other shows him playing the violin with his prosthetic arm.[49] By itself, the photograph featuring the violin and prosthetic arm presents adaptation and unhindered ability, though it is impossible to know if the veteran's musical proficiency was unaffected by his injury. Viewed together, the images indicate many of the veterans' attempts to display their altered bodies without obscuring or covering over their missing limbs. "The discourse of prosthesis"—faith in the ability of artificial limbs to make the dismembered whole, the feminized masculine, the unemployed employable—is largely absent from the contest entries. If artificial limbs enable a fictive and convincing (for both the amputee and those who encounter him) "wholeness," then the possibility of an identity that is whole despite the absence of limb(s) is cut off. Such "wholeness" also relies on restrictive social constructions of normality and masculinity.[50] While manufacturers of artificial limbs promised full functionality and "working bod[ies]" that could enter the industrial workforce, the contest did not encourage the amputees to see themselves as viable laborers or factory workers, instead outlining a less physically taxing work—one that depends solely on the worker's ability to form neat and appealing letters.[51] Cash premiums for "literary merit" and "ornamental penmanship" served as an "inducement to the class of wounded and disabled soldiers . . . to make every effort to fit themselves for lucrative and honorable positions," thus outlining the path from socioeconomic and bodily disability to gainful employment and continued masculine endeavor.[52]

* * *

Good Bye Right Arm!

Penmanship, Bourne's contests asserted, would enable one-armed veterans to support themselves and their families, despite the absence of what William Tecumseh Sherman called the "best part" of their bodies: the right arm. In his letter to Caleb Fisher, recipient of a fifty-dollar prize bestowed by the general himself, Sherman writes, "Whilst we have been accustomed to regard the loss of the right arm as almost fatal to a useful and consequently happy life, these samples show how nature substitutes wisely and well our other arm; and I hope and trust that you may enjoy a long life, crowned by the contentment which the sacrifice of the best part of your body to your country's flag and safety is calculated to give."[53]

Sherman articulates a prevalent way of understanding the loss of life and limb in the war for the Union: soldiers died and lost parts of their body in order to make the Union whole. Though thousands of men relinquished "the best part[s] of [their] body," the Union remained intact; the preserved nation existed because the veterans' right arms did not. Submitting prose and verse accounts of their service, contestants both participated in and complicated such narratives of substitution and synecdoche. The amputees engaged in, to borrow Ann Millett-Gallant's concept, "strategic acts of self-exhibition" by which "the disabled or disfigured body becomes the source of creative and intellectual productions."[54]

In substituting the left hand for the right, the contest implied, veterans would ostensibly reestablish their masculine competency and potency. Members of the Left-Armed Corps attested to the ways in which amputation impeded their ability to engage in what contestant Phineas P. Whitehouse called "manly labor": farming, taking care of livestock, and performing other household chores.[55] Losing an arm prevented veterans like Whitehouse from trading in their rifles for plows (though some amputees proudly mentioned their continued ability to manage farms) and also barred them from entering the industrial workforce, which, as the century progressed, increasingly linked masculinity to physical labor outside of the domestic space.[56] Connected implicitly to these manly labors was sexual potency—anxieties about incompetence and impotence were figured most tellingly by a number of amputee contestants in terms of romantic rejection following mutilation. David Serlin argues that "veterans whose bodies manifested physical damage . . . were men for whom disability suggested a certain level of incompetence"; at the same time, however, "the amputation stump, the artificial limb, or any other overt physical evidence of injury became shorthand for military service."[57] Megan Kate Nelson describes the efforts of "many Americans [who] created images of amputees that emphasized both their empty sleeves and their virility" to counteract depictions of "the infantilized, incomplete man."[58] Contestants attempted to negotiate competing narratives of bodily incompetence and former competence as evidenced by military service by poeticizing their stumps. The mangled right arm, then, becomes more communicative of the embodied experience of war and amputation than the empty sleeve or prosthetic limb.

A number of contestants attested to the interconnectedness of corporeal wholeness, economic stability, sexual potency, and, in some cases, racial identity. Some did so through a version of apostrophe in which the required "turn away" is necessitated by amputation or disfiguring injury but imperfect because of the remaining presence of unsightly stumps and unwieldy remaining limbs. Others personified their missing limbs by imbuing them with agency and discursive power.[59] As Barbara Johnson has suggested, apostrophe allows poets to "repossess their lost selves" via the "anthropomorphized other."[60] Left-armed veterans attempted to do just that, with varying levels of success. Apostrophe as a literary device is uniquely suited to absent limbs, since it is grounded in the irrevocable distance between the addresser and the addressee and forces a turn to a third entity.[61] Within that distance reside concerns about the potentially social, economic, and sexual castrating effects of the surgeon's knife. In apostrophizing or personifying their pre-amputation limbs, left-armed veterans had to account for what remained—misshapen and at times painful stumps. Therefore, the turn to an intact right arm or the invocation of a still powerful limb (and thus the reclamation of a masculinity based on intactness) is impeded by the maimed one. The failure of apostrophe and personification to reintegrate and re-member bodies, then, complicates the path to recovery laid out by Sherman's insistence on nature's ability to substitute one arm for the other.

In his submission to the contest, John Blanchard, formerly a private in the First Regiment Ohio Light Artillery, charts the process by which his right arm becomes a separate entity and documents the personal and interpersonal repercussions of amputation.[62] His poem, which ends with a final "Good-bye, good-bye," enacts, both in form and content, the speaker's anxiety about and acceptance of disfigurement. Personification, followed by apostrophe, fails to reconstitute and re-member his body and, by the end of the poem, Blanchard's speaker must relinquish all claim to his right arm. Before this final farewell, however, the poem moves from the fever dreams of a recent amputee to his discovery of and difficult adjustment to his post-amputation life. Along the way, the speaker makes his amputated right arm into a repository of his former existence and directly addresses the lost arm that waits in "the quiet church-yard" for its comrade.

Shifting from a disembodied dream-state to the embodied experience of amputation, the poem navigates the complicated space between the abstract and absent right arm and Blanchard's transformed body. The speaker wakes in a hospital bed with a "dim and dizzy brain." Punctuated by blank-verse moments of clarity and regularity, the speaker's stream-of-consciousness narration mimics his attempts to orient himself. He muses, "I wake / From what to what?" In an attempt to find out, the speaker observes his surroundings—the "strange odor sweet and sick" makes him "just remember" his rapid heartbeat and the sensation of "float[ing] / On pinions from [his] shoulders newly grown." The speaker's disembodied and ether-induced dreams end abruptly when a voice says, "He wakes." Brought back to his body by the words, he confronts the truth without the aid of anesthetics: "Ah, now I knew." To confirm his suspicions, the speaker asks, "Quick surgeon with your work. What, is it off?" The surgeon's response—"Ay, even so, there lies your arm"—personifies the recently amputated limb and establishes it as an entity distinct from the speaker's body. The title of the poem, "Amputated," becomes both adjective and verb; the speaker is cut off from dreams of "light and wine and love" and from his former identity as a two-armed man.

Blanchard locates this former identity in the "idle arm off yonder" by reciting its former activities and synecdochically linking it to his relationships with others. "It was the hand that long ago [his] mother held" and "laid right proudly in her lap the / Scholar's prize." It was also the hand he offered, along with his heart, to "Madeline Dubray." As such, it embodies Blanchard's fears that his marked body will adversely affect his familial and romantic relationships. Looking at his disembodied arm, he must confront his changed circumstances and renegotiate both his ability to work and his viability as a romantic partner. The speaker appeals to Madeline, proclaiming that he has brought "back the honors which [she] bid [him] win" in place of the right hand he once offered to her. The "honors" and the remaining left arm are imperfect but represent the potential for a reconstituted masculinity not dependent on corporeal completeness. The speaker implicitly ties his recovery to his remaining limb: "Pray God you do not turn away when one poor hand / With halting awkward gestures seek your own." The speaker's "awkward gestures" threaten both his ability to win Madeleine's hand and his ability to manage the "farmhouse" he mentions.[63] However, Blanchard's fears and the concerns of many of the contestants about their capacity to be full men despite their missing limbs speak to the relationship of physicality to notions of manhood.

Blanchard ends his poem by apostrophizing his lost right arm; however, he does so not in an attempt to reverse the work of the surgeon's knife but instead to surrender all mortal claims to his former appendage. He proclaims, "Good bye right arm! Your work is done / Forever." Referring to his left arm as "your [the right arm's] comrade," the speaker recruits his remaining arm for active service and "pray[s] God the left / May never shame the right." By personifying and apostrophizing his recently amputated right arm, Blanchard honors his missing limb and lays his former identity to rest; by in turn personifying his remaining appendage, he imagines his future as a left-armed man. The turn away becomes a turn back, mimicking how Blanchard awoke from dreams of "idle revel[s]" to the embodied experience of amputation.

Unlike Blanchard, Phineas P. Whitehouse, a corporal for the Sixth New Hampshire Volunteers, retained his right arm and hand. His ode to his diminished limb employs a form of personification that approaches apostrophe but never fully turns away to an idealized and intact appendage. His poem, "My Crippled Arm," which won a twenty-five-dollar prize for literary merit, emphasizes the uneasy and inherently fractured relationship between a formerly intact limb and a "shattered" remnant.[64] Both entities exist in the space of his poem, the "crippled" appendage preventing a full turn away toward the anthropomorphized uninjured right arm. In iambic pentameter quatrains, also known as heroic or elegiac stanzas, Whitehouse makes his right arm into a crippled and withering version of Keats's Grecian urn (also apostrophized in pentameter). Because Whitehouse's chosen verse form invokes both mourning and heroism, he is able to frame the loss of his arm as devastating and fundamentally significant. The poem begins with a recollection of the arm's former status as a "faithful servant": "'Twas hardy once, and strong for manly labor . . . could shoulder musket or could turn the sabre / Could wield the pen or till New England soil." A "rebel bullet's madness" destroys his right arm and makes it "a weak and feeble patient," in turn threatening his ability to perform "manly" duties and fragmenting his lifelong connection to his limb; he "watch[es] to find it stronger" and "look[s] upon the tender, child-like fingers," but the "shapeless arm" and "rough scar" refuse to heal.

Though shapeless and "feeble," the arm does not resist interpretation or obscure meaning; for Whitehouse, it is a constant reminder of the war. Whitehouse forces his readers to confront the repercussions of disfigurement: "I look at this, the feeble thing before me— / The piteous wreck of what was once an arm— / And can you wonder if a cloud comes o'er me?" Whitehouse's arm will never fully heal and thus disrupts narratives of postwar recovery and forgetting.[65] However, Whitehouse ends his poem with the hope that, with the help of Heaven, his remaining arm will "a final victory see." Whitehouse focuses on his "true and faithful, one stout arm," averring that, though his right arm is childlike and weak, "for Life's stern conflicts [he is] still defended." Tellingly, the remaining fight is removed from the battlefield; time and lack of use will "rust the rifle and the sabre." Instead, Whitehouse and his left arm fight to construct an alternative form of wholeness and masculinity—one that depends not on an artificial limb but instead on perseverance and faith in "a final victory."

Similarly to Blanchard and Whitehouse's submissions, Thomas Perrine's "Sinister Manuscripta," a title that combines the Latin words for "left" and "handwritten," addresses the somatic, economic, and interpersonal repercussions of losing his right arm.[66] However, Perrine, a member of the 140th Pennsylvania Volunteers, ties racial identity and political agency as well as masculinity to bodily wholeness. Instead of apostrophizing his missing limb, he manipulates language through wordplay so that his former right arm, the stump that remains, and his left arm all retain symbolic and discursive power. Through an interrelated series of puns that play with multiple connotations of the word "left" and the homophonic qualities of citizenship rights and right-handedness, Perrine claims that losing his right arm is tantamount to losing his identity as an enfranchised white American man. Adding insult to injury, that loss also results in romantic rejection. In describing this rejection, Perrine plays with the etymological and actual importance of hands to courtship rituals. As such, Perrine's "stump" embodies his and other contestants' concerns about impotency and fears that losing an arm has made them less of a man in more ways than one. Though a shell fragment struck his "Humerus vein," Perrine's sense of humor, as evidenced by multiple puns throughout the poem, remains intact. Taking the first line of Virgil's *Aeneid,* "Arma Virumque Cano" (I sing of arms and of a man), for the title of his poem, Perrine slyly turns the story of losing his arm into a mock epic and riffs on the etymological linkage between appendages and warfare. His choice of the ballad form, which, according to Michael Cohen, antebellum Americans associated with the formation of "political relations . . . among readers," situates his experience of injury and the anxieties that attend it within an established literary tradition of addressing large public audiences.[67] Perrine makes the personal political and presents his amputation stump as evidence of service, and extends his left hand to readers.

Perrine first mentions racial identity in relation to his romantic troubles following amputation. Poetic license allows Perrine to lose his arm on "May-day" and also lose the love of "Miss May Dey." His failed romance with the jilting Miss Dey resembles John Blanchard's interactions with Madeleine Dubray—both veterans return to the home front lacking the hands they had previously plighted to their sweethearts. Amputation, it seems, threatens traditional courtship rituals centered on the proffering, accepting, and joining of hands. "To accept my hand she had agreed," Perrine explains, "But when I lost my hand, she said, / The bargain didn't hold." Though he offers her his "other hand / Uninjured by the fight" since it is all he "ha[s] left," she tells him "'twould not be right." Playing with the association of hands and marriage, as well as the presumed correctness of right-handedness, Perrine somewhat euphemistically relates his concerns about the castrating potential of amputation. In his formulation, amputation destroys masculine viability and virility; moreover, it threatens to turn white men black. He laments, "O woful day! that took away / My arm and sweetheart too:— / An empty sleeve, an empty heart— / 'Twould make a Darkey blue." In the preceding stanza, Perrine's speaker tells his lady love to "gaze on these features," claiming "they're fair as you will see." She replies, "Without two hands . . . / You cannot handsome be." Handsomeness depends on "fair" skin and intact limbs; since Perrine lacks a right arm, his whiteness is tenuous.

Perrine equates his body's maiming and his subsequent loss and emasculation with the marks of race by comparing his plight to that of African American slaves. He does so by invoking the Supreme Court's 1857 decision regarding Dred Scott's suit for freedom: "'These negroes all,' Judge Taney said, / 'A white man's rights do lack': / The rebels left not right to me— / I might as well be black." Chief Justice Roger Taney composed the Supreme Court's decision, which declared that, among other things, "persons of African descent cannot be, nor were ever intended to be, citizens under the U.S. Const."[68] The loss of the right hand, Perrine implies, is equivalent to the loss of political rights. He portrays the decision as a type of amputation that cuts off any possibility of African American citizenship. In this way, his account of bodily loss both disrupts and reaffirms categories of racial difference: wounding can reduce a white soldier to the level of disenfranchised former slaves, but that soldier remains white. Significantly, Perrine does not claim he is like a black person; rather, he says he "might as well be," thus implying that blackness is a form of disability and vice versa. He claims that his "one consolation" is that, "when wars again shall be, / And Congressmen shall say, 'Two Arms!' / They can't say that to [him]." As a one-armed man, Perrine is safe from the "Provost marshal with his draft," his ineligibility both evidence of his reduced status and proof of his prior service.[69] His continuous punning underscores the dualities of his post-amputation existence (he is white but might as well not be, whole and fragmented within the space of the poem) and also enables him to retain a reconfigured form of agency through his continued ability to express himself through left-handed writing.

Our Other Arm

In order to write poems about their mangled or missing right arms, contestants had to adapt to using a lesser limb. "Left," derived from the Old English word for "paralysis," carries the cultural connotations of weakness, effeminacy, ineffectuality, and evil.[70] Though it is impossible to know if the erstwhile right arms of the members of the Left-Armed Corps were indeed dominant, extremely impressive specimens sent in by a number of contestants show that some men took to writing with their left hands with greater alacrity than others.[71] Significantly, the contest did not call on men who lost their left arms in battle to submit specimens of their right-hand penmanship; it assumed that right-handedness was the norm and implicitly excluded left-handed men.[72] The contest, following the lead of a federal government that barred Confederate veterans from receiving disability pensions and subsidized artificial limbs, also excluded Confederate amputees, who lost their limbs to a traitorous cause.[73] The Left-Armed Corps, according to the contest organizers and the contestants themselves, consisted of formerly right-handed men who became left-handed as a result of their loyalty to the Union.

The men who submitted specimens of their handwriting thus had to contend with the stigmas associated with left-handedness in the context of a contest that recognized the superiority of the right hand while at the same time suggesting that the left hand could be taught and shaped and made (almost) *right*. Encouraging amputees to "fit themselves for positions of honor and usefulness," the contest established the normate American male body as right-handed.[74] Contestants employed bodily puns and tongue-in-cheek invocations of the stigmas associated with left-handedness in order to confront their new, nonnormative physical reconfigurations. Apostrophic gestures to the formerly intact right arm dovetailed back to clumsy but capable left arms as contestants negotiated a left-handed form of masculine competence and economic stability.

Henry W. Palmer, a twenty-year-old veteran of the Maine Volunteers, apostrophizes his missing right arm in prose; however, the trajectory of his account shifts focus to his lesser limb. "Lost right arm!" Palmer exclaims, "thou wert a member of a perfect body, given to Country in her day of trial, and while Virginia's soil is enriched by thy decay, the remnant of that Soldier body is reserved for such further duties as Country may demand."[75] In Palmer's account, his arm is symbolic because of amputation and not because of its former status as part of his "perfect body"; though he mentions that it once "was as ready at all times to wield the pen . . . or pull the trigger," he makes clear that it is more powerful detached from his body. He trusts it has "sown seeds of loyalty" that "will generate and send forth an abundant harvest" in the formerly traitorous South. As a literary device, apostrophe enables Palmer to eulogize and commemorate. As with Blanchard, however, the turning away to an ideal and unscathed right arm is incomplete as Palmer describes his macabre search for his amputated limb: "Among the limbs amputated, I sought my own right arm. . . . strange sensations are those of him standing beside the grave of a member of his own body—strange communings between the quick and the dead." Palmer does not state whether or not he found his arm, an omission that points to the irreducible distance between the "remnant" of Palmer's body and its former "member."

Apostrophe ("Lost right arm!") followed by Palmer's inability to find his personified missing limb mimics another turning away; this time, however, Palmer returns to what remains: the "remnant of that Soldier body" and his future as a left-armed man. After a "minie ball penetrate[s] the center of the bone, pulverizing it to a powder," Palmer's left arm receives an "immediate promotion" and must take up the rifle and the responsibilities of the right. The transition proves difficult since his left arm is "no veteran at trigger pulling," and Palmer is forced to "lay down . . . arms." Palmer's punning binds together warfare and manual ability but also inspires a series of anthropomorphic actions on the part of his right arm that shift focus and agency to his left. It becomes a testator that "bequeath[s] unto the left arm, all the properties of which it died seized and possessed." The young veteran understands the loss of his arm in legal terms: "The seal of this last Will and Testament was the blood seal of amputation. Patriotism, love of Country, and Equal Rights were the subscribing witnesses to the Instrument." By personifying not only his left and right arms but also the abstract ideals of service in the Union army, Palmer makes his personal sacrifice of national importance and makes bodily loss a marker of elevated and exemplary masculinity.

While Blanchard centers his anxieties about manhood in his missing right arm, Palmer frames his as an "outward mark of devotion" that bolsters his claims to citizenship and manly ability. Having buried his right arm and settled its affairs, Palmer turns to the future and addresses "the thousands of mutilated soldiers," asking, "Shall we be indolent because we are maimed?" With "stirring brain[s] strong in growing manhood," Palmer and others can exercise the remnants of their bodies in the causes of "Patriotism—Sobriety—Zeal," their masculinity increased by their extra effort. Part of this effort will involve the development of "the spared hand." Indeed, it is Palmer's left arm—not the "artificial Lincoln arm" that seems "destitute of 'a fellow feeling'"—that is "Devisee of all . . . the right arm possessed." Though his hand writes "timidly and trembles through fear of failure," he has faith that practice will make perfect and insists that he is ready to reprise his role as the nation's defender: "all that I now am—*all that I can make my-self* is at command of Country now and ever."[76] This process makes a "nerved left arm" ready for continued service and locates the difficulties of as well as the possibilities for post-amputation adjustment.[77]

Alfred Whitehouse, who refers to himself as Bourne's "left arm soldier friend" and celebrates his membership in a community of marked veterans he calls "The Right, and Left, Arm of the Nation's Defense," enlisted in 1859 and was wounded in the first battle of the conflict.[78] "Remaining upon the battlefield about six days among [his] wounded, and dyeing [*sic*], comrades, till [his] shattered arm was full of maggots," the transplanted Englishman eventually lost his arm to amputation in Richmond before being sent under flag of truce to Baltimore. A short poem included in his second submission to the contest synecdochically ties his missing right arm (and the missing limbs of other veterans) to the redeemed Union while signaling the potential and capacity of his remaining limb: "The right arm's gone, / the Nation yet remanes [*sic*], / Tho many perished yet we are saved, / The right will triumph over wrong / Tho it leave us but one left arm strong." Rather than erasing loss, the poem creates an inverse relationship in which the right arm is absent because the Union survives and the Union survives because the right arm is absent.

Whitehouse concludes that "the Pen is mightier than the sword, and can be wield from right, to left with great efect [*sic*]." Whitehouse's slightly clumsy pun inverts the left to right movement of Western chirography and tangibly mimics his attempts to substitute his left hand for his right. The substitution may be imperfect, but, as Whitehouse argues, it is sufficient and should not prevent him from being a fully functional citizen. He demands work for himself and other left-armed veterans: "Give us Work, that we can do! / And don't be afraid of what we cant [*sic*] do, / Because one arm is not two, / So deny us the right." According to Whitehouse, labor is a God-given right regardless of a right arm's presence or absence. "Soldier's [*sic*] in War," members of the Left-Armed Corps deserve to be "Citizens in peace" with all the attendant "blessings" thereof. Whitehouse frames his changed body in terms of its competence and adaptive skills, thus constructing a form of left-handedness that is deserving of praise.

Genuine Testimony

Bourne's left-handed penmanship contests testify to survival and loss, successful adaptation and painful readjustment. Three years after the end of the war, Bourne reprinted an article titled "Left-Hand Penmanship" from *Frank Leslie's Illustrated News* that featured specimens of left-handed writing from O. O. Howard, the famous one-armed general, and two contestants.[79] Arguing that the entries are "genuine testimony to the character of our volunteer soldiers," the article echoes Bourne in his hopes that the contest will give disabled veterans evidence of their ability to live full and successful lives as American citizens. One specimen displays the "legible and superior business penmanship" of Franklin H. Durrah, the recipient of the "first premium of $200." Shortly after winning the contest, Durrah, most likely afflicted by post-traumatic stress disorder, was committed to an insane asylum; he eventually died in another institution.[80] Though his penmanship was meant to serve as a marker of survival and a promise of success, Durrah soon became another casualty of the war. The stories of Durrah and others like him, men forever marked by the Civil War, are crucial to understanding the ways in which soldiers conceptualized their service to the Union and their place in postbellum American society. Rather than seamlessly aligning themselves with the rhetoric of promised rehabilitation and recuperation propounded by the penmanship contests, they presented fragmented bodies and fractured selves. Their missing limbs could not be restored, and their left arms could never do the work of two hands; however, Left-Armed Corps veterans presented to the public reconfigured forms of masculinity and bodily ability, strategically framing their missing and remaining limbs as poetic subjects worthy of respect.

Taken as a "united production" and as solitary testimonies to trauma, the writings of the Left-Armed Corps constitute a unique body of disabled literature and are therefore invaluable cultural artifacts as well as aesthetic literary navigations of the inextricable ties between physical wholeness, masculinity, and economic and political agency. For men like R. Watson Seague, a former first lieutenant in the Michigan Volunteer Infantry who lost all use of his right arm at Gettysburg, the penmanship contests served as forums for self-expression and, if the pun can be excused, as a call to arm(s).[81] Seague, in a letter to Bourne, writes, "I hope my manuscript may recommend itself for the first credit of the well known gentlemen who compose your committee, but it if proves second to others I shall at least be encouraged to renewed diligence and perseverance in my left hand labors." These "labors" do significant cultural and literary work; Seague and other members of the Left-Armed Corps offered personal accounts of amputation and adaptation by proposing new ways of conceptualizing heroic masculinity and bodily disfigurement. The left-handed papers produced by Bourne's contests make available a more representative canon that uncovers what lies beneath the empty sleeve.

CHAPTER FOUR

Spirit Wounds and Invisible Bullets

Families of the Left-Armed Corps almost certainly learned of their soldiers' grievous injuries via letter, newspaper, or telegram. "Tangled and Raveled," a story published in *Harper's Weekly* in 1862, describes the rapid spread of information after a battle: "It flashed along the wires, and heart-strings quivered in sympathy."[1] In a number of stories and poems published in newspapers and periodicals during the war, heartstrings and telegraph wires connect the front to the home, tangling the two. The narrator of "Only One Killed," also published in *Harper's Weekly* in 1862, describes a similar relationship between telegraph wires and heart-strings.[2] After hearing a casualty report for a recent engagement—"One killed and three wounded"—the narrator callously remarks, "That all! . . . Hardly worth the cost of a telegram." He subsequently witnesses the deterioration and torment of the mother, father, and sweetheart of the "one killed." Having learned his lesson, the narrator declares, "Away from every battle-field, from every skirmishing ground, heart-cords stretch, in single lines, to as many hearts and homes as there are individuals, and death, or wounding, thrill these sympathetic lines, each with its own wild fear and anguish." In his pronouncement, the narrator echoes and revises Abraham Lincoln's final sentiments in his first inaugural address. "The mystic chords of memory," the new president urged, "stretching from every battlefield and patriot grave to every living heart and hearthstone all over this broad land, will yet swell the chorus of the Union, when again touched, as surely they will be, by the better angels of our nature."[3] As better angels failed to prevent civil strife, chords became cords, intangible memories became fresh wounds, and telegraph lines served as concrete proof of new connections between households and battlefields.

In telegrams and telegraph lines, technology integral to the waging of war and the dissemination of news and information, popular fiction writers and poets found an analogue for the inextricability of battlefield violence and home-front anguish, and a nation at war became a nation of interconnected lines by which death and wounding traveled with telegraphic speed. A significant trope in Civil War fiction and poetry—the embodied effects of telegrams from the front and newspaper casualty lists—demonstrates how reading had corporeal consequences and the process of reading about the war became tantamount to participating in it. In literature of the conflict, the home front and the battlefield were equally important, mutually constitutive, and at times indistinguishable. As a result, both male and female bodies were emblematic of the stakes and ramifications of the struggle. News entered the home and corporeally transformed those within. Southern homes, even more so than northern ones due to geographical proximity to the seat of war, were vulnerable to the encroachment of battlefield violence, and fictional southern women faced the threat of rapacious invaders. "Spartan" women who armed their husbands for the fight against Yankee hordes followed the war news closely and dedicated their bodies to the cause, as did the wives, mothers, sisters, and sweethearts of the Union soldiers so detested by southern ladies.[4]

The advent of telegraphic technology also obliterated the already porous line between the domestic space and the public sphere and allowed women and their bodies access to the sights, sounds, and sensations of the battlefield. Remembered as the conflict that pitted brother against brother, the Civil War was not a predominantly masculine phenomenon or undertaking. Indeed, the beleaguered and at times war-torn bodies of (predominantly) white women appeared on the pages of the periodical press as often as the wounded bodies of soldiers.[5] If a bullet can wound or kill women and men alike, and if men go to battle thinking of and encouraged by the women they left behind, most of whom voraciously read the news and imagine the horrors of combat, then home front and battlefield cannot be mutually exclusive. In actuality, the battlefield and the home, and experiences therein, were of course fundamentally different in many ways; nevertheless, Civil War writers portrayed them as inextricably linked and subject to pain and wounding. Scholarly studies of Civil War literature often implicitly embrace and perpetuate distinct lines between the front and the domestic space, masculine physical endeavor and feminine emotional experience.[6] Alice Fahs insists on the "domestic" quality of women's suffering in "feminized war literature" while Kathleen Diffley argues that, in popular literature, "domestic rhetoric and narrative strategies tried to contain [the war's] disruption.[7] However, the home front was not necessarily masculinized by incursions of violence, nor was the battlefield domesticated by the presence of women. Instead, the battlefield and the home front, as represented in print, became increasingly attached and similar realms that were male and female, domestic and public.[8]

I argue for a reappraisal of so-called "feminized war literature" and "domestic war fiction."[9] Stories and poems about women appeared on the pages of local newspapers, periodicals marketed to soldiers, regimental histories, and major northern and southern periodicals; they were written by, marketed to, and read by women and men, and exhibit generic and thematic similarities, thus creating a war literature that is simultaneously male and female, private and public. Stories that portray women reading and responding to newspaper reports, casualty lists, and telegrams appeared on the pages of actual newspapers, next to descriptions of battles, lists of wounded and killed soldiers, and information from the front sent via telegraph.[10] These texts illuminate an alternative form of wounding—one that kills and maims without bullets and bayonets. Telegraphic wounding, the process by which news of the war invades the domestic space and corporeally marks female bodies, collapses distinctions between public and domestic, soldier and noncombatant. It embodies what Shirley Samuels finds in wartime fiction, namely that the "battlefield and home appear tensely joined, each unsettling the role of the other."[11] Telegraph wires replace (or augment) the so-called heartstrings (or "mystic chords of memory") central to sentimental fellow-feeling, allowing for direct communication between the front and the home. The conventions of antebellum sentimental literature provided a foundation for this communion, but the telegraph in particular embodied the experience of shared feeling, sympathy, and suffering during the conflict.[12] Characters receive instruction on how to read news sentimentally—to extrapolate from lists of names and casualty statistics the emotional and somatic effects of the war and, more importantly, the physical repercussions of *reading* about the war. The result is a reconfigured form of sentimentality that does not attempt to "blo[t] out the uglier details of life" by containing, eliding, or mitigating suffering and destruction, but instead underlines the disruptive and damaging influence of widespread violence.[13]

The Home and the Camp So Inseparable

This is not to say that the battlefield and the home were in actuality the same place—indeed, their geographical distance, especially for northern households, made telegraphic technology necessary—but instead to elucidate the ways in which popular literature imagined them as such. Hundreds (and perhaps thousands) of poems and stories imbued campfires and hearth fires with the same glowing warmth; the forces that shaped and influenced the home had a place on the battlefield, as the men who traveled to the front carried with them mementos of home and the loved ones they never quite left behind them. Writing two years after the end of the war, "A Lady," inspired by the fifth anniversary of the battle of Antietam, recounted her experiences as a Union nurse by extolling the glory of "our volunteer soldiery."[14] Walking the battlefield and its environs, she happens upon "some of the very stones of our queer little fire-place, made by 'Company H.'" The stones evoke memories of a campfire that "lighted the earnest faces grouped around it"—soldiers with "singing books, striving to beguile some weary hours." The fire, outdoors on a battlefield, is barely distinguishable from the hearth fires at home, celebrated in domestic and sentimental fiction. Civil War writers often associated the campfire and the domestic fireside, as soldiers longed for the hearth, women imagined their loved ones around a makeshift fireplace, and the "kindled fire" of Whitman's "By the Bivouac's Fitful Flame" evoked "tender and wondrous thoughts" of home.[15] As a communal spot, the fireplace warmed the bodies and souls of homesick soldiers.

Happening upon other battlefield landmarks, the former nurse remembers her encounter with an off-duty soldier who kindled a fire: "As we came up, he started, and, rising, showed us the treasure he had kindled the fire to see—his wife's picture with baby on her knee. We saw something else, and deeper, as well as the pretty picture—the influence of the home affection, keeping the soldier brave and true through all the stern discipline of war—the home and the camp so inseparable." This soldier, like many on the pages of Civil War periodicals, carried his home to the front. Somewhat ironically, Antietam, remembered as the bloodiest battlefield of the struggle, provides the setting for an intimate scene pervaded by "home affection."

The influences of home and family permeate the front in wartime literature, drowning out the siren calls of alcohol, impiety, licentiousness, and playing cards. In one poem, the arrival of a mother's letter prevents three disillusioned and dissolute soldiers from deserting and becoming Copperheads; similarly, in a short piece by Timothy Shay Arthur titled "The Soldier's Letter," a "restless and brooding" soldier reforms after receiving a letter from a young woman of his acquaintance.[16] Sweethearts and mothers served as moral compasses as well as inspiration for bellicosity. John Antrobus, writing at the headquarters of the Ninth Regiment Louisiana Volunteers, invoked the home front as an impetus for battlefield aggression:

> In battle's bloody hour
> These pictures shall arise,
> Of mothers, sisters, wives, and homes,
> And red and streaming eyes;
> And every arm shall stronger be,
> For home, for God, for liberty,
> And strike, while mercy dies.[17]

Instead of relegating women to symbolic status, mementos of home operate as tangible (letters and photographs) and intangible (imagined "pictures") indicators of feminine involvement and agency.

Stories featuring heroines who travel to the battlefield via psychic connections with the soldiers they love make the close ties between women and the war even more explicit. Seemingly embowered in the domestic space of the home, southern women move beyond the confines of plantation boudoirs and country cottages, communing with their soldier sons or sweethearts and witnessing the horrors of war. In Rosa Wild's poem "The Parting," written for and published in the *Southern Illustrated News* in 1863, "a maiden sits by her window" and contemplates the imminent departure of her sweetheart.[18] Though "evening air / Falls tenderly upon her brow," as evening air is wont to do in poems featuring fair maidens, the young woman is unmoved. With "quivering lips," she implores God for the strength to bravely send her lover to battle. Her resolve weakens when she "think[s] of the marshalled host's array" and "the battlefield appears"; she hears "the clash of steel" and "the cannon's fearful peal / Booming o'er the gory field." The confined space of her bedroom, as well as the limited space of the poem, contains all the sights and sounds of battle and its attendant sensations. The maiden's struggle to relinquish her lover is a physical one, informed by her ability to access the "gory field."

Similarly, the speaker of "A Mother's Prayer," a poem published in northern and southern newspapers during the war and a number of Confederate poetry anthologies after, appeals to the almighty for strength and seems to travel to the battlefield.[19] Her "sad heart wanders back / To tented field and bivouac" in search of her son. "Often in my troubled sleep," she explains,

> Waking,—wearily to weep—
> Often dreaming *he* is near,
> Calming every anxious fear,—
> Often startled by the flash
> Of hostile swords that meet and clash,
> Till the cannon's smoke and roar
> Hide him from my eyes once more.

As the speaker peers through the "cannon's smoke," so can we look past the generic hallmarks of Civil War poetry (the clashing swords and roaring cannons) and recognize a literary trope that is integral to understanding the inextricability of the home and the front: women's ability to intellectually, emotionally, and, perhaps most significantly, physically experience the battlefield. Telegraphic technology both enables this communion and mimics its immediacy.

Telegraphic Wounding

The speed with which women imaginatively travel to the battlefield parallels the rapidity with which information traveled along telegraph lines. The political cartoon "The First Telegraphic Message from California" (fig. 27), published in *Harper's Weekly,* celebrates the inaugural telegram sent to President Lincoln from San Francisco on October 24, 1861. The sender, Horace W. Carpenter, president of the Overland Telegraph Company, announced the completion of the telegraph, writing, "May it be a bond of perpetuity between the states of the Atlantic and those of the Pacific."[20] In the cartoon, Columbia strides along a telegraph wire bearing a scroll that reads, "May the Union be Perpetual."[21] Ostensibly, telegraph wires are tangible proof of nationhood—they constitute a direct conduit between opposite coasts—and augur the eventual reconciliation of a nation divided; if a man in San Francisco could send the president a message in a matter of minutes, then surely the seceding states could be brought back into the national fold. Telegraph lines resemble heartstrings in their ability to connect people across long distances, and their appearance in Civil War stories and poems creates a community that is simultaneously divided and united, battlefield and home front, masculine and feminine.

The word "telegraph," derived from the Greek words for distance and writing, collapses the space between sender and receiver; in this compression of space and often time, Civil War writers found an analogue for the communicability and immediacy of wartime suffering.[22] Though the Union and Confederate armies regularly tampered with each other's telegraph lines and the speed with which people could receive telegrams often depended on their proximity to a telegraph machine, telegraph lines, in conjunction with newspaper reports derived from telegraphed information sent primarily by members of the United States Military Telegraph Corps, provided civilians with exhaustive war coverage.[23] Eliza

FIG. 27 "The First Telegraphic Message from California." *Harper's Weekly* 5, no. 256 (November 23, 1861): 752. Library of Congress Prints and Photographs Division, LC-USZ62-116943.

Richards has indicated how the "new mass-media networks," comprising technological advances like the telegraph and the rail system, shaped how Civil War–era poets wrote. According to Richards, "linear words and images" are central tropes in wartime popular poetry and display the "radical abstraction entailed by transmitting news of physical conflict over large distances."[24] However, telegraph lines and casualty lists constitute a direct (though at times imperfect) link between the home and the battlefield and become the vehicles by which the wounds of soldiers are transferred onto the bodies of women at home.

Winslow Homer's 1862 illustration for *Harper's Weekly,* "News from the War" (fig. 28), portrays the act of reading as both a communal and a solitary endeavor, and one that takes place at the front, at home, and in-between.[25] Telegraph wires frame the illustration, surrounding and linking the various spaces portrayed and indicating the means by which ship deck, camp, and home are connected to one another. The article accompanying the illustration announces that one of the paper's "most ingenious artists" has "done justice" to the "thrilling effects" of war news.[26] "*News of the war!*" the article proclaims, "We all live on it. Few of us but would prefer our newspaper . . . to our breakfast." Different categories of news produce different corporeal results: news describing daring missions and victories "fires the heart and makes the eye glisten and the cheek redden with patriotic ardor"; news of "slaughter and massacre" blanches the cheek and "nerves the brave man's heart to further encounters." As the illustration demonstrates, both men and women consume dispatches; sailors (who transport and read mail), soldiers (who peruse *Harper's Weekly* and fight over recent editions), and women confront the conflict via print.

The image at top center, offset by a wooden frame but linked by telegraph wires to the outside world, features a woman clasping a piece of paper. "Wounded" appears beneath the frame, situated atop lines radi-

FIG. 28 Winslow Homer, "News from the War."
Harper's Weekly 6, no. 285 (June 14, 1862): 378. Image courtesy of the House Divided Project at Dickinson College.

ating from a bugle-blowing soldier. The woman, though alone at home, is not immune to the forces outside of the frame. The article alludes to the woman's condition: "To many tender hearts news of the war, be it of victory or defeat, merely means the death or wounding of some dear soldier. How little they think, whose lovers or brothers are reported in the fatal list of killed and wounded, of the triumphs or the perils of the Union cause! Little she recks, whose face is buried in her handkerchief in an agony of anguish, of the utter discomfiture of the rebels!" Together, article and illustration simultaneously point to women's distance from the progress of the struggle (victory or defeat are irrelevant when a loved one dies) while underscoring their physical and emotional participation in it. The telegraph, the newspaper, and the casualty list pervaded the home and the texts that appeared alongside "war news."

Whether casualty lists are incomplete or incorrect, letters fail to reach their destinations, or living soldiers are confused with similarly named dead ones, war news marks those who receive or fail to receive it.[27] A number of stories end with the miraculous reappearances of soldiers presumed dead due to battlefield confusion or bureaucratic error; female characters whose health was destroyed by the initial tidings of death recuperate after their lovers return.[28] Clara, a "dreadfully pretty" coquette and the heroine of "Fortune Favors the Brave," a story published in *Harper's Weekly* in 1862, "had been wont to declare that she never could understand how people read the war news with such avidity; but she never missed a single paragraph of it now."[29] Having toyed with and bid farewell to Philip Preston, a suitor who mistakenly assumes Clara loves his rival and dejectedly rides off to the front, Clara grows "pale and thin," her "heart throb[bing] wildly" when she hears "news-boys calling 'Extras.'" When news of the Battle of "Fairoaks" [*sic*], better known as the Battle of Seven Pines, arrives, Clara reads with "palpitating heart" the list of wounded but avoids "a more terrible list." The narrative, previously past tense, shifts to present as Clara forces her "cowardly eyes" to read the list of killed: "Quickly she scans the dreadful column—breathes freely a great sigh of relief—then a sob, a gasp, a thrill of anguish, and three words are graven on her heart. 'Philip Preston, killed.'"

The narrative immediately returns to the past tense, isolating the moment of initial wounding and emphasizing the instantaneous bodily effects of reading: "a deathly feeling of sickness came over her, and the light died out of her eyes—the color from her cheeks and lips." Affliction removes the attributes—a complexion of "pearls and roses" and lips the "tint of ripe cherries"—that make her "dreadfully pretty" prior to her devastation. Philip's miraculous return (the death of another Philip Preston in his regiment led to a "blunder") restores "into her face such a color as had not graced it for twelve months," but Clara shudders when she remembers the initial moment of revelation; even the memory of reading, it seems, is embodied.

The act of "waiting for news"—a phrase that appears in the titles of poems and stories—could be better described as searching for or demanding news. By seeking out information—eagerly reading telegrams, casualty lists, and newspapers—women actively participate in and are not passive observers of the war. "The Tuberose," an 1861 story about a recently orphaned young woman named Jessie who supports herself by selling nosegays while her sweetheart is away fighting, describes the influence of battle news sent via telegraph: "Terror and dismay spread with lightning speed from city to city. A great battle had been fought and lost. Who were the dead? who the maimed and crippled for life? were the questions that with sickening dread were asked by many. Women, wailing and weeping, besieged the news and telegraph offices—not a home but feared to know all, not a heart that did not beat with sorrow."[30]

Despite their removal from the geographical location of the "great battle," women, struck by news that travels with lightning speed, resemble soldiers as they besiege communication centers and demand answers. "A Mother Waiting for the News," a poem published in the Unionist *Natchez Courier* in 1863, uses a similar metaphor for telegraphic communication: "How wearily the hours pass, / Since through the ambient air / The lightning flashed the startling fact, / A battle has been there."[31] Lightning, which strikes suddenly and without mercy, proves a fitting analogue for telegraphic wounding.

"The Tuberose" transitions from generalized furor caused by the lightning-fast delivery of war news to individualized suffering; Jessie's experience of the arrival of news is one of pain and wounding. "The first news [strikes] with one scathing blow," and Jessie remains still and silent, "as when lightning strikes a tree through the centre, leaving it standing though deprived of life." The same metaphor appears in "Morven and Linda," a poem by Confederate chaplain Adolphus Williamson Mangum.[32] Upon Morven's miraculous return, Linda explains her sensations upon reading of his death:

> I never shall forget the day
> A paper came, in which were given
> The names of all our Southern slain.
> How tremblingly I read that list. . . .
> I can't remember what I felt
> For 'twas a shock which rent my heart
> As lightning rends the stricken tree.

Reading war news, as the poem and story display, is an embodied act that has embodied results. While Linda's eyes "hurr[y] almost madly on," Jessie initially sees only dancing letters; eventually, however, she confronts the list "with throbbing temples." After learning that her lover is a prisoner, she becomes a "shadow of herself" and, confined to her bed, longs to be "where wars and rumors of wars can not reach." Fortunately, her lover returns, as does "new life."

Not all women were so lucky; in the relatively circumscribed and regimented space of lyric poems, women wait for and receive news, faith their only comfort. The anonymous author of "List of the Killed," a poem published in multiple newspapers after first appearing in *Harper's Weekly* in 1861, invokes a community of women who read the war news and dread discovering the names of their soldiers on the list.[33] Quotation marks surround the printed title, ostensibly intended to clarify that the poem, which at first glance resembles an actual list of wounded, is not an official casualty report. The speaker addresses women who read casualty lists and also read poems about women reading casualty lists. Reading war news, in the context of the poem, is a specifically feminine undertaking that connects mothers to each other and, to paraphrase the speaker, the boys they sent away.

The speaker addresses the "mothers who sit in dumb terror and dread / Holding that terrible list" in the second person; "I pity you," she tells them, "sitting with faces so white, / Striving to parry the blow." Reading "the name of the boy you have kissed" is an act inherently violent and corporeal. The speaker recognizes in the "shudder and start" of other mothers her own ordeal, identifying "the pang that's rent *my* desolate heart, / By this crushing weight of despair." Collective reading begets collecting suffering; however, the poem ends with the speaker's personal pain—"the boy you kissed" becomes "the boy I kissed"—and a hope that resembles Emily Dickinson's "repealess list."[34] "Above there's a glorified list," the speaker intones, finding comfort in an intangible and unprinted column of names. The act of reading occurs in the home but transcends its walls, encompassing heaven and the battlefield.

Even domestic spaces that initially seem intact and imperturbable open to any hint of war information. Letters and telegrams sent from the front arrive at home and bring disruption and bodily harm with them. Many of the poems and stories that foreground the ubiquity of war news and its effects on women's lives and homes begin with invocations of deceptively closed-off rooms and homes amidst typically pastoral scenes. The central figure of Harriet M'Ewen Kimball's poem "Woman—1862" mumbles prayers while "patriot-shouts" disrupt the "blessed summer days glid[ing] by in sweet succession."[35] Though the surrounding "Nature's palace-walls" are immune to human strife, the woman "plies the threaded steel" and "thinks of those whose wounds are fresh." Despite her seeming isolation, she thinks of bayonets and bullets and "shudders while the words of fate along the wires are chasing," telegraph wires physically anchoring her to the battlefield. God, Kimball's speaker intones, "who alone can clearly read the human, / Traces the hero's autograph through tear-blots of the Woman." Women, the poem implies, read and write "words of fate."

Refugitta's "Implora Pace," published in the *Southern Illustrated News* in 1863, also begins in a seemingly circumscribed domestic space.[36] A woman "is sitting in the twilight / All her work is laid aside, / And around the scene before her / Shines the light of eventide." Irregular in structure—an extra seventh syllable in every second line disrupts the ubiquitous ballad stanza pattern—the poem is at once familiar and altered. The recognizable domestic "scene," complete with "sweet uprising odors / Borne from flower-bells afar," begins to disintegrate with an abrupt "But" in the first line of the second stanza; the odors "fall on senses deadened," and the fourth and fifth stanzas gradually disclose the agent of disruption. The woman "clasps a paper," her eyes straining to read; "'Tis a list of dead and wounded!" the fifth stanza proclaims, and her lover's name is "mid the first." A single piece of paper leaves her heart "like to burst."

Constance Cary Harrison, who published extensively in southern periodicals using the pen names "Refugitta" (a persona exiled from her native South) and "Secessia" (a citizen of Baltimore), never explicitly refers to her poem's title in the poem itself.[37] The title perhaps alludes to Lord Byron's desired epitaph, which he encountered in Italian cemeteries and requested in multiple letters to friends; "there is all the helplessness," he explained, "and humble hope, and deathlike prayer, that can arise from the grave—'implora pace.'"[38] The doubling of "pace" as signifying both peace and eternal rest mirrors the "Death-in-Life" that results from reading the casualty list. This doubling extends to the woman's body and her geographical location; never moving from her chair, she is already entombed. Stars "shin[ing] stilly downward" replace the "trembling" twilight star of the first stanza and illuminate "the death-place of the brave, / And a woman's heart lies buried / In the soldier's lonely grave!" For the woman, there is no rest or peace; Harrison's poem implicitly critiques a war that makes neither possible.

The speed with which telegrams and newspapers wounded and altered was not a phenomenon confined to newspaper stories and poems. Walt Whitman's "Come Up from the Fields Father" begins with the arrival of a letter from a "dear son" and a daughter calling her father and mother to meet on the threshold of their home.[39] Before they can, however, Whitman's speaker interrupts and describes a bucolic and Edenic scene in which "apples ripe in the orchards hang." Inviting the reader to smell "the grapes on the vines," Whitman's poem and the home it depicts seem immune from the influence of conflict until line 20 reveals the letter's contents. "Sentences broken," the telegraphic shorthand of war, reach the mother's ears: "*gunshot wound in the breast, cavalry skirmish, taken to hospital, / At present low, but will soon be better.*" The bucolic scene vanishes, leaving only a "single figure . . . Sickly white in the face and dull in the head, very faint." Whitman's prescient speaker knows that "while they stand at home at the door he is dead already, / The only son is dead." Like her son, the mother, "her thin form presently drest in black," needs to be better but isn't. The temporal anomalies of the poem—Pete is simultaneously wounded, recovering, and already dead—mirror the temporal logic of telegraphic wounding.

Telegraphic Sentimentality

Stories featuring characters reading telegrams and newspapers reflected anxiety about the potential for abstraction inherent in the transmission of war information via dots and dashes. By teaching readers how to interpret casualty lists and newspaper accounts of battles, these stories engaged in the sentimental trope of reader instruction—the cultivation of readers who feel and read compassionately.[40] Telegrams and casualty lists, unlike sentimental texts, did not describe pain or present bodies to spectators. Necessarily brief, they could not provide the particulars of a soldier's experience of wounding. Unlike sentimental writing, war news was not intended to disseminate emotional pain to spectators or allow readers to appropriate the suffering of soldiers.[41] Readers had to extrapolate when faced with statistics and humanize terse descriptions of battles. Physical alteration often resulted from this intense process of reading and interpreting.

"Missing," a story published in *Harper's Weekly* in 1862, features a female narrator named Agnes whose affliction upon finding her fiancé's name on a list of missing soldiers mirrors battlefield wounding.[42] At first, the cause of Agnes's distress is unclear. This withholding of important information mimics the uncertainty and suspense of waiting for war news. Clear from the beginning is Agnes's close connection to the battlefield and its sights and sounds. Despite her geographical distance from the seat of war, she hears "the roll of drums" in "the reverberation of the crowd of carriages and omnibuses on Broadway." The sound, she explains, has been her constant companion "day and night, for five weeks." The phantom drums become the muffled drums of a "Dead March" for a fallen soldier; attempting to rid herself of visions of a "dear form . . . unburied" with a "ghastly, blackened face, upturned to the scorching sun," Agnes hears the "sad dirge" as tribute to an unnamed "him."

As swiftly as a telegram, the revelation of the cause of Agnes's despair abruptly interrupts her musings on the comforts of "a low, quiet grave." A month before, she cheerfully awaited the arrival of a letter from her soldier husband, ignoring the "morning paper" and the "carefully-worded telegraphs of the War Department." Young and "over-confident of our cause," she received her "first warning" from the "white, fixed look in [her] uncle's face"; his alteration presages hers and exhibits mature men's susceptibility to the vicissitudes of war. Before divulging the actual content of the newspaper, Agnes directly addresses the reader with an indictment and instructions:

> You take up the papers day after day, and read those dreadful lists without a thought. Those names are no more to you than the columns of a directory, or a list of advertised letters. You have a kind heart, and you sigh, and say, "Poor fellows!" as you lay them down. How little do you understand of the sickening anxiety, the appalling shock, which those very columns carry to a thousand households! How eager eyes dilate with horror and unbelief as fearing, and hoping, and praying they come upon the name they seek for staring them in the face with such persistent reality—staring them into blindness.

Casualty lists and official reports, Agnes's appeal implies, enable detachment and abstraction for those without personal interest in the soldiers listed. As such, they fail to communicate suffering while simultaneously causing it. The "columns" are immaterial for some and material for others. After reading "*Missing—Arthur L. Grant*" at the top of a list, Agnes realizes she is not exempt from suffering and a "veil of self-delusion" falls from her eyes. What is "missing" for the detached reader is physically present for the attached reader; the "blighted life in [Agnes's] thin, worn face" testifies to her confrontation with "persistent reality."

Stories and poems like "Missing" called on readers to resist detachment enabled by statistics and official reports, encouraging them to recognize a new and widespread form of injury. An adjusted way of reading, one that looks at numbers and lists of unknown names and sees bodies and souls, was necessary. Informed in part by what Carolyn Sorisio calls "the sentimental assumption that corporeal pain is a universally understandable and translatable experience," the hermeneutic approach advocated by these texts draws attention to bodies without abstracting or appropriating the pain of others.[43] Wounding proliferates via "swift-winged messengers" but remains tied to the original sufferer. Agnes reads her own pain as a symptom of being unable to nurse Arthur and decides to leave her "sheltered home," despite her weakened state, and "devote [herself] to the wearing, self-sacrificing life of nurse among the hospitals." Agnes's dedication to others enables her to find what is missing and to recognize in "a wan and wasted figure"—Arthur, taken prisoner while delirious with fever—the name she read on the list. Arthur avoids "lying among the crowded unknown dead of a soldiers' burial-ground" and Agnes returns home with her husband. The incursion of information in the form of telegrams and newspapers threatens to cause detachment and callousness but instead ties the battlefield to the home and enables concrete interaction between the two.

Virginia F. Townsend's "Wounded and Killed" (1862), a short piece by the coeditor of *Arthur's Home Magazine* that appeared in northern and southern newspapers, illustrates the importance of casualty lists and newspaper reports in Civil War Americans' daily lives while warning against casual and unfeeling reading that sees only letters on a page; the antidote to abstraction, in Townsend's formulation, is a sentimentally framed recognition of emotional and, most significantly, embodied pain: "WOUNDED AND KILLED.—It takes but little space in the columns of the daily papers; but O! what long household stories and biographies are every one of these strange names, that we read over and forget! . . . 'Wounded and Killed!' Every name in that list is a lightning stroke to some heart, and breaks like thunder over some home, and falls a long, black shadow upon some hearthstone."[44]

The "little" columns of newspapers and casualty lists, like the dots and dashes of Morse code, had big spatial and material effects on the home and the bodies of those within it. As Shirley Samuels contends, sentimentalism comprises "a set of cultural practices designed to evoke a certain form of emotional response, usually empathy, in the reader or viewer."[45] "Wounded and Killed," in highlighting the failure of empathy in the face of disembodied lists of names, encourages acknowledgment of the bodily impact of psychological torment.

Invisible Bullets

The short story "Wounded," also published in 1862, brings together the interconnected tropes of telegraphic wounding and telegraphic sentimentality, presenting a new form of reading that accounts for the rapidity with which information traveled and for the process by which war news transmitted pain from one body to another.[46] First published anonymously in *Harper's Weekly* in July 1862, the story subsequently appeared in the August 8, 1862, edition of Oskaloosa, Kansas's *Independent*; Lewiston, Pennsylvania's *Gazette* on August 13, 1862; the *Nashville Daily Union* (a Tennessee unionist paper) on September 11, 1862; and *Arthur's Home Magazine* in September 1863.[47] Timothy Shay Arthur, the editor of *Arthur's Home Magazine,* later published the story in multiple collections: as "Wounded" in *Home-Heroes, Saints, and Martyrs* (1865), "Messengers of Death" in *Home Heroines: Tales for Girls* (1867), and "Wounded" in *Heroes of the Household* (1887).[48] Its publishing history constitutes a test case for rethinking dichotomous understandings of "feminized" and "masculinized" Civil War literature. The titles of Shay's collections frame the story as domestic fiction intended, primarily, for young women. However, "Wounded" was also included in *Skedaddle, by Our "Special Correspondent,"* a collection printed in London and edited by one Lieutenant Robert Warneford of the Royal Navy.[49]

Librarians and scholars have listed Warneford as a pseudonym for William Russell, a "miscellaneous writer" of naval and detective stories, and, occasionally, for Sir William Howard Russell, widely recognized as the first war correspondent.[50] After gaining fame as a correspondent for the London *Times* during the Crimean War, Sir William Howard Russell traveled to the United States to report on the Civil War.[51] It is perhaps unlikely that the prolific correspondent found time to edit a collection of Civil War newspaper and magazine fiction; however, Warneford, a military man, and Russell, a war correspondent, were both closely associated with the supposedly masculine realm of battle, indicating the generic ambiguity of war stories.

A notice preceding the narrative and signed by Warneford discloses little about the lieutenant's identity. Instead, it frames the collection as a favor: "A LITERARY friend has asked me to see this volume of Tales through the press, making such emendations as I might deem expedient. I have done so to the best of my ability, and here only further to remark that, having no claim to the merit of the Authorship, I must not be held responsible for the political or social opinions expressed or implied in this very interesting volume. Robert Warneford, Lieut, R.N. Dec, 1864." Indicative of what Meredith L. McGill terms the nineteenth century's "culture of reprinting," the notice underscores the stories' political and societal implications.[52] Each of the stories in the collection (except for the first piece, which begins during a retreat) commences in or near the home and predominantly features female characters as well as soldiers and male noncombatants. *Skedaddle* presents "Wounded" and other seemingly domestic stories culled from popular periodicals as works closely associated with the battlefield.

The narrator of the collection's first piece, "The Gallant Lads of Missouri," claims to be "William Benton, of Hertfordshire, England, M.R.C.S., and M.D."[53] Working as an assistant surgeon in Nashville, Benton encounters "a young officer, who had been brought into the hospital, mortally wounded." A friendship ensues and, when the soldier dies, he leaves Benton "a collection of manuscripts, describing events of much interest and pathos, which have been arranged in the form of the ensuing tales." *Skedaddle,* framed by multiple masculine narrative voices, binds together war stories about women and a representative male soldier body. As such, the stories themselves are tangible links between the front and the home, both of which appear as important sites of discursive production.

"Wounded" follows "The Gallant Lads of Missouri" and connects the battlefield and military hospital to the home via telegraph lines. The narrative begins with a husband reading a casualty list to his wife; to his report of "six hundred and forty-three wounded," she responds, "If that were all." The narrator, "referring again to the newspaper which [he] h[olds] in [his] hand," confirms that the information comes from an "official return; signed by the commanding general." The narrator holds a casualty list in his hand but fails to physically register its significance. His wife, however, *feels* the news and attempts to make tangible for her husband the influence of telegrams and reports from the front. "From every battle-field," she explains, "go swift-winged messengers that kill or wound at a thousand miles instead of a thousand paces; bullets invisible to mortal eyes, that pierce loving hearts." The narrator's wife employs a number of metaphors to describe how soldiers' wounds and deaths are transmitted to women at home: war news, transmitted by telegraph and printed in newspapers, is spread by "invisible messengers of pain and death," "invisible bullets," and "such missives as pain and death." Battlefield wounds, she argues, are communicable, regardless of geographical distance. Bullets, in this story and others like it, are like telegrams: tangible and intangible, immaterial yet potent, and, most importantly, transferable; they bridge the gap between battlefield and home front.

Tellingly, the narrator's wife continues her explanation of the true significance of casualty lists by "tak[ing] the matter home"; as parents of a soldier son, she insists, the couple faces the threat of battlefield violence: "The ball that strikes him strikes us. If in that list of killed and wounded we had found his name, would there have been no bayonet point or shattering bullet in our flesh?" Echoing the grammatical structure of Shylock's plaintive "If you prick us, do we not bleed?" she references concrete agents of violence (bayonets and minié balls) to explain the pervasive corporeal and spiritual effects of wounding. She is more attuned to the outward signs of psychological suffering while her husband must learn to recognize the less visible symptoms of war's destruction. Confronted with the possibility of finding his son's name among the wounded and killed, the narrator sees instead his neighbor's name on the casualty list. His education continues when he witnesses the physical effects of casualty reports on his wife and Mrs. Harley, the wife of his wounded friend. Upon hearing the news of Harley's wounding, the narrator's wife becomes "slightly pale" and places "her hand over her heart." Her observant husband interprets her movement for the reader, connecting corporeal change to interior emotion—it is "a sign that she fe[els] pain there." Urged on by fellow-feeling, she rushes to Mrs. Harley's side and later reports back to her husband. Mrs. Harley, she tells him, "was in most intense pain. Every line in her face exhibited suffering. One hand was pressed all the while tightly over heart." Pressing their hands to their chests, Mrs. Harley and the narrator's wife resemble soldiers who clutch bullet wounds in an attempt to hold themselves together.

As the lines on telegrams Mrs. Harley receives become lines on her prematurely aged face, her husband, almost fully recovered and eager to rejoin his regiment, seems unequipped to read them. Like the narrator, Mr. Harley must learn to recognize wounds on bodies that are not "bearded and in male attire." When Mr. Harley, with "wounding, and the pain of wounding all forgotten," enthusiastically remarks that he will be with his regiment in three weeks, the narrator's wife, witnessing Mrs. Harley's distress, explains, "When you were struck she was struck also." Mr. Harley's enlightenment is instantaneous: "He turned quickly toward his wife, and saw in her face what had been unseen before, the wasting and exhaustion that come only from deep-seated pain. He had thought the paleness of her countenance, the weakness that made her step slow and cautious, only the result of overtaxed muscles and nerves. But he knew better now." Mr. Harley recognizes in his wife not a fragile woman beset by "nerves" but a fellow soldier. In cases like Mrs. Harley's, the narrator's wife explains, "the healing, if it follows, is never, as the surgeons say, by first intention, but always slow, and often through abscess and ulceration." Women like Mrs. Harley "may linger for years, but do not lose the marks of suffering." These marks—lines, pallor, abscesses, ulcers—are texts that must be interpreted correctly and compassionately. The narrator and Mr. Harley must learn to read bodies instead of statistics—to recognize in pale faces and wasted forms the pervasive influence of battlefield wounding and death.

Separating emotional experience from physical experience, the story implies, is impossible and irresponsible. The narrator recognizes that he lacked "any realizing sense of what [casualty lists] involved" when reading statistics. Using the third person to indict his audience, the narrator reflects, "We read of the killed and wounded, and sum up the figures as coldly, almost, as if the statistics were simply commercial. We talk of our losses as indifferently as if men were crates and bales." Detachment, coupled with an increasingly industrialized and capitalistic understanding of the world, leads to abstraction and heartlessness. Significantly, the narrator fears that "all sensibility, all sympathy for human suffering, has died out of [his] heart." In short, the narrator recognizes his detachment and the dangers of abstraction and learns to read correctly corporeal signs of inner torment.

Having learned the lesson his wife preaches and practices, the narrator reads a "long list of killed and wounded" and, after "counting the numbers," moves from contemplating the "bloody field and suffering hospital" to echoing his wife's sentiments at the beginning of the story. "These are not all," he exclaims. "The ball struck twice, thrice; sometimes oftener. There is pain, there is anguish, there is wounding even unto death, in many, many homes within a thousand miles of that gory place. Some are alone and neglected—dying on their battle-field with none to put even a cup of water to their lips—some are with loving friends who yet fail to stanch the flow of blood, or bandage the shattered limb—some cover their wounds, hiding them from all eyes, and bear the pain in chosen solitude." In application and effect, soldiers' bullet wounds resemble women's "invisible bullet" wounds. Rather than emphasizing the distance between home and battlefield, the casualty list allows for a complete breakdown of the line between the two as women die "on *their* battlefield," alone and untended.[54] As Drew Gilpin Faust and others have noted, Civil War Americans were troubled by the thought of their loved ones dying anonymously, far removed from the loving comforts of home and family.[55] Here, however, the home provides no such comfort. All the hallmarks of death on the battlefield—the unquenched thirst, the flowing blood, the shattered limb—exist within the domestic space.

It is the reader's responsibility, the narrator argues, to look "beyond the hospitals" for "our wounded." It is necessary to read each name on a casualty list—to resist abstraction and statistical detachment and read compassionately and corporeally—and just as necessary to understand that the news of war is as tangible and invasive as the war itself. The narrator's education enables him to teach others, namely the reader, whom he addresses as "you" and "Sir" in an imagined dialogue: "Did you notice Mrs. D—in church last Sunday? 'Yes; and now I remember that she was pale, and had an altered look.' One of our wounded!" The men in the story, and imagined male readers, must learn to read as the narrator's wife and Mrs. Harley do—to recognize alteration not only as an outward sign of inner suffering, but also as a record of embodied participation in a war fought at the front and at home. Telegraphs, casualty lists, and official reports are as lethal as bullets and kill both men and women, on the battlefield and "their battlefield." "Wounded" does not "feminize" the process of wounding but instead implies that bullets, traveling along telegraph lines, know no gender.

Invisible bullets are far-reaching and extremely destructive; they mimic the immediacy of telegraphic technology in their ability to penetrate the home and prove especially potent against the flesh and the spirit. The narrator's wife explains the severity of Mrs. Harley's condition by contrasting wounds of the body and wounds of the soul; however, her diagnosis firmly anchors spiritual wounding to the corporeal. "Flesh wounds," she argues, "close readily, but spirit wounds are difficult to heal. These invisible bullets are almost sure to reach some vital part." Her use of the word "vital" is telling: the "vital part" is simultaneously immaterial and material, related to both the essential spark of life and the organs that enable life. Mrs. Harley's spiritual pain registers as physical pain and alteration and enables Mr. Harley to understand "that two balls left the rifle when he was struck, one of them reaching to his distant home."

The bodily, spatial, and temporal logic of "Wounded"—that telegraphically transmitted war news and casualty lists resemble bullets in their ability to strike multiple individuals across long distances and at different times—appeared in stories and poems on both sides of the Mason-Dixon Line.[56] As a trope, telegraphic wounding allowed writers to understand and express the pervasive influence of violence on noncombatants while also reflecting the mutually constitutive relationship between the home and the battlefield. Mrs. Harley's literary counterparts, both female and male, endure the pain of receiving tidings of war and waiting for news of their beloved soldier boys. These texts provide another answer to Herman Melville's reflection on the dead of Shiloh—"What like a bullet can undeceive!" Causing the same effects as bullets, telegraphs and casualty lists utterly destroy assumptions about the relative safety of the home or the individual from the incursions of war.

Afterword

In his poem "Lo, Victress on the Peaks," Walt Whitman claims that he brings "no poem proud" to the triumphant Union. Though the war is over and the North has won, Whitman gives to his country "a little book containing night's darkness and blood-dripping wounds / And psalms of the dead."[1] Whitman was not alone. Lesser-known poets and authors confronted and accounted for the vicissitudes of battle and the long-lasting scars of internecine warfare. The canon has come a long way since Edmund Wilson's *Patriotic Gore,* but it is due for an influx of embodied accounts of the concrete effects of violence that reveal the real war *did* in many cases "get in the books." Any survey course about or scholarly study of nineteenth-century American literature should attend to the primacy of print culture and to popular literature's influence on the canonical texts we still read and remember today.

The canonical implications and pedagogical possibilities of disruptive bodies in Civil War print culture are indicated by how two fundamentally canonical American authors, Walt Whitman and Herman Melville, engage with a key concept: the allegorical feminine. Whitman's *Drum-Taps* and *Sequel to Drum-Taps,* and Melville's *Battle-Pieces and Aspects of the War* participate in and draw from wartime print culture and are populated by bodies; most of these bodies, however, are Caucasian and male.[2] Both poets mention war's effects on women—Melville's "A Mound by the Lake" and Whitman's "Come Up from the Fields Father" feature unnamed but symbolic women—but most feminine elements in their poems are allegorical. Attending to the rhetorical implications of female personifications in Whitman's and Melville's responses to the conflict provides a convenient entry point into the lesser-known print culture that informed the work of both poets; it also further underscores the widespread and fundamental role the allegorical feminine played in literary representations of the war, and the ways in which such allegorical representation obscured the actual contributions of real American women.

In poems like "Beat! Beat! Drums!" Whitman urged the North to war, the preservation of the nation foremost in his mind. His time in Washington, D.C., hospitals, tending to the soldiers he loved, tempered his enthusiasm; nevertheless, he remained supremely confident in the Union and its cause.[3] Whitman regularly invoked the allegorical feminine, and therefore provides further proof of Columbia's dominance as national representative and mother. The "Victress" Whitman invokes is none other than Columbia, this time in the guise of "Libertad." She surveys the world with "mighty brow," having "thwart[ed]" all attempts to destroy her. Columbia's "immortal soundness and bloom" stand in stark contrast to the aforementioned "blood-dripping wounds"; she, unlike the children who fought on her behalf, is unscathed and "unharm'd." Whitman's Columbia is far removed (standing on pedestal-like peaks) from the vicissitudes of war due to her status as an allegorical construct. Ostensibly, the "little book" Whitman brings will constitute her closest contact with the conflict.

"Over the Carnage Rose Prophetic a Voice" features another remote Columbia as inspirer of and impetus for male action.[4] Calling on the "sons of the Mother of All!" Whitman's prophetic poetic persona avers, "you shall yet be victorious." Victory, the prophecy implies, will come only through collective masculine action on behalf of Columbia, who occupies the roles of mother *and* lover. At her most allegorical, she sponsors and requires the comradeship of men: "those who love each other shall become invincible—they shall yet make Columbia victorious." The homosocial bonds between fighting men—"manly affection" in the streets between those linked "with the love of lovers"—occur under the auspices of a removed but loving maternal feminine. The prophetic voice makes no mention of Columbia's daughters, but any discussion of allegorical femininity during the Civil War should account for the equal importance of symbolic femininity—the substantial presence of real women's real wars in print culture. Whitman's Columbia, though monumental and triumphant, is detached from the lived experiences of American women.

For the most part, actual women are also absent from Melville's *Battle-Pieces*. "The Scout Toward Aldie" mentions a doomed "sunny bride" and a "sister-rebel" who teaches Union soldiers a valuable lesson about "woman's wiles in wiles of war," but the women and their wiles are secondary to the drama of Melville's lyrical interludes. The allegorical feminine, however, appears often, under the guise of "Hope," "the Past," "Israel," "Authority," and a monstrous maternal "South" who "with heat of her hate . . . hatched the egg with the cockatrice." The allegorical feminine provides Melville with a convenient means by which to invoke what he sees as the major forces, concepts, and stakes shaping the war.

In "America," Melville personifies the titular figure in a fashion surprisingly similar to S.J.A.'s poem "Not Dead," published in *Harper's Weekly* in 1861. The latter poem took its inspiration from a motto printed on a "New York banner": "The Union is not dead but sleeping." Melville's poem begins with a description of "a Banner in gladsome air," floating above "a sunny Dome" in peacetime. The personified banner is inextricably tied to the allegorical and feminine representative of the nation, the "young Maternity" invoked at the end of the first stanza; its changing environments and roles mirror the progress of the country during the war. The second stanza finds the banner "stream[ing] in fight," witness to the "lorn Mother . . . pale at the fury of her brood," while in the third the banner has become a shroud for the Union's "fair cold form." The "shining shroud" fails to rouse the national mother, but a "watcher" reports that she "sleeps, but sleeps, she is not dead." The unnamed watcher echoes S.J.A.'s poem; this similarity is perhaps not surprising, since Melville lived in New York during the war and eagerly read newspapers to learn about its progress.[5] Whether or not Melville was familiar with the poem or with the New York banner, he finds in the Union's temporary and nightmarish "trance" a fitting analogy for the nation's temporary and nightmarish dissolution.

Moving from peace to war and back to peace, Melville's poem ends with the somewhat subdued triumph of the now mature and unthreatened national mother. In other words, "America" ends where "Lo, Victress on the Peaks" begins. Having survived the national struggle, Melville's version of Columbia is not emotionally unscathed. Her "look" speaks of pain that "purifies from stain," but her fair form is intact; in her recent purification, America resembles the Columbia cleansed of the national sin by "hero-blood" in Charles A. Barry's "Columbia's Invocation." Having survived a conflict that threatened to destroy her, America wears "law on her brow and empire in her eyes." Whitman's triumphant and "unharm'd" Victress also boasts an impressive and "mighty brow regarding the world" as she stands "dominant" in the "dazzling sun." "America" ends with a similar final vision of the mother-nation:

> So she, with graver air and lifted flag;
> While the shadow, chased by light,
> Fled along the far-drawn height,
> And left her on the crag.

"The crag" is Melville's version of Whitman's "peaks"; given his earlier invocation of a "Dome," Melville potentially refers to the Statue of Freedom, added to the top of the Capitol dome in 1863. Both the statue and Melville's America stand apart from and above the fray; as representatives of legality and liberty, they are largely distant from their female children. Melville's Columbia, like Whitman's, witnesses the conflict and registers its effects but remains physically intact, unlike the wounded and scarred symbolic women and the marked men discussed earlier; "no trace of passion or of strife" mars her. Melville's maternal feminine turns her "aspect" to heaven while Whitman's "regard[s] the world," both prepared for what comes next by what came before.

Invoking the allegorical feminine enabled Melville and Whitman to tell a cohesive story about the United States during the Civil War and to imagine its postwar future—to manifest in one entity the entire course of the struggle and the significance of Union victory. In doing so, they participated in one of the most prevalent tropes of Civil War print culture. By putting their poems into conversation with each other and with representative examples from widely read newspapers and periodicals, we can broaden our understanding of the relationship between print culture and canonical works while we tell a more comprehensive story about representations of the conflict that shaped American society, culture, and literature.

In a prose supplement appended to *Battle-Pieces,* Melville wrote, "It is more than a year since the memorable surrender, but events have not yet rounded themselves into completion."[6] The cruel war was finally over, but the process of recovery, reconciliation, Reconstruction, and remembering was not. Memoirs, regimental histories, and official accounts would come later; initially, periodicals were the primary forum for constructing and contesting the Civil War's significance and legacy. In its immediacy and accessibility, print culture presents us with the opportunity to chronologically and thematically follow the ways in which Civil War Americans responded to utter defeat, total surrender, and staggering bloodshed. It also reveals a significant group of ostensibly marginalized bodies closely tied to the major issues of the conflict: Columbia, the allegorical feminine; her real-life daughters; the black soldiers who fought to save the Union and secure their freedom; and the amputee veterans of the Left-Armed Corps. The corpses of soldiers and wounded women are buried and covered by grass and the passing of time, but their broken bodies speak to us in the lines of poems and stories. Though the wounds no longer bleed, the scars remain.

NOTES

Introduction

1. Frederika Macky White, Commonplace Book, Frederica Holmes Trapnell Papers, Virginia Historical Society.

2. Dorothy Denneen Volo and James M. Volo describe antebellum literacy and newspaper consumption in *Daily Life in Civil War America* (Westport, Conn.: Greenwood Press, 1998), 203–11. For information on newspaper circulation during the war, see Brayton Harris, *Blue & Gray in Black & White* (Washington, D.C.: Brassey's, 1999).

3. Benedict Anderson, *Imagined Communities: Reflections on the Origin and Spread of Nationalism* (London: Verso, 1983), 34–35; 62–63.

4. Edmund Wilson, *Patriotic Gore: Studies in the Literature of the American Civil War* (New York: Oxford University Press, 1966), 470. Daniel Aaron, *The Unwritten War: American Writers and the Civil War* (New York: Alfred A. Knopf, 1973).

5. Timothy Sweet, *Traces of War: Poetry, Photography, and the Crisis of the Union* (Baltimore: Johns Hopkins University Press, 1990).

6. Shirley Samuels, *Facing America: Iconography and the Civil War* (New York: Oxford University Press, 2004), 6.

7. James Dawes, *The Language of War: Literature and Culture in the U.S. from the Civil War Through World War II* (Cambridge, Mass.: Harvard University Press, 2002), 1.

8. Alice Fahs, *The Imagined Civil War: Popular Literature of the North & South, 1861–1865* (Chapel Hill: University of North Carolina Press, 2001). For a recent study of canonical authors during the Civil War, see Cody Marrs, *Nineteenth-Century American Literature and the Long Civil War* (New York: Cambridge University Press, 2015).

9. Faith Barrett, *To Fight Aloud Is Very Brave* (Amherst: University of Massachusetts Press, 2012), 6–13.

10. Timothy Sweet, "Introduction," in *Literary Cultures of the Civil War*, ed. Timothy Sweet (Athens: University of Georgia Press, 2016), 8.

11. Sweet, *Traces of War*, 165, 110.

12. Franny Nudelman, *John Brown's Body: Slavery, Violence, and the Culture of War* (Chapel Hill: University of North Carolina Press, 2004), 2.

13. Ibid., 1.

14. Ibid., 98, 72.

15. Lisa A. Long, *Rehabilitating Bodies: Health, History, and the American Civil War* (Philadelphia: University of Pennsylvania Press, 2004).

16. Ibid., 9.

17. Ibid., 7.

18. Cynthia Wachtell claims that "the Civil War . . . was an idealized war," noting that "poetry's adaptability as an antiwar tool . . . was rarely on display" (*War No More: The Antiwar Impulse in American Literature, 1861–1914* [Baton Rogue: Louisiana State University Press, 2010], 31).

19. Bruce Burgett, *Sentimental Bodies: Sex, Gender, and Citizenship in the Early Republic* (Princeton, N.J.: Princeton University Press, 1998), 15.

20. Ibid.

21. See Karen Sánchez-Eppler, *Touching Liberty: Abolition, Feminism, and the Politics of the Body* (Berkeley: University of California Press, 1997); Carolyn Sorisio, *Fleshing Out America: Race, Gender, and the Politics of the Body in American Literature, 1833–1879* (Athens: University of Georgia Press, 2002); Joan Burbick, *Healing the Republic: The Language of Health and the Culture of Nationalism in Nineteenth-Century American* (Cambridge, U.K.: Cambridge University Press, 1994); Jennifer Putzi, *Identifying Marks: Race, Gender, and the Marked Body in Nineteenth-Century America* (Athens: University of Georgia Press, 2006).

22. Russ Castronovo, *Necro Citizenship: Death, Eroticism, and the Public Sphere in the Nineteenth-Century United States* (Durham, N.C.: Duke University Press, 2001), xiii.

23. Ibid., xiii.

24. Ibid., 1.

25. Sánchez-Eppler, *Touching Liberty*, 1.

26. *Chronicling America: Historic American Newspapers*, Library of Congress, chroniclingamerica.loc.gov/.

27. Paula Bernat Bennett, *Poets in the Public Sphere: The Emancipatory Project of American Women's Poetry* (Princeton, N.J.: Princeton University Press, 2003), 4–5.

28. Franco Moretti, *Distant Reading* (London: Verso, 2013).

29. J. David Hacker, "A Census-Based Count of the Civil War Dead," *Civil War History* 57, no. 4 (2011): 307. Prior to Hacker's study, the consensus on Civil War casualties hovered around 620,000 deaths.

30. James M. McPherson, *Battle Cry of Freedom: The Civil War Era* (New York: Oxford University Press, 1988), 472. For a discussion of military tactics prevalent at the outset of the war, see Herman Hattaway and Archer Jones, *How the North Won: A Military History of the Civil War* (Urbana: University of Illinois Press, 1983), 11–17. For historical overviews of the conflict, see Allan Nevins, *The War for the Union: The Improvised War* (New York: Charles Scribner's Sons, 1959); William C. Davis, *The Imperiled Union: 1861–1865* (New York:

Doubleday, 1982–83); J. G. Randall and David Donald, *The Civil War and Reconstruction* (Boston: D. C. Heath and Co., 1961).

31. For information on Civil War medicine and mortality rates, see Richard H. Shyrock, "A Medical Perspective on the Civil War," *American Quarterly* 14, no. 2 (Summer 1962); Frank R. Freemon, *Gangrene and Glory: Medical Care During the American Civil War* (Madison, N.J.: Fairleigh Dickinson University Press, 1998), Alfred J. Bollet, *Civil War Medicine: Challenges and Triumphs* (Tucson, Ariz.: Galen Press, 2002), Harold E. Straubing, *In Hospital and Camp: The Civil War Through the Eyes of Its Doctors and Nurses* (Harrisburg, Pa.: Stackpole Books, 1993).

32. Hacker, "A Census-Based Count of the Civil War Dead," 332; McPherson, *Battle Cry of Freedom,* 487.

33. See Fahs's discussion of Civil War print culture in *The Imagined Civil War,* 19.

34. "Printing Press," *Big Blue Union* (Marysville, Kans.), vol. 1, no. 7 (May 10, 1862): 1.

35. Volo and Volo, *Daily Life in Civil War America,* 214.

36. "Stonewall Jackson's Way," *Southern Literary Messenger* 37, no. 2 (February 1, 1863): 116, Daniel Lucas Bedinger Papers, Virginia Tech Archives.

37. "A Southern Publishing House," *Southern Illustrated News* 1, no. 3 (September 20, 1862): 4.

38. Volo and Volo, *Daily Life in Civil War America,* 211.

39. "The Only Reliable War Illustrations," *Frank Leslie's Illustrated Newspaper* 11, no. 283 (April 27, 1861): 1.

40. "Wanted Immediately," *Southern Illustrated News* 1, no. 3 (September 20, 1862): 4.

41. "Salutatory," *Southern Illustrated News* 1, no. 1 (September 6, 1862): 4.

42. George Sullivan, *In the Wake of Battle: The Civil War Images of Mathew Brady* (New York: Prestel, 2004), 6.

43. Qtd. in Sweet, *Traces of War,* 116.

44. Sullivan, *In the Wake of Battle,* 7.

45. For a discussion of the relationship of nineteenth-century Americans with death and the role that photography played, see Nudelman's *John Brown's Body*; for specific information on corpse photography, see page 104. See also Mark Schantz, *Awaiting the Heavenly Country: The Civil War and America's Culture of Death* (Ithaca, N.Y.: Cornell University Press, 2008).

46. Nudelman, *John Brown's Body,* 105.

47. "Some Uses of a Civil War," *Continental Monthly* 6, no. 4 (October 1864): 361.

Chapter One

1. S.J.A., "Not Dead," *Harper's Weekly* 5, no. 230 (May 25, 1861): 322.

2. E. McClung Fleming argues that the early nineteenth century "saw both the Indian Princess and the Greek goddess replaced, in popular arts, by the masculine figures of

Brother Jonathan and Uncle Sam." He also asserts that the advent of male personifications added "a missing flexibility, vitality, and robustness to the American image" ("The American Image as Indian Princess," *Winterthur Portfolio* 2 [1965]: 65–66). For more about Uncle Sam and Brother Jonathan, see Alton Ketchum, "In Search of Uncle Sam," *History Today* 40, no. 4 (1990): 20–26; Winifred Morgan, *An American Icon: Brother Jonathan and American Identity* (Cranbury, N.J.: Associated University Presses, 1988).

3. For information on Civil War cartoons and the differences between northern and southern cartoons, see Kristen M. Smith, *The Lines Are Drawn: Political Cartoons of the Civil War* (Athens, Ga.: Hill Street Press, 1999).

4. John Higham identifies Columbia as the "most common personification of the Union" in humor magazines published during the war ("Indian Princess and Roman Goddess: The First Female Symbols of America," *Proceedings of the American Antiquarian Society* 100, no. 1 [1990]: 79). Kristen Smith, in her collection of Civil War cartoons, argues that Columbia "symbolized the American people until the appearance of Brother Jonathan who became Uncle Sam." However, Brother Jonathan and Uncle Sam appear as separate entities in Civil War cartoons, and the absorption of one by the other is a later phenomenon. Columbia continued to reign supreme despite the advent of symbolic masculinity. For Smith's claim, see *Lines Are Drawn*, xviii.

5. These statistics are based on my survey of both publications between the years 1861 and 1865.

6. Drew Gilpin Faust, *Southern Stories: Slaveholders in Peace and War* (Columbia: University of Missouri Press, 1992), 112.

7. Samuels, *Facing America*, 87.

8. For representative social histories, see Elizabeth D. Leonard, *Yankee Women: Gender Battles in the Civil War* (New York: W. W. Norton & Co., 1995); Drew Gilpin Faust, *Mothers of Invention: Women of the Slaveholding South in the American Civil War* (Chapel Hill: University of North Carolina Press, 1996); Jeanie Attie, *Patriotic Toil: Northern Women and the American Civil War* (Ithaca, N.Y.: Cornell University Press, 1998); Jane E. Schultz, *Women at the Front: Hospital Workers in Civil War America* (Chapel Hill: University of North Carolina Press, 2004); Nina Silber, *Daughters of the Union: Northern Women Fight the Civil War* (Cambridge, Mass.: Harvard University Press, 2005); Judith Giesberg, *Army at Home: Women and the Civil War on the Northern Home Front* (Chapel Hill: University of North Carolina Press, 2009).

9. Frank Moore, *Women of the War: Their Heroism and Self-Sacrifice* (Hartford, Conn.: S. S. Scranton & Co., 1866); Linus Pierpont Brockett and Mary C. Vaughan, *Woman's Work in the Civil War: A Record of Heroism, Patriotism and Patience* (Philadelphia: Zeigler, McCurdy, & Co., 1867). In 1906, a former Confederate chaplain "presented the heroism of the women of the Confederacy" (J. L. Underwood, *The Women of the Confederacy* [New York: Neale Publishing Co., 1906]).

10. Alice Fahs, "The Feminized Civil War: Gender, Northern Popular Literature, and the Memory of the War, 1861–1900," *Journal of American History* 85, no. 4 (March 1999): 1493.

11. Ibid.

12. Barbara Johnson, "Women and Allegory," in *The Wake of Deconstruction* (Cambridge, Mass.: Blackwell Publishers, 1994), 54.

13. Paul de Man, "The Rhetoric of Temporality" in *Blindness and Insight: Essays in the Rhetoric of Contemporary Criticism* (Minneapolis: University of Minnesota Press, 1983), 187–228.

14. Johnson, "Women and Allegory," 73.

15. Samuels, *Facing America*, 87.

16. Mary P. Ryan, *Women in Public: Between Banners and Ballots, 1825–1880* (Baltimore: Johns Hopkins University Press, 1990), 52. Elizabeth Young, *Disarming the Nation: Women's Writing and the American Civil War* (Chicago: University of Chicago Press, 1999), 49.

17. Anne Norton, *Alternative Americas: A Reading of Antebellum Political Culture* (Chicago: University of Chicago Press, 1986).

18. Focusing on artistic and novelistic depictions of familial violence, Shirley Samuels traces the interconnectedness of family, sex, politics, and race in the formation of American identity in *Romances of the Republic: Women, the Family, and Violence in the Literature of the Early American Nation* (New York: Oxford University Press, 1996), 13.

19. C. Dallett Hemphill, *Siblings: Brothers and Sisters in American History* (New York: Oxford University Press, 2011), 131. Drew Gilpin Faust notes that southerners employed "metaphors of family and of organic duty" (*The Creation of Confederate Nationalism: Ideology and Identity in the Civil War South* [Baton Rouge: Louisiana State University Press, 1988], 84).

20. Amy Murrell Taylor, *The Divided Family in Civil War America* (Chapel Hill: University of North Carolina Press, 2005), 2.

21. Patricia Vettel-Becker, "Sacagawea and Son: The Visual Construction of America's Maternal Feminine," *American Studies* 50, no. 1–2 (Spring–Summer 2009): 27–50.

22. Latin for "stood the mournful Mother weeping." See Julia Kristeva's "The Female Body in Western Culture: Semiotic Perspectives," trans. Arthur Goldhammer, *Poetics Today* 6, no. 1–2 (1985): 133–52.

23. See Fleming's discussion of the prevalence of personified nations and continents in art in "From Indian Princess to Greek Goddess: The American Image, 1783–1815," *Winterthur Portfolio* 3 (1967): 50. For a discussion of female allegories, see Marina Warner, *Monuments and Maidens: The Allegory of the Female Form* (Berkeley: University of California Press, 1985).

24. For a discussion of the racial politics of artistic portrayals of a Native American America, see Samuels, *Romances of the Republic*, 3–10.

25. Samuels, *Romances of the Republic*, 12. Fleming, "The American Image as Indian Princess," 65.

26. According to John Higham, "Americans spoke almost interchangeably" of the two figures, and this interchangeability is reflected in the pictorial and literary record ("Indian Princess and Roman Goddess: The First Female Symbols of America," *Proceedings of the American Antiquarian Society* 100, no. 1 [1990]: 63, 79).

27. Samuels, *Facing America*, 4. Samuels claims that Columbia "gradually disappears" by the end of the nineteenth century (15). My study of the figure indicates otherwise.

28. Joshua C. Taylor, with a contribution by John G. Cawelti, *America as Art* (Washington, D.C.: Smithsonian Institution Press, 1976), 7.

29. For a discussion of personifications of the goddess of Liberty, see Maurice Algulhon, *Marianne into Battle: Republican Imagery and Symbolism in France, 1789–1880*, trans. Janet Lloyd (Cambridge, U.K.: Cambridge University Press, 1981); Martha Banta, *Imaging American Women: Idea and Ideals in Cultural History* (New York: Columbia University Press, 1987).

30. Taylor, *The Divided Family in Civil War America*, 1.

31. Oliver Wendell Holmes Sr., "Brother Jonathan's Lament For Sister Caroline," *Atlantic Monthly* 7, no. 43 (May 1861): 613.

32. G.E.D., "Two Pictures of the South," *The Liberator* 31, no. 27 (July 5, 1861): 108.

33. "Mistress Columbia, Who Has Been Taking a Nap, Suddenly Wakes Up and Calls Her Noisy Scholars to Order," *Harper's Weekly* 4, no. 158 (January 7, 1860): 16.

34. "The Great Union Meeting at New York," *Harper's Weekly* 4, no. 158 (January 7, 1860): 2, 8–9.

35. Eleanor Flexner and Ellen Frances Fitzpatrick, *Century of Struggle: The Woman's Rights Movement in the United States* (Cambridge, Mass.: Harvard University Press, 1996), 99–100.

36. "Out of a Situation," *Vanity Fair* 1, no. 15 (April 7, 1860): 233.

37. Samuels, *Facing America*, 41.

38. According to Drew Gilpin Faust, "communities gathered en masse to wish the soldiers farewell and often to present them with uniforms or flags sewn by local ladies" (*Mothers of Invention*, 15). See also Attie's discussion of flags in *Patriotic Toil*, 26–27.

39. "Woman in the Ascendant," *Saturday Evening Post*, September 13, 1862, 4.

40. For accounts of women's work related to sewing during the war, see Francis Butler Simkins and James Welch Patton, *The Women of the Confederacy* (Richmond, Va.: Garrett and Massie, 1936), 23–26; Marilyn Mayer Culpepper, *Trials and Triumphs: Women of the American Civil War* (East Lansing: Michigan State University Press, 1991), 245–48; Attie, *Patriotic Toil*, 33–35. Judith Giesberg discuss women in the Civil War workplace in *Army at Home*, 68–91.

41. "The War—Making Havelocks for the Volunteers," *Harper's Weekly* 5, no. 235 (June 29, 1861): 401. Attie describes "havelock mania" at the outset of the conflict (*Patriotic Toil*, 35).

42. Harriet N. Babb, "Maggie Morton's Mittens; or, Working for the Soldiers and What Came of It," *Ladies' Repository* 22, no. 4 (April 1862): 219–22.

43. "Flag-Presentation at New Orleans," *Harper's Weekly* 6, no. 292 (August 2, 1862): 487.

44. "Presentation of a Flag to the Thirteenth Connecticut Regiment by Loyal Ladies of New Orleans," *Harper's Weekly* 6, no. 292 (August 2, 1862): 493.

45. "A Story of Patriotism," *Douglass' Monthly* 5, no. 10 (August 1863): 856–57.

46. Cora, "To a Company of Volunteers Receiving Their Banner at the Hands of the Ladies," *Southern Literary Messenger* 33, no. 1 (July 1861): 17–19.

47. Emphasis in original.

48. Emphasis in original.

49. Emphasis mine.

50. "Columbia Awake At Last," *Harper's Weekly* 5, no. 232 (June 8, 1861): 368.

51. *Come, patriots, all that hate oppression, Assist in putting down Secession* (1861–65) American Broadsides and Ephemera, series 1, American Antiquarian Society no. 25148. The words "Columbia awake at last" appear beneath the same image on another envelope, *Columbia awake at last* (1861) American Broadsides and Ephemera, series 1, American Antiquarian Society no. 25147.

52. Samuels, *Facing America*, 42.

53. Untitled cartoon, *Harper's Weekly* 5, no. 232 (June 8, 1861): 368.

54. See Elizabeth D. Leonard, *All the Daring of the Soldier: Women of the Civil War Armies* (New York: W. W. Norton & Co., 1999); DeAnne Blanton and Lauren M. Cook, *They Fought Like Demons: Women Soldiers in the American Civil War* (Baton Rouge: Louisiana State University Press, 2002); Larry G. Eggleston, *Women in the Civil War: Extraordinary Stories of Soldiers, Spies, Nurses, Doctors, Crusaders, and Others* (Jefferson, N.C.: McFarland & Co., 2003); *An Uncommon Soldier: The Civil War Letters of Sarah Rosetta Wakeman, alias Pvt. Lyons Wakeman, 153rd Regiment, New York State Volunteers, 1862–1864*, ed. Lauren Cook Burgess (New York: Oxford University Press, 1994).

55. For examples, see "Deborah Sampson, the Woman Soldier," (Augusta) *Maine Farmer* 30, no. 22 (May 15, 1862): 4; "A Female Soldier," *Circular* (Brooklyn, N.Y.) 1, no. 1 (March 21, 1864): 8; "A Wounded Female Soldier," *Camden* (S.C.) *Daily Journal* 1, no. 20 (July 25, 1864): 1; "Another Woman Soldier," *Public Ledger* (Memphis, Tenn.) 10, no. 41 (April 16, 1870): 1.

56. S. Annie Frost, "The Soldier's Sister," *Godey's Lady's Book and Magazine* 63 (August 1861): 135.

57. I found reporting on Frances Louisa Clayton, who served in the Thirteenth Missouri Cavalry (Union), in three newspapers: "Eventful History of a Soldier Woman," *Highland Weekly News* (Hillsborough, Ohio), 27, no. 24 (October 8, 1863): 1; "Eventful History of a Soldier Woman," (New Philadelphia) *Ohio Democrat* 24, no. 47 (November 6, 1863): 1; "A Heroine," *White Cloud Kansas Chief* 7, no. 21 (November 26, 1863): 1. I found articles about Loretta De Caulp, who formed her own cavalry in Louisiana and eventually earned the rank of first lieutenant while serving as "T. Buford" in the Confederate army, in five publications: "A Female Confederate Officer," *Wilmington* (N.C.) *Journal* 22, no. 16 (May 24, 1866): 1 (rpt. from *Mobile Times*); "A Woman's Adventures in the Rebel Army," (Philadelphia) *Daily Evening Telegraph* 5, no. 128 (May 29, 1866): 2 (rpt. from "a Savannah paper"); "A Woman's Adventures in the Rebel Army," *Rutland* (Vt.) *Weekly Journal* 72, no. 23 (rpt. from "a Savannah paper"); "A Woman's Adventures in the Rebel Army," *Cleveland Daily Leader* 20, no. 141 (June 16, 1866): 2; "An Adventurous Woman," *Pulaski* (Tenn.) *Citizen* 8, no. 39 (September 28, 1866): 4 (rpt. from "the St. Louis *Republican*").

58. "The Female Sold-uier," *Vanity Fair* 4, no. 81 (July 13, 1861): 16.

59. Blanton and Cook, *They Fought Like Demons*, 5, 7.

60. For a representative example of women urging unwilling men to battle, see "A Loyal Woman's No," *Atlantic Monthly* 12, no. 73 (December 1863): 726–28. For a representative example of women urging willing men to battle, see "Go, My Boy, Where Duty Calls You," *Harper's Weekly* 6, no. 286 (June 21, 1862): 395–96.

61. "An Unwelcome Return," *Harper's Weekly* 5, no. 241 (August 10, 1861): 510.

62. "Scene, Fifth Avenue," *Harper's Weekly* 6, no. 296 (August 30, 1862): 560.

63. Harriet N. Babb, "Jennie Jewitt, the Young Recruiting Officer," *Ladies' Repository* 23, no. 4 (April 1863): 241–44.

64. William Cullen Bryant, "Our Country's Call," in *Poems of American History*, ed. Burton Egbert Stevenson (Boston: Houghton Mifflin Co., 1908), 410–11, originally published in *New York Ledger*, November 2, 1861. William Cullen Bryant, "Not Yet," *The Liberator* 31, no. 34 (August 23, 1861): 136, also published in *Smoky Hill and Republican Union* (Junction City, Kans.), September 12, 1861.

65. James Ryder Randall, "My Maryland," *Southern Literary Messenger* 36 (January 1, 1862): 40.

66. Richard E. Mezo, "Randall, James Ryder," American National Biography Online, www.anb.org/articles/16/16-01342.html (2000). I found the poem in *Southern Literary Messenger, Jacksonville Republican* (May 23, 1861), and on two broadsides published during the war.

67. For Randall and his composition of the "My Maryland," see John Wilber Jenkins, "The Poems of James Ryder Randall," *South Atlantic Quarterly* 7 (January–October 1908): 242–47.

68. "Our Women and Children," rpt. from *Memphis Avalanche* in *Liberator* 31, no. 24 (June 14, 1861): 1. For a scholarly discussion of the perceived and actual threat and occurrence of rape in the South during the Civil War, see Crystal N. Feimster, "General Benjamin Butler and the Threat of Sexual Violence During the Civil War," *Dædalus* 138, no. 2 (Spring 2009): 126–34.

69. Crystal N. Feimster, *Southern Horrors: Women and the Politics of Rape and Lynching* (Cambridge, Mass.: Harvard University Press, 2009), 20. For other scholarly discussions of sexual violence during the war, see E. Susan Barber and Charles F. Ritter, "Dangerous Liaisons: Working Women and Sexual Justice in the American Civil War," *European Journal of American Studies* 10, no. 1 (2015): 1–16; Kim Murphy, *I Had Rather Die: Rape in the Civil War* (Batesville, Va.: Coachlight Press, 2014); Thomas P. Lowry, *The Story the Soldiers Wouldn't Tell: Sex in the Civil War* (Mechanicsburg, Pa.: Stackpole Books, 1994): 123–31. These studies complicate or reject earlier claims that the Civil War was a "low rape war." For examples of the "low rape" claim, see Susan Brownmiller, *Against Our Will: Men, Women and Rape* (New York: Fawcett Columbine, 1975): 416; Reid Mitchell, *The Vacant Chair: The Northern Soldier Leaves Home* (New York: Oxford University Press, 1993): 109; Michael Fellman, "Women and Guerilla Warfare" in *Divided Houses: Gender and the Civil War*, ed. Catherine Clinton and Nina Silber (New York: Oxford University Press, 1992): 150.

70. Lisa Tendrich Frank attests to the rampant fears of sexual violence during Sherman's march to the sea: "the realization that Confederate soldiers could do little to protect women

from Union soldiers fostered a dread of sexual assault across the Southern home front" (44). According to Frank, "reports of physical rape of white women were rare," but Sherman's troops did enter and loot private homes, "verbally insulted women, threatened rape, [and] destroyed personal items" (*The Civilian War: Confederate Women and Union Soldiers During Sherman's March* [Baton Rouge: Louisiana State University Press, 2015], 52, 4).

71. Estelle B. Freedman, *Redefining Rape: Sexual Violence in the Era of Suffrage and Segregation* (Cambridge, Mass.: Harvard University Press, 2013): 31.

72. The appeal appeared under various titles in a number of publications: "Prepare for the Winter Campaign—Make the Soldier Comfortable," *Daily Nashville Patriot* 22, no. 1751 (August 20, 1861): 2; "Prepare for the Winter Campaign—Make the Soldier Comfortable," *Memphis Daily Appeal* 12, no. 192 (August 23, 1861): 2; "A Well-Timed Hint," *Semi-Weekly Standard* (Raleigh, N.C.) 11, no. 82 (September 14, 1861): 2; "A Good Suggestion," *Yorkville* (S.C.) *Enquirer* 7, n. 46 (November 14, 1861): 1. Various publications attribute the appeal to the *Richmond Examiner,* though one attributes it to the *Southern Field and Fireside.*

73. "rape, n.3.," *OED Online.* Oxford University Press.

74. The adjective "rapacious" modifies Yankees quite often, even in modern accounts of the Civil War. A Google Books search of the phrase produces 148 results.

75. T. Hulbert Underwood, "Now," *Liberator* 31, no. 40 (October 4, 1861): 160.

76. "Maryland in Fetters" (1861), Confederate Broadside Poetry Collection, WakeSpace Digital Archive, hdl.handle.net/10339/164.

77. Howard Glyndon [Laura Redden Searing], "The Legend of Our Victories," in *Idylls of Battle and Poems of the Rebellion* (New York: Hurd and Houghton, 1864), 27–32. For further examples of articles and poems that depict Columbia as stained or impure, see Mary G. Harpine, "Our Country's Guilt," *Liberator* 31, no. 42 (October 18, 1861): 168; Mary E. Wilcox, "Our Country," *Ladies' Repository* 21, no. 12 (December 1861): 733; Gerrit Smith, "Another Proof That the Nation Is Ruined," *Douglass' Monthly* 5, no. 6 (June 1863): 845.

78. Howard Glyndon [Laura Redden Searing], "Union Forever," in *Idylls of Battle and Poems of the Rebellion* (New York: Hurd and Houghton, 1864), 48–52.

79. Charles A. Barry, "Columbia's Invocation," *New South* 1, no. 6 (September 13, 1862): 1.

80. "The Union and Slavery," *New South* 1, no. 6 (September 13, 1862): 1. *New South* paraphrases Horace Greeley's August 20, 1862, letter to Lincoln, printed originally in Greeley's *New York Tribune,* which accuses the president of waging war with "deference to slavery." Lincoln's reply appears in full.

81. Schultz, *Women at the Front,* 21.

82. Both Jane E. Schultz and Libra R. Hilde articulate the difficulty of ascertaining how many southern women worked in hospitals. For explanations of the difficulties and estimates, see Schultz, *Women at the Front,* 21; Hilde, *Worth a Dozen Men: Women and Nursing in the Civil War South* (Charlottesville: University of Virginia Press, 2012), 4.

83. "The Women of the South," University of North Carolina Archive, Confederate Papers, Scrapbook clippings, 172.

84. Drew Gilpin Faust, "Altars of Sacrifice: Confederate Women and Narratives of the War," *Journal of American History* 76, no. 4 (March 1990): 1217.

85. *Journal of the Congress of the Confederate States of America: 1861–1865* (Washington, D.C.: Government Printing Office, 1904), vol. 2: 152.

86. Ibid., vol. 1: 726.

87. Libra R. Hilde notes in her study of southern nurses that "hospital work in its various forms . . . allowed women to function as political actors in a manner not available to them before the war" (*Worth a Dozen Men,* 4).

88. "Abduction of the Yankee Goddess of Liberty," *Southern Punch* 1, no. 14 (November 14, 1863): 4.

89. William Shakespeare, *Macbeth*, 5.1.36.

90. "Check-Mate!" *Harper's Weekly* 9, no. 440 (June 3, 1865): 337.

91. Andrew McCallum, "The Court-Room at the Old Penitentiary, Washington, During the Trial of the Conspirators," *Harper's Weekly* 9, no. 440 (June 3, 1865): 344–45.

92. "Trial of the Conspirators," *Harper's Weekly* 9, no. 440 (June 3, 1865): 341–43.

93. Peter S. Duval, *In Defence of the Union and the Constitution* (Philadelphia: P. S. Duval and Son, 1861), Library of Congress Prints and Photographs Online Catalog, hdl.loc.gov/loc.pnp/pga.03676.

94. Ehrgott, Forbriger, & Co., lithographer, *The Union Defenders Certificate* (1863), Library of Congress Prints and Photographs Online Catalog, hdl.loc.gov/loc.pnp/cph.3b37096.

95. For the wartime work of women abolitionists, see Wendy Hamand Venet's *Neither Ballots Nor Bullets: Women Abolitionists and the Civil War* (Charlottesville: University Press of Virginia, 1991), 2.

96. For the participation of free African American women in the antislavery movement, see Shirley J. Yee's *Black Women Abolitionists: A Study in Activism, 1828–1860* (Knoxville: University of Tennessee Press, 1992).

97. William Lloyd Garrison, "Our National Visitation," *Liberator* 32, no. 28 (July 11, 1862): 112.

98. "National Ode: Suggested by the President's Proclamation of January 1, 1863," *Continental Monthly* 3, no. 5 (May 1863): 554.

99. George Lansing Taylor, "The Promise Must Be Kept," *Liberator* 34, no. 8 (February 19, 1864): 32.

100. Kristeva, "The Female Body in Western Culture," 134.

101. "November 8, 1864." *Harper's Weekly* 8, no. 413 (November 26, 1864): 754.

102. "Columbia to Lincoln," *Harper's Weekly* 7, no. 314 (January 3, 1863): 16.

103. J. E. Baker, "Columbia Demands Her Children" (Boston, 1864), Library of Congress Prints and Photographs Online Catalog, hdl.loc.gov/loc.pnp/ppmsca.15768.

104. "The Soldier's Grave," *Freedom's Champion* (Atchinson City, Kans.), September 20, 1862, 1.

105. Thomas Nast, "Honor the Brave," *Harper's Weekly* 7, no. 356 (October 24, 1863): 680–81.

106. Thomas Nast, "Compromise with the South," *Harper's Weekly* 8, no. 401 (September 3, 1864): 572.

107. Drew Gilpin Faust, *This Republic of Suffering: Death and the American Civil War* (New York: Knopf, 2008), 149.

108. "Grounds at Andersonville, Georgia, Where Are Buried Fourteen Thousand Union Soldiers Who Died in Andersonville Prison," *Harper's Weekly* 9, no. 458 (October 7, 1865): 633.

109. "Confederate Cemetery, Franklin, Tennessee," *Harper's Weekly* 10, no. 516 (November 17, 1866): 721.

110. For the advent of Decoration Day, which later became Memorial Day, see David W. Blight, "Decoration Days: The Origins of Memorial Day in North and South," in *The Memory of the Civil War*, ed. Alice Fahs and Joan Waugh (Chapel Hill: University of North Carolina Press, 2004), 94–129.

111. "Abraham Lincoln's Coffin," *Harper's Weekly* 9, no. 435 (April 29, 1865): 267–68.

112. "A Dirge—April 15, 1865," *Liberator* 35, no. 9 (May 12, 1865): 76.

113. Thomas Nast, "Our Arms Victorious," *Harper's Weekly* 9, no. 443 (June 24, 1865): 392–93.

114. Charles Kimmel, *The End of the Rebellion in the United States, 1865* (New York: Kimmel and Foster, 1866), Library of Congress Prints and Photographs Online Collection, hdl.loc.gov/loc.pnp/cph.3a15123.

115. For further examples of the close alignment of the allegorical feminine and Union victory, see Thomas Nast, "The Blessing of Victory," *Harper's Weekly* 3, no. 404 (September 4, 1864): 616; Bayard Taylor, "Comments," *Liberator* 34, no. 29 (July 15, 1864): 116; "America Is Free," *Crutch* 2, no. 71 (May 13, 1865): 1; W. J. Linton, "Columbia Victrix," *Liberator* 35, no. 24 (June 16, 1865): 96; Mrs. A. D. T. Whitney, "Peace," *Liberator* 35, no. 33 (August 18, 1865): 132.

116. Linton, "Columbia Victrix," 96.

117. Taylor, "Comments," 116.

118. Augusta Cooper Kimball, "Shout!" *Liberator* 35, no. 29 (July 21, 1865): 116.

119. Mrs. E. A. Kidder, "The Peace Jubilee," *Liberator* 35, no. 29 (July 21, 1865): 116.

120. "The Return Home," *Harper's Weekly* 9, no. 438 (May 20, 1865): 320.

121. Mrs. P. R. Woodbury, "The Statue of Freedom," *Liberator* 34, no. 3 (January 15, 864): 12.

122. "The Statue of Freedom," Architect of the Capitol, www.aoc.gov/cc/art.

123. Eugene Walton, "Philip Reed: Slave Caster of Freedom," *Examiner* (Washington), March 1, 2005, rpt. in *Chicken Bones: A Journal for Literary and Artistic African-American Themes*, www.nathanielturner.com.

124. *Statue of Liberty.* National Park Service, 2014. www.nps.gov/stli/historyculture/people.htm.

Chapter Two

1. "A Man Knows a Man," *Harper's Weekly* 9, no. 434 (April 22, 1865): 256.

2. Thomas Nast, "Pardon and Franchise," *Harper's Weekly* 9, no. 449 (August 5, 1865): 488–89. For biographical information on Nast, see Brooks D. Simpson, "Nast, Thomas," *American National Biography Online*, www.anb.org/articles/17/17-00616.html (2000).

3. For enlistment numbers, see John David Smith, "Introduction," in *Black Soldiers in Blue: African American Troops in the Civil War Era*, ed. John David Smith (Chapel Hill: University of North Carolina Press, 2002), xiii. For historical studies of African American military service during the Civil War, see James McPherson, *Marching Toward Freedom* (New York: Knopf, 1968); James McPherson, *The Negro's Civil War: How American Negroes Felt and Acted during the War for the Union* (New York: Vintage Books, 1967); Dudley Taylor Cornish, *The Sable Arm: Negro Troops in the Union Army, 1861–1865* (New York: W.W. Norton, 1966); Benjamin Quarles, ed., *The Negro in the Civil War* (New York: Russell & Russell, 1968); Ervin L. Jordan Jr., *Black Confederates and Afro-Yankees in Civil War Virginia* (Charlottesville: University Press of Virginia, 1995); Joseph T. Glatthaar, *Forged in Battle: The Civil War Alliance of Black Soldiers and White Officers* (New York: Free Press, 1990); Noah Andre Trudeau, *Like Men of War: Black Troops in the Civil War, 1862–1865* (Boston: Little, Brown, 1998).

4. Frederick Douglass, "Enlistment of Colored Men." *Douglass' Monthly* 5, no. 15 (August 1863): 852.

5. Christopher Hager, "'if we Ever Expect to be a Pepple': The Epistolary Culture of African American Soldiers," in *Literary Cultures of the Civil War*, ed. Timothy Sweet (Athens: University of Georgia Press, 2016), 26.

6. For historical studies of shifting conceptions of black manhood during the Civil War, see Margaret Humphreys, *Intensely Human: The Health of the Black Soldier in the American Civil War* (Baltimore: Johns Hopkins University Press, 2008); Leann Whites, "The Civil War as a Crisis in Gender," in *Divided Houses*, ed. Clinton and Silber, 3–21.

7. Fahs, *The Imagined Civil War*, 181, 166.

8. Jennifer James, *A Freedom Bought with Blood: African American War Literature from the Civil War to World War II* (Chapel Hill: University of North Carolina Press, 2007), 48, 52.

9. Fahs, *The Imagined Civil War*, 161.

10. Ibid., 172.

11. James, *A Freedom Bought with Blood*, 17.

12. Carole Emberton, *Beyond Redemption: Race, Violence, and the American South after the Civil War* (Chicago: University of Chicago Press, 2013), 133.

13. McPherson, *Marching Toward Freedom*, 123.

14. Emberton, *Beyond Redemption*, 104. After the passage of the Conscription Act in 1863, white men who could not afford a substitute were subject to the draft, a form of forced enlistment. For the draft, see Iver Bernstein, *The New York City Draft Riots: Their Significance for American Society and Politics in the Age of the Civil War* (New York: Oxford University Press, 1990), 7–9.

15. Emberton, *Beyond Redemption*, 126, 117.

16. Elaine Scarry, *The Body in Pain: The Making and Unmaking of the World* (New York: Oxford University Press, 1985), 24.

17. Putzi, *Identifying Marks*, 123.

18. In her discussion of Walt Whitman's revisions to *Drum-Taps*, Christanne Miller finds in the 1871 *Leaves of Grass* an "unproblematized reconciliation [that] can take place

only through the erasure of the memory of slavery." According to Miller, African American poets continue to write about black soldiers after the war, but "Northern white poets . . . many of whom condemned slavery and Confederate betrayal . . . now write of reconciliation" ("Drum-Taps: Revisions and Reconciliation," *Walt Whitman Quarterly Review* 26, no. 4 [Spring 2009]: 186. John A. Casey Jr. contends that many post-Reconstruction African American writers purposefully avoided the topic of black soldiers in the Civil War in order to dissociate black men and violence (*New Men: Reconstructing the Image of the Veteran in Late-Nineteenth-Century American Literature and Culture* [New York: Fordham University Press, 2015], 130–62).

19. Karen Sánchez-Eppler, "Bodily Bonds: The Intersecting Rhetorics of Feminism and Abolition," *Representations* 24 (Fall 1988): 39. Samuels, *Romances of the Republic*, 113.

20. For a derogatory depictions of black soldiers, see Fahs, *The Imagined Civil War*, 150–94.

21. McPherson, *Marching Toward Freedom*, 12.

22. See Ella Forbes, *African American Women During the Civil War* (New York: Routledge, 1998).

23. McPherson, *Marching Toward Freedom*, 123.

24. *Taking an Observation from a Dark Point* (Philadelphia: Magee, 1861), American Broadsides and Ephemera, series 1, American Antiquarian Society no. 24742, Archive of Americana, infoweb.newsbank.com.

25. "Dark Artillery; or, How to Make the Contrabands Useful," *Frank Leslie's Illustrated News* 12, no. 309 (October 26, 1861): 368.

26. Casey, "An Illustration of the New Yankee Doctrine About the Darkey," *Southern Illustrated News* 3, no. 20 (June 11, 1864): 160.

27. McPherson, *Marching Toward Freedom*, 12.

28. For the image's dissemination, see Marcus Wood, *Blind Memory: Visual Representations of Slavery in England and America: 1780–1865* (New York: Routledge, 2000), 268–71. For analyses of the image, see Fahs, *The Imagined Civil War* 169–71; James, *A Freedom Bought With Blood*, 16–18; Marcus Wood, *Black Milk: Imagining Slavery in the Visual Cultures of Brazil and America* (Oxford, U.K.: Oxford University Press, 2013), 247; Emberton, *Beyond Redemption*, 103–4.

29. "A Typical Negro," *Harper's Weekly* 7, no. 340 (July 4, 1863): 429–30.

30. David Silkenat, "'A Typical Negro': Gordon, Peter, Vincent Colyer, and the Story behind Slavery's Most Famous Photograph," *American Nineteenth Century History* 15, no. 2 (2014): 183.

31. Ibid., 179. The revision of the date complicates Marcus Wood's claim that "Gordon's status is not one of martyrological elevation but of secular victimhood" (*Blind Memory*, 268).

32. Wood, *Blind Memory*, 268; James, *A Freedom Bought With Blood*, 17; Emberton, *Beyond Redemption*, 104.

33. See Fahs, *The Imagined Civil War*, 169–71; Putzi, *Identifying Marks*, 100.

34. "A Typical Negro," *Harper's Weekly* 7, no. 340 (July 4, 1863): 429–30.

35. “The Escaped Slave and the Union Soldier,” *Harper’s Weekly* 8, no. 392 (July 2, 1864): 422 (text), 428 (image).

36. Fahs, *The Imagined Civil War*, 176.

37. Jennifer Putzi’s claim seems to overlook an important counternarrative produced by texts like the ones I discuss in this chapter in order to account for postwar reconciliationist and reactionary rejections of black men’s claims to manhood and citizenship. See *Identifying Marks*, 123.

38. “The Black Heroes,” *Liberator* 33, no. 6 (February 5, 1864): 24.

39. Emphasis in the original.

40. Howard Glyndon [Laura Redden Searing], “Butler’s Black Brigade,” *Idylls of Battle and Poems of the Rebellion* (New York: Hurd and Houghton, 1864), 142–44.

41. For information on the riots, see Bernstein, *New York City Draft Riots.*

42. For Benjamin Butler and the formation of the U.S.C.T., see John David Smith, “Let Us All Be Grateful That We Have Colored Troops That Will Fight,” in *Black Soldiers in Blue: African American Troops in the Civil War Era*, ed. John David Smith (Chapel Hill: University of North Carolina Press, 2002), 22.

43. For more on the Fort Pillow massacre, see Richard L. Fuchs, *Unerring Fire: The Massacre at Fort Pillow* (Mechanicsburg, Pa.: Stackpole Books, 2002).

44. *Henry V* 4.3.61–63.

45. “The Negro Regiment—Meeting of the Colored Citizens,” *Douglass’ Monthly* 5, no. 10 (March 1863): 809.

46. Scarry, *The Body in Pain*, 24.

47. F. M. Adlington, “The Heroic Black,” *Liberator* 34, no. 11 (March 11, 1864): 44.

48. Sarah E. Shuften, “Ethiopia’s Dead,” *Colored American* 1, no. 3 (December 30, 1865): 4.

49. For Shuften, see a brief biography in Faith Barrett and Cristanne Miller, *“Words for the Hour”: A New Anthology of American Civil War Poetry* (Amherst: University of Massachusetts Press, 2005), 391.

50. Thomas B. Wester, Letter 93, in *A Grand Army of Black Men: Letter from African-American Soldiers in the Union Army, 1861–1865*, ed. Edwin S. Redkey (New York: Cambridge University Press, 1992), 216–18; originally published in *Christian Recorder* 5, no. 1 (January 7, 1865): 2.

51. William H. Watson, Letter 94 in *A Grand Army of Black Men*, ed. Redkey, 216–18. Originally published in *Christian Recorder* 5, no. 12 (March 18, 1865): 41.

52. For African American soldiers and literacy, see Heather Andrea Williams, “‘Commenced to Think Like a Man’: Literacy and Manhood in African American Civil War Regiments,” in *Southern Manhood: Perspectives on Masculinity in the Old South*, ed. Craig Thompson Friend and Lorri Glover, 196–219 (Athens: University of Georgia Press, 2004).

53. Hager, “‘if we Ever Expect to be a Pepple,’” 26.

54. Jim Cullen, “‘I’s a Man Now’: Gender and African American Men,” in *Divided Houses*, ed. Clinton and Silber, 77.

55. William Waters, “Letter from the 26th U.S.C.T.” *Christian Recorder* 5, no. 15 (April 15, 1865).

56. James M. McPherson's *For Cause and Comrades: Why Men Fought in the Civil War* (Oxford, U.K.: Oxford University Press, 1997) is a helpful study of the motivations of Civil War soldiers; see 117–30 for Union soldiers' views on emancipation.

57. "A Colored Private," Letter 26 in *A Grand Army of Black Men*, ed. Redkey, 65–66. Originally published in *Liberator* 34, no. 29 (July 15, 1864): 114.

58. William Wells Brown, *The Negro in the American Rebellion: His Heroism and His Fidelity* (Boston: Lee and Shepard, 1867), 379–80.

59. Brian Matthew Jordan writes of Edmonds's first entry only, using it as evidence that "disfigured veterans became especially committed to the cause of emancipation and racial equality." Edmonds's second submission complicates Jordan's generalization. See Brian Matthew Jordan, *Marching Home: Union Veterans and their Unending Civil War* (New York: Liveright Publishing Corp., 2014), 121.

60. Charles A. Edmonds, Contest Entry, 1st series, no. 51, William Oland Bourne Papers, Manuscript Division, Library of Congress, Washington, D.C.

61. Casey, *New Men*, 131.

62. For the battle of Port Hudson and the participation of two Louisiana black regiments, see Hondon B. Hargrove, *Black Union Soldiers in the Civil War* (Jefferson, N.C.: McFarland & Co., 1988), 131–39.

63. "Battle of Port Hudson," *Frank Leslie's Illustrated News* 16, no. 404 (June 27, 1863): 209.

64. See Emberton, *Beyond Redemption*, 371–72.

65. Hargrove, *Black Union Soldiers in Blue*, 86.

66. "Assault of the Second Louisiana (Colored Regiment) on the Rebel Works at Port Hudson, May 27," *Frank Leslie's Illustrated News* 16, no. 404 (June 27, 1863): 216–17.

67. George H. Boker, "The Second Louisiana," *Frank Leslie's Illustrated News* 16, no. 404 (June 27, 1863): 209–10; broadside version: *The Second Louisiana* (Philadelphia: Union League of Philadelphia, 1863), American Broadsides and Ephemera, series 1, American Antiquarian Society no. 11388, Archive of Americana, infoweb.newsbank.com.

68. *Officer and Members of the Philadelphia Union League* (Philadelphia: Henry B. Ashmead, 1863), Ann Arbor: ProQuest I&L Research Collections. For a biography of Boker, see Claudia Durst Johnson, "Boker, George Henry," American National Biography Online, www.anb.org/articles/16/16–00142.html (2000).

69. Daniel Hack, "The Canon in Front of Them: African American Deployments of the 'The Charge of the Light Brigade,'" in *Early African American Print Culture*, ed. Lara Langer Cohen and Jordan Alexander Stein (Philadelphia: University of Pennsylvania Press, 2012), 185.

70. "Charge of the Black Brigade," *Chicago Daily Tribune* 16, no. 299 (June 12, 1863): 3.

71. George H. Boker, *Das Zweite Louisiana Regiment* (Philadelphia, 1863), American Broadsides and Ephemera, series 1, American Antiquarian Society no. 11387, Archive of Americana, infoweb.newsbank.com.

72. "The Drama," *Chicago Daily Tribune* (August 25, 1901): 39.

73. I found Boker's poem in a number of publications: "The Second Louisiana," *Daily Intelligencer* (Wheeling, W.Va.) 11, no. 251 (June 11, 1863): 4; "The 2D Louisiana," *Union*

County Star and Lewisburg (Pa.) *Chronicle* (June 23, 1863): 2; "The Second Louisiana," *Littell's Living Age* (Boston) 996 (July 4, 1863): 2; "The Second Louisiana," *Ashtabula* (Ohio) *Weekly Telegraph* 13, no. 26 (July 11, 1863): 1; "The Second Louisiana," *Weekly Perrysburg* (Ohio) *Journal* 11, no. 11 (July 15, 1863): 1; "The Black Regiment," *Free South* (Beaufort, S.C.) 1, no. 29 (July 25, 1863): 1; "The Second Louisiana," *Cecil Whig* (Elkton, Md.) 23, no. 17 (October 31, 1863): 1; "The Black Regiment," *Potter Journal* (Potter County, Pa.) 16, no. 5 (February 24, 1864): 1; "The Black Regiment," *New National Era and Citizen* (Washington, D.C.) 4, no. 23 (June 12, 1873): 4; "The Black Regiment," *Mitchell* (S.Dak.) *Capital* 19, no. 29 (April 22, 1898): 3. I found excerpts of the poem in the following publications: "Indiana Legion in Camp," *Indianapolis Journal* (July 23, 1889): 8; "The Negro as a Soldier," *Indianapolis Journal* (November 15, 1890): 8; "Echoes of the Battle," *Washington* (D.C.) *Bee* 10.12 (August 15, 1891): 2.

74. Ringwalt & Brown, *In Commemoration of Emancipation in Maryland, November 1, 1864* (Philadelphia: Ringwalt & Brown, ca. 1864), Gilder Lehrman Collection GLC05701, www.americanhistory.amdigital.co.uk/Documents/Images/GLC05701/0?searchId=e8afca55-9a3b-4792-a488-74491fdf8fe6.

75. Ibid., verso.

76. "Speech of Hon. Henry P. Cheatham, at Raleigh, N.C., on January 1, 1898," *Gazette* (Raleigh, N.C.) 9, no. 48 (January 15, 1898): 2.

77. "A Pleasant Incident," *Colored American* 8, no. 9 (June 2, 1900): 7.

78. "Lest We Forget: Some History Now Quite Pertinent and More Than Interesting," *Washington Post,* November 12, 1901, 6; "*New York Sun* Says Noble Record of Colored Regiments Should be Considered," *Sedalia Weekly Conservator* 4, no. 24 (November 26, 1906): 2.

79. John D. Weaver, *The Brownsville Raid* (College Station: Texas A&M University Press, 1992).

80. For the Twenty-Fourth Regiment and African American soldiers in the Spanish-American War, see Roger D. Cunningham, "'A Lot of Fine, Sturdy Black Warriors': Texas's African American 'Immunes' in the Spanish-American War," in *Brothers to the Buffalo Soldiers: Perspectives on the African American Militia and Volunteers, 1865–1917*, ed. Bruce A. Glasrud (Columbia: University of Missouri Press, 2011): 186–208; and Marvin E. Fletcher, "The Black Volunteers in the Spanish-American War," in *Brothers to the Buffalo Soldiers,* ed. Glasrud, 129–42. For a contemporary account of black regiments at the Battle of San Juan Hill, see T. G. Steward, *Buffalo Soldiers: The Colored Regulars in the United States Army* (1904; rpt. Mineola, N.Y.: Dover Publications, 2014), 191–219.

81. Addie W. Hunton and Kathryn M. Johnson, *Two Colored Women with the American Expeditionary Forces* (Brooklyn, N.Y.: Brooklyn Eagle Press, 1920), 75–76.

82. "The Black Regiment," *Kansas City* (Mo.) *Sun* 10, no. 43 (June 22, 1918): 1.

83. "Literature," *Crisis* 17, no. 6 (April 1919): 288. "Kettle Hill" refers to the Battle of San Juan Hill.

84. Frederick Douglass, "Men of Color, to Arms!" *Douglass' Monthly* 5, no. 11 (April 1863): 826–27.

Chapter Three

1. Civil War reminiscences by soldiers and sailors in Central Park Hospital, New York City, William Oland Bourne Papers.

2. Biographical information on Bourne from obituary: "Death List of a Day," *New York Times*, June 7, 1901, 9. Bourne published *Poems of the Republic* in 1864. He also published poems and descriptions of the war written by members of the "Left Hand Corps" in his newspaper, the *Soldier's Friend*.

3. Faith Barrett indicates the "flexibility" of poetry as one reason Civil War Americans chose to write verse in response to the conflict. In her study of popular poetry, Barrett focuses particularly on the "poet-speaker's personal 'I' and the vital collective 'we' of military experience," two perspectives that reflect "conflicting aesthetic and political aims" (*To Fight Aloud Is Very Brave*, 3, 43).

4. "An Attractive Book: Battle Memories of the Left-Armed Corps," *Soldier's Friend* 2, no. 9 (September 1866): 2.

5. "specimen, n.," *OED Online*.

6. For the relationship of disability to capitalism and industrialization, see Harlan Hahn, "Advertising the Acceptably Employable Image: Disability and Capitalism," in *The Disability Studies Reader*, ed. Lennard Davis (New York: Routledge, 2010), 172–186; Lennard Davis, "Constructing Normalcy: The Bell Curve, the Novel, and the Invention of the Disabled Body in the Nineteenth Century," in *The Disability Studies Reader*, ed. Davis, 9–28.

7. Frances M. Clarke, *War Stories: Suffering and Sacrifice in the Civil War North* (Chicago: University of Chicago Press, 2011), 145.

8. Jordan, *Marching Home*, 111.

9. "Left-Hand Penmanship," *Soldier's Friend* 4, no. 9 (September 1868): 1.

10. Walt Whitman, *Specimen Days*, in *Complete Prose Works* (Philadelphia, 1892), 80.

11. Aaron, *The Unwritten War*, xvii; Sweet, *Traces of War*, 46–51; Nudelman, *John Brown's Body*, 72–73; Dawes, *The Language of War*, 7–8.

12. Clarke, *War Stories*, 145–46. Clarke looks at "three dominant narratives of redemptive suffering": political, religious, and personal. Benjamin Cooper, "Franklin H. Durrah, John William De Forest, and the Varieties of Military Experience," *Arizona Quarterly* 67, no. 2 (Summer 2011): 42.

13. Whitman, *Specimen Days*, in *Complete Prose Works* (Philadelphia, 1892), 81.

14. Ibid., 81.

15. Walt Whitman, *Specimen Days* (New York: Barnes and Noble, 2007), 225n.

16. Walt Whitman, *Memoranda During the War* (Camden, N.J., 1875), whitmanarchive.org/published/other/memoranda.html. 4.

17. Whitman, *Specimen Days*, in *Complete Prose Works* (Philadelphia, 1892), 81.

18. Castronovo, *Necro Citizenship*, 10.

19. Wilson, *Patriotic Gore*.

20. Jordan, *Marching Home*, 109.

21. Frances M. Clarke argues that depictions of Civil War amputees presented a "singular class"—men who deserved recognition but failed to become "a rallying point for structural changes to address poverty or warfare." My approach distinguishes between depictions of empty sleeves and amputation stumps, thus challenging Clarke's "singular class" designation; see Clarke, *War Stories*, 151. For representative examples of empty sleeves in the popular press, see J. M. Letts, "Our Disabled Veterans," *Soldier's Friend* 3, no. 9 (September 1867): 4; August H. Penn, "A Story of the War," *Soldier's Friend* 3, no. 9 (August 1867): 1; Dr. G. W. Bagby, "The Empty Sleeve," *Southern Illustrated News* 1, no. 14 (December 13, 1862): 5; Britomarte, "Empty Sleeves," *Soldier's Friend* 4, no. 2 (February 1868): 8.

22. The word "apostrophe" is derived from the Greek words for "turn" and "away" ("apostrophe, n.1.," *OED Online.*)

23. James Dawes argues that efforts to transform individual suffering into collective recovery "subdue violence with language" (*The Language of War*, 11). Collective traumas, posits Jeffrey C. Alexander, "are reflections of neither individual suffering nor actual events, but symbolic renderings that reconstruct and imagine them" (*Trauma: A Social Theory* [Malden, Mass.: Polity Press, 2012], 4).

24. For the ways in which pain resists "verbal or visual representation" and "objectification," see Elaine Scarry, *Resisting Representation* (New York: Oxford University Press, 1994), 20.

25. "Empty Sleeves," *Soldier's Friend* 4, no. 10 (October 1868): 1.

26. Laurann Figg and Jane Farrell-Beck, "Amputation in the Civil War: Physical and Social Dimensions," *Journal of the History of Medicine and Allied Sciences* 48 (October 1993): 459.

27. Figg and Farrell-Beck note that "one-and-a-half times more men survived the War with upper extremity amputations than lower extremity amputations" ("Amputation in the Civil War," 460).

28. David Barker, "The Empty Sleeve," *Frank Leslie's Illustrated News* 16, no. 399 (May 30, 1863): 149; also published in *Crutch* 2, no. 70 (May 6, 1865): 1, Archives of Maryland Online, aomol.net.

29. John C. Buttre, *The Empty Sleeve* (Boston: N. Y. & B. B. Russell & Co., 1866), Southern Methodist University, Central University Libraries, DeGolyer Library Collection, digitalcollections.smu.edu/cdm/ref/collection/civ/id/424.

30. David Barker, "The Empty Sleeve," *Soldier's Friend* 3, no. 9 (September 1867): 8.

31. "Literary and Artistic Items," *Ladies' Repository* 36, no. 20 (October 1866): 316.

32. G. P. Critcherson, *The Empty Sleeve* (1870), Southern Methodist University, Central University Libraries, DeGolyer Library Collection, digitalcollections.smu.edu. *The Railsplitter: A Journal for the Lincoln Collector* identifies Henry H. Meacham as the soldier in the image (www.railsplitter.com/sale10/imprints.html).

33. Mrs. P. A. Hanaford (words) and Rev. J. W. Dadmun (music), "The Empty Sleeve" (Boston: Oliver Ditson & Co., 1866), Johns Hopkins University, Levy Street Music Collection, box 087, item 139, jhir.library.jhu.edu/handle/1774.2/25685. For analysis of the close connection of song and verse during the Civil War, see Barrett, *To Fight Aloud Is Very Brave*,

17–40; Michael Cohen, "Contraband Singing: Poems and Songs in Circulation during the Civil War," *American Literature* 82, no. 2 (June 2010): 271–304.

34. In her study of the discursive implications of the wartime practice by which draftees hired substitutes to fight in their place, Colleen Glenney Boggs argues that the empty sleeve "becomes an emblem of and mechanism for a set of substitutions that tie the bodily to the political and make disability a key condition of American subjectivity" ("The Civil War's 'Empty Sleeve' and the Cultural Production of Disabled Americans," *J19: The Journal of Nineteenth-Century Americanists* 3, no. 1 [Spring 2015]: 51, 61–62).

35. "Left-Handed Penmanship," *Harper's Weekly* 10, no. 448 (July 29, 1865): 467.

36. "List of Competitors for the Prizes for Left-Hand Penmanship," *Soldier's Friend* 4, no. 1 (January 1868): 2; William Oland Bourne, "Left-Hand Writing by Disabled Soldiers and Sailors of the War," *Soldier's Friend* 4, no. 1 (January 1868): 4.

37. Handbills, William Oland Bourne Papers.

38. "To the Left-Armed Corps of the Union," *Soldier's Friend* 3, no. 6 (June 1867): 2.

39. Martha Stoddard Holmes, *Fictions of Affliction: Physical Disability in Victorian Culture* (Ann Arbor: University of Michigan Press, 2004), 94–136.

40. George Bucknam, Contest Entry, 2nd series, no. 47, William Oland Bourne Papers.

41. Alfred D. Whitehouse, Contest Entry, 1st series, no. 163, William Oland Bourne Papers.

42. Famous nineteenth-century "armless wonder" performers like Ann E. Leak Thompson and Charles Tripp were photographed writing and drinking tea with their feet; showmen used such portraits to portray performers as morally upstanding personages who overcame hardship while at the same time presenting them as fascinating spectacles of difference that assured spectators of their own bodily wholeness and normality. For freak shows, see Rachel Adams, *Sideshow U.S.A.: Freaks and the American Cultural Imagination* (Chicago: University of Chicago Press, 2001); Rosemarie Garland-Thomson, *Extraordinary Bodies: Figuring Physical Disability in American Culture and Literature* (New York: Columbia University Press, 1997), 55–80. For freak-show photography, see Ann Millett-Gallant, *The Disabled Body in Contemporary Art* (New York: Palgrave Macmillan, 2010).

43. David Serlin, "Crippling Masculinity: Queerness and Disability in U.S. Military Culture, 1800–1945," *Gay and Lesbian Quarterly* 9, no. 1–2 (2003): 161. Serlin also discusses Civil War photography in *Replaceable You: Engineering the Body in Postwar America* (Chicago: University of Chicago Press, 2004), 33–35. Kim E. Neilsen notes that "disabled veterans embodied a unique disability status" since their military service confirmed their manhood (*A Disability History of the United States* [Boston: Beacon Press, 2012], 87).

44. For literary representations of the demobilization and reintegration into civilian life of Civil War soldiers, see Casey, *New Men*, 17–47.

45. "Exhibition of Left-Hand Penmanship," William Oland Bourne Papers.

46. Clarke, *War Stories*, 144–45.

47. Erin O'Connor, *Raw Material: Producing Pathology in Victorian Culture* (Durham, N.C.: Duke University Press, 2000), 124.

48. Jennifer Davis McDaid claims that "many veterans considered prosthetic arms and legs noisy, uncomfortable, and cumbersome" ("'How a One-Legged Rebel Lives': Confederate Veterans and Artificial Limbs in Virginia," in *Artificial Parts, Practical Lives: Modern Histories of Prosthetics*, ed. Katherine Ott, David Serlin, and Stephen Mihm [New York: New York University Press, 2002], 122). Laurann Figg and Jane Farrell-Beck also note that many amputees complained of uncomfortable and ill-fitting artificial limbs ("Amputation in the Civil War," 464). For more on the prosthetics industry after the war, see Stephen Mihm, "'A Limb Which Shall Be Presentable in Polite Society': Prosthetic Technologies in the Nineteenth Century," in *Artificial Parts, Practical Lives*, ed. Ott, Serlin, and Mihm, 282–99. Mihm, noting the difficulty Confederate veterans had obtaining artificial limbs, argues that in the North an empty sleeve often inspired derision and revulsion while in the South it inspired respect and recognition. A number of contestants, choosing to send pictures of themselves with empty sleeves, complicate this bifurcation.

49. I am unable to verify the veteran's identity. However, he appears to be Burritt Stiles of Connecticut (Burritt Stiles, Contest Entry, 1st series, William Oland Bourne Papers).

50. For norms and the formation of the "normal," see Davis, "Constructing Normalcy," 9–28.

51. O'Connor, *Raw Material*, 126.

52. "Premium $500 to the Left-Armed Soldiers of the Union," *Soldier's Friend* 1, no. 7 (August 1865): 2. The list of entrants for the first competition names 270 veterans, including 30 commissioned officers, 52 noncommissioned officers, 185 privates, and two members of the United States Colored Troops ("List of Contributors," *Soldier's Friend* 2, no. 3 [March 1866]: 2–3).

53. William Tecumseh Sherman, Letter to Caleb Fisher, William Oland Bourne Papers; also published in *Soldier's Friend*. Bourne, "Left-Hand Writing by Disabled Soldiers and Sailors of the War."

54. Millett-Gallant, *The Disabled Body in Contemporary Art*, 10.

55. Phineas P. Whitehouse, Contest Entry, 1st series, no. 136, William Oland Bourne Papers.

56. For nineteenth-century American conceptions of masculinity and physical labor, see Gregory L. Kaster, "Labour's True Man: Organised Workingmen and the Language of Manliness in the USA, 1827–1877," *Gender and History* 13, no. 1 (April 2001): 24–64.

57. Serlin, "Crippling Masculinity," 160–61. Lisa Marie Herschbach similarly argues that "the 'empty-sleeve' was both a badge of courage and a mark of permanent disability; of manly heroism and effeminate dependency; of patriotic sacrifice and inability to care for family" ("Prosthetic Reconstructions: Making the Industry, Re-Making the Body, Modelling the Nation," *History Workshop Journal* no. 44 [Autumn 1997]: 24).

58. Megan Kate Nelson, *Ruin Nation: Destruction and the American Civil War* (Athens: University of Georgia Press, 2012), 197.

59. Frances M. Clarke claims that personification allowed amputee writers to "grieve without relating grief to a permanent state inherent to their injuries." Combining personification with apostrophe, however, complicates this distinction. See Clarke, *War Stories*, 158.

60. Barbara Johnson, "Apostrophe, Animation, and Abortion," *Diacritics* 16, no. 1: 30, 32.

61. See J. Mark Smith, "Apostrophe, or the Lyric Art of Turning Away," *Texas Studies in Literature and Language* 49, no. 4 (Winter 2007): 411–37.

62. John Blanchard, Contest Entry, 1st series, no. 75, William Oland Bourne Papers.

63. By 1880, Blanchard had two children with his wife, Mary, and worked as a school-teacher, his ability to support his family unaffected by his disability (U.S. Census Bureau, *U.S. Census, 1880: Elyria, Lorain, Ohio,* roll 1042, Ancestry.com).

64. Phineas P. Whitehouse, Contest Entry, 1st series, no. 136. Noticeably more writerly than most of the other contestants, Whitehouse left a poetic message expressing his gratitude in Bourne's hospital-reminiscence book and later published a biographical sketch of another soldier in Bourne's newspaper ("A True Patriot," *Soldier's Friend* 3, no. 2 [February 1867]: 1).

65. For Frances M. Clarke's reading of Whitehouse's poem as a journey from "anguish to acceptance," see *War Stories*, 157.

66. Thomas A. Perrine, Contest Entry, 1st series, no. 50, William Oland Bourne Papers.

67. Michael Cohen, "Whittier, Ballad Reading, and the Culture of Nineteenth-Century Poetry," *Arizona Quarterly* 64, no. 3 (Autumn 2008): 3.

68. *Scott v. Sandford,* 60 U.S. 393 (1856).

69. Perrine went on to work a dairy farm with his wife, a woman who, unlike the fictional May Dey, accepted his remaining hand (U.S. Census Bureau, *U.S. Census, 1880: Douglas, Colorado,* roll 90, Ancestry.com).

70. "left, adj. 1, adv., and n.," *OED Online.* Lauren Julius Harris notes that the word for "left" in other languages, including French, German, and Greek, connotes weakness and clumsiness ("Cultural Influences on Handedness: Historical and Contemporary Theory and Evidence," in *Left-handedness: Behavioral Implications and Anomalies*, ed. Stanley Coren [New York: North-Holland Elsevier Science Publishing Co., 1990], 202). For other examinations of the cultural meanings of the left side and the left hand, see Chris McManus, *Right Hand, Left Hand: The Origins of Asymmetry in Brains, Bodies, Atoms, and Cultures* (London: Weidenfeld & Nicolson, 2002); Michael Barsley, *An Investigation into the Sinister History of Left-Handedness* (New York: Hawthorn Books, Inc., 1966); Anne Harrington, *Medicine, Mind, and the Double Brain: A Study in Nineteenth-Century Thought* (Princeton, N.J.: Princeton University Press, 1987). For the relationship between left-handedness and femininity, see Anne Harrington, "Unfinished Business: Models of Laterality in the Nineteenth Century," in *Brain Asymmetry*, ed. Richard J. Davidson and Kenneth Hugdahl (Cambridge, Mass.: MIT Press, 1995).

71. Contestant John Bryson sent a signed affidavit attesting to both the loss of his right arm and the fact that he had "never used [his] Lefthand in writing, prior to losing [his] right" (Contest Entry, 2nd series, no. 18, William Oland Bourne Papers).

72. Scientists and historians estimate that 10 percent of the global population is and has historically been left-handed; however, one study reports that the number of left-handed people dropped to only 2 percent in 1860. Attempting to explain a nadir in left-handedness during the Victorian period, I. C. McManus suggests that the Industrial Revolution increased the "visibility and stigmatization of left-handers"; included in this stigmatization

was the common practice of forcing schoolchildren to write with their right hands even if they demonstrated a preference for the left ("The History and Geography of Human Handedness," in *Language Lateralization and Psychosis*, ed. Iris E. C. Sommer and René S. Kahn [New York: Cambridge University Press, 2009], 37, 40). For more on forced right-handedness, see Howard I. Kushner, "Retraining Left-handers and the Aetiology of Stuttering: The Rise and Fall of an Intriguing Theory," *Laterality* 17, no. 6 (2012): 673–93; Harris, "Cultural Influences on Handedness," 197–201. Kushner outlines early twentieth-century pseudo-scientific conceptions of handedness and sidedness in "Deficit or Creativity: Cesare Lombardo, Robert Hertz, and the Meanings of Left-Handedness," *Laterality* 18, no. 4 (2013): 416–36.

73. Because they had fought against the Union, Confederate amputees had to rely on their state governments for support (Figg and Farrell-Beck, "Amputation in the Civil War," 462). For the experiences of Confederate amputees, see McDaid, "'How a One-Legged Rebel Lives': Confederate Veterans and Artificial Limbs in Virginia," 119–43; R. B. Rosenburg, "'Empty Sleeves and Wooden Pegs': Disabled Confederate Veterans in Image and Reality," in *Disabled Veterans in History*, ed. David A. Gerber (Ann Arbor: University of Michigan Press, 2000), 204–28.

74. For Rosemarie Garland-Thomson's formulation of the "normate," see *Extraordinary Bodies*, 8.

75. Henry W. Palmer, Contest Entry, 1st series, no. 73, William Oland Bourne Papers.

76. Emphasis in original.

77. Fifty-four years old and unmarried in 1900, Palmer worked as a bookkeeper, a profession advocated by the organizers of the contest as fitting for members of the Left-Arm Corps (U.S. Census Bureau, *U.S. Census, 1900: Boston Ward 12, Suffolk, Massachusetts*, roll 681, Ancestry.com).

78. Alfred D. Whitehouse, Contest Entry, 1st series, no. 163.

79. "Left-Hand Penmanship," *Soldier's Friend* 4, no. 9 (September 1868): 1.

80. For Franklin Durrah's postwar life, see Jalynn Olsen Padilla, "Army of 'Cripples': Northern Civil War Amputees, Disability, and Manhood in Victorian America," PhD diss., University of Delaware, 2007, ProQuest (3277826), 57–58; Clarke, *War Stories*, 169–70.

81. R. Watson Seague, Contest Entry, 1st series, no. 4, William Oland Bourne Papers.

Chapter Four

1. "Tangled and Raveled," *Harper's Weekly* 6, no. 266 (February 1, 1862): 78. Also published in *American Mail-Bag, or Tales of the War* (London: Ward and Lock, 1863): 271–89.

2. "Only One Killed," *Harper's Weekly* 6, no. 282 (May 24, 1862): 330–31; also published in *Weekly Perrysburg* (Ohio) *Journal* 10, no. 5 (June 4, 1862): 1. In an article for the *Pittsburg Post-Gazette*, Len Barcousky notes that the story was also printed in the *Pittsburg Post* on July 3, 1862. Barcousky reports that the death of Capt. Leopold Sahl Jr. in 1861 "echoed" the

events of the story. Leopold Sahl Sr. died six months after his son. See Barcousky, "Eyewitness 1862: Life Follows Fiction in Civil War Deaths," *Pittsburgh Post-Gazette*, July 8, 2012.

3. Abraham Lincoln, "First Inaugural Address" (1861), *The Avalon Project*, avalon.law.yale.edu/19th_century/lincoln1.asp.

4. Kathleen Diffley notes that southern magazine stories, more so than northern ones, portrayed the disruption of domestic rituals. She also argues, however, that "threats to homesteads" in southern literature were "remarkably similar" to those in northern literature (*Where My Heart Is Turning Ever: Civil War Stories and Constitutional Reform, 1861–1876* [Athens: University of Georgia Press], 17, 20). For southern women as Spartan women, see "The Rose and the Ring," *Harper's Weekly* 6, no. 293 (August 9, 1862): 506; "The Women of Sparta," *Weekly Register* (Lynchburg, Va.) 1, no. 1 (January 2, 1864): 8.

5. Alice Fahs collated war stories published by *Harper's Weekly* on a yearly basis during the war, and found that more than half of the published stories featured female heroines and "feminized themes" ("The Feminized Civil War," 1463). In her survey of 321 wartime stories, Kathleen Diffley notes that 41 "center on the home" and 75 invoke the "Old Homestead" (*Where My Heart Is Turning Ever*, 15).

6. As Cathy N. Davidson and others have indicated, organizing nineteenth-century American culture and society into two "separate spheres" simplifies and at times misrepresents social, cultural, racial, gendered, and economic complexities. For an overview of "separate spheres," see Cathy Davidson, "No More Separate Spheres!" *American Literature* 70, no. 3 (September 1998): 443–63; Dana D. Nelson, "Women in Public," in *The Cambridge Companion to Nineteenth-Century American Women's Writing*, ed. Dale M. Bauer and Philip Gould (Cambridge, U.K.: Cambridge University Press, 2001): 38–68.

7. Fahs, *The Imagined Civil War*, 132; Diffley, *Where My Heart Is Turning Ever*, xii.

8. In her analysis of domestic ideology prior to the Civil War, Nina Baym argues that "the domestic ideal meant not that woman was to be sequestered from the world in her place at home but that everybody was to be placed in the home, and hence that home and the world would become one" (*Woman's Fiction: A Guide to Novels by and about Women in America, 1820–1870*, 2nd ed. [Champaign: University of Illinois Press], xxvii).

9. Shirley Samuels differentiates between "war fiction," in which "violence within the home might mirror or present a complicated engagement with violence outside the home," and "domestic fiction," which "locates its violence in a complicated uneasiness about women's roles within the home." Samuels, "Women at War," in *The Cambridge Companion to Nineteenth-Century American Women's Writing*, ed. Bauer and Gould, 144. The stories I discuss here resist such categorization, as there is little difference between the domestic space and the battlefield. "Feminized" is Fahs's term (*The Imagined Civil War*, 121–49).

10. Most newspapers regularly printed columns entitled "Telegraphic News" and "By Telegraph." The masthead of the *Daily Green Mountain Freeman* of Montpelier, Vermont, boasts that "each edition will contain the latest telegraphic news to the time of going to press" (C. W. Willard, "A Daily Freeman," *Daily Green Mountain Freeman* 1, no. 231 (January 11, 1862): 2.

11. Samuels, *Facing America*, 87.

12. Gillian Silverman argues that "the ability of reading to produce experiences of mental and bodily contact was typical of nineteenth-century American life" (2). For her discussion of reading and what she terms "fantasies of communion," see *Bodies and Books: Reading and the Fantasy of Communion in Nineteenth-Century America* (Philadelphia: University of Pennsylvania Press, 2012).

13. Jane Tompkins, *Sensational Designs: The Cultural Work of American Fiction, 1790–1860* (New York: Oxford University Press, 1985), 151–52.

14. A Lady, "Antietam," *Soldiers' Friend* 3, no. 11 (November 1867): 1.

15. Walt Whitman, "By the Bivouac's Fitful Flame," *Drum-Taps* (New York, 1865), 16, www.whitmanarchive.org/published/other/DrumTaps.html.

16. "The Mother's Letter," *Harper's Weekly* 7, no. 326 (March 28, 1863): 194. T. S. Arthur, "The Soldier's Letter," *Daily Ohio Statesman* 9, 269 (April 24, 1863): 1; *Soldier's Friend, and Grand Army of the Republic* 5, no. 7 (July 1869): 4.

17. John Antrobus, "Gone to the Battlefield," *New Orleans Daily Crescent* 14, no. 260 (January 20, 1862): 1, *Chronicling America: Historic American Newspapers,* Library of Congress. Also published in *Rebel Rhymes and Rhapsodies*, ed. Frank Moore (New York: George P. Putnam, 1864): 211–13; *Songs and Ballads of the Southern People, 1861–1865* ed. Frank Moore (New York: D. Appleton and Co., 1886): 196–99.

18. Rosa Wild, "The Parting," *The Southern Illustrated News* 2, no. 19 (November 14, 1863): 150.

19. "A Mother's Prayer," attributed to "Faith" by some publications. *Lewiston* (Pa.) *Gazette* 16, no. 29 (May 21, 1862): 1; *Civilian and Telegraph* (Cumberland, Md.) 35, no. 31 (July 31, 1862): 1; *Gallipolis* (Ohio) *Journal* 27, no. 40 (August 28, 1862): 4; *Natchez* (Miss.) *Weekly Courier* 33, no. 37 (September 3, 1862): 1; *Potter Journal* (Potter County, Pa.) 15, no. 29 (July 15, 1863): 1. Also published in *Lays of the South: Verses Relative to the War Between the Two Sections of the American States* (Liverpool: Printed for the Liverpool Bazaar, in Aid of the Southern Prisoner's Relief Fund, 1864): 63–65; *The Rebellion Record: A Diary of American Events*, ed. Frank Moore (New York: G.P. Putnam, 1864), vol. 6: 21–22; *War Lyrics and Songs of the South*, ed. Abram Joseph Ryan (London: Pottiswoode & Co., 1866): 42–43; *The Southern Poems of the War*, ed. Emily V. Mason (Baltimore: John Murphy & Co., 1889): 169–71.

20. Alice L. Bates, "The History of the Telegraph in California," *Annual Publication of the Historical Society of Southern California* 9, no. 3 (1914): 185.

21. "The First Telegraphic Message from California," *Harper's Weekly* 5, no. 256 (November 23, 1861): 752. John Gast's painting *American Progress* (1872) features a telegraph-wire-toting Columbia connecting the East and the West.

22. "telegraph, n.," *OED Online.*

23. For the USMTC, see Lewis Coe, *The Telegraph: A History of Morse's Invention and Its Predecessors in the United States* (Jefferson, N.C.: McFarland & Co., 2003), 52–53. For telegraphic technology during the Civil War, see William R. Plum, *The Military Telegraph During the Civil War in the United States* (Chicago: Jansen, McClurg & Co., 1882).

24. Eliza Richards, "Correspondent Lines," *ESQ: A Journal of the American Renaissance* 54, no. 1–4 (2008): 149.

25. Winslow Homer, "News from the War," *Harper's Weekly* 6, no. 285 (June 14, 1862): 376–77.

26. "News from the War," *Harper's Weekly* 6, no. 285 (June 14, 1862): 378.

27. Drew Gilpin Faust notes that casualty lists "were notoriously inaccurate and incomplete" (*This Republic of Suffering*, 104).

28. For examples, see Carry Stanley, "The Volunteer's Wife," *Peterson's Magazine* 11, no. 4 (October 1861): 256; Emma Garrison Jones, "Coming Home at Christmas; or, The Soldier's Pocket Bible," *Frank Leslie's Illustrated Newspaper* 16, no. 406 (July 11, 1863): 245–47; C.D.G., "The Dead Alive," *United States Service Magazine* 2, no. 6 (December 1864): 579.

29. "Fortune Favors the Brave," *Harper's Weekly* 6, no. 294 (August 16, 1862): 519.

30. "The Tuberose," *Harper's Weekly* 5, no. 255 (November 16, 1861): 731–32; also published in *American Mail-Bag, or Tales of the War* (London: Ward and Lock, 1863), 199–208.

31. David H. Menamin, "A Mother Waiting for the News," *Natchez Courier*, October 16, 1863, 3.

32. Adolphus Williamson Mangum, *Morven and Linda; or The Token Star* (Raleigh, N.C.: Branson, Farrar, & Co., 1863). Mangum served as chaplain for the Sixth North Carolina Regiment. For Mangum, see Josephus Daniels, "Adolphus Williamson Mangum: Memorial Address Delivered in the Chapel of the University," *North Carolina University Magazine* 10, no. 1 (1891): 1–22.

33. "List of the Killed," *Harper's Weekly* 5, no. 261 (December 28, 1861): 826; also published in *Big Blue Union* (Marysville, Kans.) 1, no. 6 (May 3, 1862): 1; *Bradford Reporter* (Bradford County, Pa.) 22, no. 52 (May 29, 1862); *Jeffersonian Democrat* (Chardon, Ohio) 13, no. 24 (June 13, 1862); *McArthur* (Ohio) *Democrat* 10, no. 44 (June 19, 1862): 1; (Madison) *Wisconsin Farmer* 14, no. 7 (July 1, 1862): 268; *Pomeroy* (Ohio) *Weekly Telegraph* 5, no. 35 (September 5, 1862): 1. (All publications except *Wisconsin Farmer* found via *Chronicling America: Historic American Newspapers*, Library of Congress.) Also published (with subtitle "Fight at Bunker Hill, VA, July 15, 1861") in *Poetical Pen-Pictures of the War: Selected From Our Union Poets*, ed. J. Henry Hayward (New York: J. Henry Hayward, 1864), 79.

34. Emily Dickinson, "They dropped like flakes," in *The Complete Poems of Emily Dickinson*, ed. Thomas H. Johnson (New York: Little, Brown and Co., 2013), 409.

35. Harriet M'Ewen Kimball, "Woman—1862," *Liberator* 32, no. 46 (November 14, 1862): 184. The *Liberator* reprints the poem from the *New York Independent*. Also published in *Pomeroy* (Ohio) *Weekly Telegraph* 5, no. 29 (July 25, 1862): 1; *Gallipolis Journal* 27, no. 50 (November 6, 1862): 4; *St. Cloud Democrat* 5, no. 29 (February 12, 1863): 1; (West Brattleboro) *Vermont School Journal* 5, no. 6 (June 1863) 132–33.

36. Refugitta (Constance Cary Harrison), "Implora Pace," *Southern Illustrated News* 1, no. 38 (May 30, 1863): 3. For more on Constance Cary Harrison, see *Refugitta of Richmond: The Wartime Recollections, Grave and Gay, of Constance Cary Harrison*, ed. Nathaniel Cheairs Hughes Jr. and S. Kittrell Rushing (Knoxville: University of Tennessee Press, 2011).

37. For Harrison's description and definition of her pseudonyms, see Hughes and Rushing, eds., *Refugitta of Richmond*, 84.

38. George Gordon, Lord Byron, *The Works of Lord Byron: With His Letters and Journals, and His Life*, ed. Thomas Moore (London: John Murray, 1836), vol. 4: 158–62.

39. Walt Whitman, "Come Up from the Fields Father," *Drum-Taps*, 39–40, www.whitman archive.org/published/other/DrumTaps.html.

40. See Shirley Samuels's introduction to *The Culture of Sentiment: Race, Gender, and Sentimentality in Nineteenth-Century America* (New York: Oxford University Press, 1992), 5, for a discussion of sentimental literature and the formation of readers who "feel right."

41. Nudelman discusses the process by which abolitionist sentimentality proliferates suffering (*John Brown's Body*, 21–22). For discussions of sentimentalism, appropriation, and exploitation (especially of African American bodies), see Sánchez-Eppler, "Bodily Bonds," 28–59; Marianne Noble, "The Ecstasies of Sentimental Wounding in *Uncle Tom's Cabin*," *Yale Journal of Criticism* 10, no. 2 (1997): 295–320; Carolyn Sorisio, "The Spectacle of the Body: Torture in the Antislavery Writing of Lydia Maria Child and Frances E. W. Harper," *Modern Language Studies* 30, no. 1 (Spring 2000): 45–66. As white men, the soldiers in the texts I discuss are obviously less vulnerable to the exploitation these critics examine.

42. "Missing," *Harper's Weekly* 6, no. 303 (October 16, 1862): 662–63. Also published in *Delaware Gazette* 44, no. 33 (November 14, 1862): 1.

43. Sorisio, "The Spectacle of the Body," 47.

44. Virginia F. Townsend, "Wounded and Killed," *Arthur's Home Magazine* 19 (May 1862): 320. Also published in *Big Blue Union* (Marysville, Kans.) 1, no. 14 (June 1862): 1, *Democratic Press* (Eaton, Ohio) 3, no. 107 (September 18, 1862): 1; *Daily Dispatch* (Richmond, Va.) 23, no. 145 (December 19, 1862): 2; *Athens* (Tenn.) *Post* 15, no. 744 (December 26, 1862): 3; *Dollar Weekly Bulletin* (Maysville, Ky.) 2, no. 16 (October 1, 1863): 2.

45. Samuels, *The Culture of Sentiment*, 5.

46. "Wounded," *Harper's Weekly* 6, no. 289 (July 12, 1862): 442–43.

47. "Wounded," *Lewistown* (Pa.) *Gazette* 16, no. 41 (August 13, 1862): 1; *Nashville Daily Union* 1, no. 131 (September 11, 1862): 1; *Independent* (Oskaloosa, Kans.) 3, no. 50 (August 8, 1863): 1; *Arthur's Home Magazine* 22 (September 1863): 118.

48. T[imothy]. S. Arthur, *Home-Heroes, Saints, and Martyrs* (Philadelphia: J. B. Lippincott Co., 1865): 132–43; *Heroes of the Household* (Philadelphia: J. B. Lippincott Co., 1887): 132–43. "Messengers of Death," *Home Heroines: Tales for Girls* (Edinburgh: William P. Nimmo, 1873), 210–18.

49. "Wounded," in *Skedaddle, by "Our Special Correspondent,"* ed. Lieutenant Warneford (London: G. Vickers, 1865): 26–33.

50. The publishing history of "Wounded" is quite complicated, and I am unable to definitively link Sir William Howard Russell to Lieutenant Warneford. In 1871, Samuel Austin Allibone attributed a number of Warneford's books, not including *Skedaddle*, to William Howard Russell. See Allibone, *A Critical Dictionary of English Literature and British and American Authors, Living and Deceased, from the Earliest Accounts to the Latter Half*

of the Nineteenth Century: Containing Over Forty-six Thousand Articles (Philadelphia: J. B. Lippincott Company, 1871), vol. 3: 2584. Emil Weller identifies William Howard Russell as Lieutenant Warneford. See Weller, *Lexicon Pseudonymorum* (Hildesheim, Germany: Georg Olms Verlagsbuchhandlung, 1963): 606. For identification of Warneford as a pseudonym for William Russell, not Sir William Howard Russell, see Victor E. Neuburg, *The Popular Press Companion to Popular Literature* (Bowling Green, Ohio: Bowling Green State University Popular Press, 1983): 196; Samuel Halkett, ed., *Catalogue of the Printed Books in the Library of the Faculty of Advocates* (Edinburgh: William Blackwood and Sons, 1877), vol. 5: 864. A twentieth-century version of Samuel Halkett and John Laing's *Dictionary of Anonymous and Pseudonymous English Literature* (1882) identifies *Skedaddle* as the edited work of "Lieut. Warneford, R.N., *i.e.* William Howard Russell?" See *Dictionary of Anonymous and Pseudonymous English Literature*, ed. James Kennedy, W. A. Smith, and A. F. Johnson (Edinburgh: Oliver and Boyd, 1927), vol. 5: 281.

51. For Sir William Howard Russell as a war correspondent, see Alan Hankinson, *Man of War: William Howard Russell of* The Times (London: Heinemann, 1982); James M. Perry, *A Bohemian Brigade: The Civil War Correspondents—Mostly Rough, Sometimes Ready* (New York: John Wiley & Sons, 2000), 1–18.

52. Meredith L. McGill, *American Literature and the Culture of Reprinting* (Philadelphia: University of Pennsylvania Press), 2003.

53. "The Gallant Lads of Missouri," in *Skedaddle*, ed. Warneford, 2.

54. My emphasis.

55. Faust, *This Republic of Suffering*, 102–36.

56. Alice Fahs notes that the ability of bullets to wound multiple times was "a much repeated trope in the North during the war." However, bullets penetrate northern *and* southern homes by traveling along telegraph lines (*The Imagined Civil War*, 135).

Afterword

1. Walt Whitman, *Sequel to Drum-Taps* (New York, 1866), 23, whitmanarchive.org/published/other/DrumTapsSequel.html.

2. Whitman, *Drum-Taps*; *Sequel to Drum-Taps*; Herman Melville, *Battle-Pieces and Aspects of the War* (New York: Harper & Brothers, 1866).

3. Whitman, *Drum-Taps*, 38.

4. Ibid., 49.

5. Stanton Garner, *The Civil War World of Herman Melville* (Lawrence: University Press of Kansas, 1993), 31.

6. Melville, *Battle-Pieces*, 259.

BIBLIOGRAPHY

Primary Works

"Abduction of the Yankee Goddess of Liberty." *Southern Punch* 1, no. 14 (November 14, 1863): 4.

"Abraham Lincoln's Coffin." *Harper's Weekly* 9, no. 435 (April 29, 1865): 267–68.

Adlington, F. M. "The Heroic Black." *Liberator* 34, no. 11 (March 11, 1864): 44.

"America Is Free." *Crutch* 2, no. 71 (May 13, 1865): 1.

Antrobus, John. "Gone to the Battlefield," *New Orleans Daily Crescent* 14, no. 260 (January 20, 1862): 1. *Chronicling America: Historic American Newspapers.* Library of Congress.

Arthur, T[imothy]. S[hay]. *Heroes of the Household.* Philadelphia: J. B. Lippincott Co., 1887.

———. *Home-Heroes, Saints, and Martyrs.* Philadelphia: J. B. Lippincott Co., 1865.

———. *Home Heroines: Tales for Girls.* Edinburgh: William P. Nimmo, 1873.

———. "The Soldier's Letter." *Daily Ohio Statesman* 9, no. 269 (April 24, 1863): 1.

"Assault of the Second Louisiana (Colored Regiment) on the Rebel Works at Port Hudson, May 27." *Frank Leslie's Illustrated News* 16, no. 404 (June 27, 1863): 216–17.

"An Attractive Book: Battle Memories of the Left-Armed Corps." *Soldier's Friend* 2, no. 9 (September 1866): 2.

Babb, Harriet N. "Jennie Jewitt, the Young Recruiting Officer." *Ladies' Repository* 23, no. 4 (April 1863): 241–44.

———. "Maggie Morton's Mittens; or, Working for the Soldiers and What Came of It." *Ladies' Repository* 22, no. 4 (April 1862): 219–22.

Bagby, Dr. G. W. "The Empty Sleeve." *Southern Illustrated News* 1, no. 14 (December 13, 1862): 5.

Baker, J. E. "Columbia Demands Her Children." Boston, 1864. Library of Congress Prints and Photographs Online Catalog. hdl.loc.gov/loc.pnp/ppmsca.15768.

Barker, David. "The Empty Sleeve." *Frank Leslie's Illustrated News* 16, no. 399 (May 30, 1863): 149.

Barry, Charles A. "Columbia's Invocation." *New South* 1, no. 6 (September 13, 1862): 1.

"Battle of Port Hudson." *Frank Leslie's Illustrated News* 16, no. 404 (June 27, 1863): 209.

"The Black Heroes." *Liberator* 33, no. 6 (February 5, 1864): 24.

"The Black Regiment." *Kansas City* (Mo.) *Sun* 10, no. 43 (June 22, 1918): 1.

Blanchard, John. Contest Entry. 1st series, no. 75. William Oland Bourne Papers.

Boker, George H. "The Second Louisiana." *Frank Leslie's Illustrated News* 16, no. 404 (June 27, 1863): 209–10. Broadside version: *The Second Louisiana.* Philadelphia: Union League of Philadelphia, 1863. American Broadsides and Ephemera, series 1, American Antiquarian Society no. 11388, Archive of Americana, infoweb.newsbank.com.

———. *Das Zweite Louisiana Regiment.* Philadelphia, 1863. American Broadsides and Ephemera, series 1, American Antiquarian Society no. 11387, Archive of Americana, infoweb.newsbank.com.

Bourne, William Oland. "Left-Hand Writing." *Soldier's Friend* 1, no. 10 (October 1865): 2.

———. "Left-Hand Writing by Disabled Soldiers and Sailors of the War." *Soldier's Friend* 4, no. 1 (January 1868): 4.

———. Papers. Manuscript Division, Library of Congress, Washington, D.C.

Britomarte. "Empty Sleeves." *Soldier's Friend* 4, no. 2 (February 1868): 8.

Brown, William Wells. *The Negro in the American Rebellion: His Heroism and His Fidelity.* Boston: Lee and Shepard, 1867.

Bryant, William Cullen. "Not Yet." *Liberator* 31, no. 34 (August 23, 1861): 136.

———. "Our Country's Call." In *Poems of American History,* ed. Burton Egbert Stevenson, 410–11. Boston: Houghton Mifflin Co., 1908.

Bryson, John. "Lines." *Soldier's Friend* 2, no. 7 (July 1866): 1.

Bucknam, George. Contest Entry. 2nd series, no. 47. William Oland Bourne Papers.

Buttre, John C. *The Empty Sleeve.* Boston: N. Y. & B. B. Russell & Co., 1866.

Byron, George Gordon, Lord. *The Works of Lord Byron: With His Letters and Journals, and His Life.* Vol. 4. Ed. Thomas Moore. London: John Murray, 1836.

Casey. "An Illustration of the New Yankee Doctrine About the Darkey." *Southern Illustrated News* 3, no. 20 (June 11, 1864): 160.

C.D.G. "The Dead Alive." *United States Service Magazine* 2, no. 6 (December 1864): 579.

"Charge of the Black Brigade." *Chicago Daily Tribune* 16, no. 299 (June 12, 1863): 3.

"Check-Mate." *Haper's Weekly* 9, no. 440 (June 3, 1865): 337.

Civil War reminiscences by soldiers and sailors in Central Park Hospital, New York City. William Oland Bourne Papers.

"A Colored Private." Letter 26. In *A Grand Army of Black Men*, ed. Redkey, 65–66.

"Columbia Awake At Last." *Harper's Weekly* 5, no. 232 (June 8, 1861): 368.

"Columbia to Lincoln." *Harper's Weekly* 7, no. 314 (January 3, 1863): 16.

"Confederate Cemetery, Franklin, Tennessee." *Harper's Weekly* 10, no. 516 (November 17, 1866): 721.

Cora. "To a Company of Volunteers Receiving Their Banner at the Hands of the Ladies." *Southern Literary Messenger* 33, no. 1 (July 1861): 17–19.

Critcherson, G. P. *The Empty Sleeve*. 1870. Southern Methodist University, Central University Libraries, DeGolyer Library Collection. digitalcollections.smu.edu/cdm/singleitem/collection/civ/id/357/rec/1.

"Dark Artillery; or, How to Make the Contrabands Useful." *Frank Leslie's Illustrated News* 12, no. 309 (October 26, 1861): 368.

"Death List of a Day." *New York Times*. June 7, 1901, 9.

Dickens, Charles. *Our Mutual Friend*. London: Chapman and Hall, 1865.

Dickinson, Emily. "They dropped like flakes." In *The Complete Poems of Emily Dickinson*, ed. Thomas H. Johnson, 409. New York: Little, Brown and Co., 2013.

"A Dirge—April 15, 1865." *Liberator* 35, no. 9 (May 12, 1865): 76.

Douglass, Frederick. "Enlistment of Colored Men." *Douglass' Monthly* 5, no. 15 (August 1863): 850–52.

———. "Men of Color, to Arms!" *Douglass' Monthly* 5, no. 10 (March 1863): 801; no. 11 (April 1863).

"The Drama," *Chicago Daily Tribune* (August 25, 1901): 39. ProQuest.

Duval, Peter S. *In Defence of the Union and the Constitution*. Philadelphia: P. S. Duval and Son, 1861. Library of Congress Prints and Photographs Online Catalog. hdl.loc.gov/loc.pnp/pga.03676.

Edmonds, Charles A. Contest Entry. 1st series, no. 51. William Oland Bourne Papers.

Ehrgott, Forbriger, & Co., lithographer. *The Union Defenders Certificate*. 1863. Library of Congress Prints and Photographs Online Catalog. hdl.loc.gov/loc.pnp/cph.3b37096.

"Empty Sleeves." *Soldier's Friend* 4, no. 10 (October 1868): 1.

"The Escaped Slave." *Harper's Weekly* 8, no. 392 (July 2, 1864): 428.

"The Escaped Slave and the Union Soldier." *Harper's Weekly* 8, no. 392 (July 2, 1864): 422.

"The Escaped Slave in the Union Army." *Harper's Weekly* 8, no. 392 (July 2, 1864): 428.

"Exhibition of Left-Hand Penmanship." William Oland Bourne Papers.

"Extracts from Letters." *Soldier's Friend* 3, no. 10 (October 1867): 6.

"The Female Sold-uier." *Vanity Fair* 4, no. 81 (July 13, 1861): 16.

"The First Telegraphic Message from California." *Harper's Weekly* 5, no. 256 (November 23, 1861): 752.

"Flag-Presentation at New Orleans." *Harper's Weekly* 6, no. 292 (August 2, 1862): 487.

"Fortune Favors the Brave." *Harper's Weekly* 6, no. 294 (August 16, 1862): 519.

Frost, S. Annie. "The Soldier's Sister." *Godey's Lady's Book and Magazine* 63 (August 1861): 135.

"The Gallant Lads of Missouri." In *Skedaddle,* ed. Warneford, 1–25.

Garrison, William Lloyd. "Our National Visitation." *Liberator* 32, no. 28 (July 11, 1862): 112.

Glyndon, Howard [Laura Redden Searing]. "Butler's Black Brigade." In *Idylls of Battle and Poems of the Rebellion,* 142–44. New York: Hurd and Houghton, 1864.

———. "The Legend of Our Victories." In *Idylls of Battle and Poems of the Rebellion,* 27–32. New York: Hurd and Houghton, 1864.

———. "Union Forever." In *Idylls of Battle and Poems of the Rebellion,* 48–52. New York: Hurd and Houghton, 1864.

"A Good Suggestion." *Yorkville* (S.C.) *Enquirer* 7, no. 46 (November 14, 1861): 1.

"The Great Union Meeting at New York." *Harper's Weekly* 4, no. 158 (January 7, 1860): 2, 8–9.

"Grounds at Andersonville, Georgia, Where Are Buried Fourteen Thousand Union Soldiers Who Died in Andersonville Prison." *Harper's Weekly* 9, no. 458 (October 7, 1865): 633.

Hanaford, Mrs. P. A. (words), and Rev. J. W. Dadmun (music). "The Empty Sleeve." Boston: Oliver Ditson & Co., 1866. Johns Hopkins University, Levy Street Music Collection, box 087, item 139. jhir.library.jhu.edu/handle/1774.2/25685.

Handbills. William Oland Bourne Papers.

Harrison, Constance Cary. *Refugitta of Richmond: The Wartime Recollections, Grave and Gay, of Constance Cary Harrison,* ed. Nathaniel Cheairs Hughes Jr. and S. Kittrell Rushing. Knoxville: University of Tennessee Press, 2011.

Holmes, Oliver Wendell, Sr. "Brother Jonathan's Lament For Sister Caroline." *Atlantic Monthly* 7, no. 43 (May 1861): 613.

Homer, Winslow. "News from the War." *Harper's Weekly* 6, no. 285 (June 14, 1862): 376–77.

Jones, Emma Garrison. "Coming Home at Christmas; or, The Soldier's Pocket Bible." *Frank Leslie's Illustrated Newspaper* 16, no. 406 (July 11, 1863): 245–47.

Kimball, Harriet M'Ewen. "Woman—1862." *Liberator* 32, no. 46 (November 14, 1862): 184.

Kimmel, Charles. *The End of the Rebellion in the United States, 1865*. New York: Kimmel and Foster, 1866. Library of Congress Prints and Photographs Online Collection. hdl.loc.gov/loc.pnp/cph.3a15123.

A Lady. "Antietam." *Soldiers' Friend* 3, no. 11 (November 1867): 1.

"Left-Hand Penmanship." *Soldier's Friend* 4, no. 9 (September 1868): 1.

"Left-Handed Penmanship." *Harper's Weekly* 10, no. 448 (July 29, 1865): 467.

"Lest We Forget: Some History Now Quite Pertinent and More Than Interesting." *Washington Post*, November 12, 1901, 6.

Letts, J. M. "Our Disabled Veterans." *Soldier's Friend* 3, no. 9 (September 1867): 4.

Lincoln, Abraham. "First Inaugural Address" (1861). *The Avalon Project*. avalon.law.yale.edu/19th_century/lincoln1.asp.

Linton, W. J. "Columbia Victrix." *Liberator* 35, no. 24 (June 16, 1865): 96.

"List of Competitors for the Prizes for Left-Hand Penmanship." *Soldier's Friend* 4, no. 1 (January 1868): 2.

"List of Contributors." *Soldier's Friend* 2, no. 3 (March 1866): 2–3.

"List of the Killed." *Harper's Weekly* 5, no. 261 (December 28, 1861): 826.

"Literature." *Crisis* 17, no. 6 (April 1919): 288.

"Literary and Artistic Items." *Ladies' Repository* 36, no. 20 (October 1866): 316.

Lucas, Daniel Bedinger. Commonplace Book. Daniel Bedinger Lucas papers. Virginia Tech Archives.

"A Man Knows a Man." *Harper's Weekly* 9, no. 434 (April 22, 1865): 256.

Mangum, Adolphus Williamson. *Morven and Linda; or The Token Star*. Raleigh, N.C.: Branson, Farrar, & Co., 1863.

"Maryland in Fetters." 1861. Confederate Broadside Poetry Collection. WakeSpace Digital Archive. hdl.handle.net/10339/164.

McCallum, Andrew. "The Court-Room at the Old Penitentiary, Washington, During the Trial of the Conspirators." *Harper's Weekly* 9, no. 440 (June 3, 1865): 344–45.

Melville, Herman. *Battle-Pieces and Aspects of the War*. New York: Harper & Brothers, 1866.

Menamin, David H. "A Mother Waiting for the News." *Natchez Courier*, October 16, 1863, 3.

"Missing." *Harper's Weekly* 6, no. 303 (October 16, 1862): 662–63.

"Mistress Columbia, Who Has Been Taking a Nap, Suddenly Wakes Up and Calls Her Noisy Scholars to Order." *Harper's Weekly* 4, no. 158 (January 7, 1860): 16.

"The Mother's Letter." *Harper's Weekly* 7, no. 326 (March 28, 1863): 194.

Nast, Thomas. "The Blessing of Victory." *Harper's Weekly* 3, no. 404 (September 4, 1864): 616.

———. "Compromise with the South." *Harper's Weekly* 8, no. 401 (September 3, 1864): 572.

———. "Honor the Brave." *Harper's Weekly* 7, no. 356 (October 24, 1863): 680–81.

———. "Our Arms Victorious." *Harper's Weekly* 9, no. 443 (June 24, 1865): 392–93.

———. "Pardon and Franchise." *Harper's Weekly* 9, no. 449 (August 5, 1865): 488–89.

"National Ode: Suggested by the President's Proclamation of January 1, 1863." *Continental Monthly* 3, no. 5 (May 1863): 554.

"The Negro Regiment—Meeting of the Colored Citizens." *Douglass' Monthly* 5, no. 10 (March 1863): 809.

"News from the War." *Harper's Weekly* 6, no. 285 (June 14, 1862): 378.

"November 8, 1864." *Harper's Weekly* 8, no. 413 (November 26, 1864): 754.

Officer and Members of the Philadelphia Union League. Philadelphia: Henry B. Ashmead, 1863. Ann Arbor: ProQuest I&L Research Collections.

"One-Legged Men." *Galaxy* 11, no. 3 (March 1871): 353–62.

"Only One Killed." *Harper's Weekly* 6, no. 282 (May 24, 1862): 330–31.

"The Only Reliable War Illustrations." *Frank Leslie's Illustrated Newspaper* 11, no. 283 (April 27, 1861): 1.

"Our Women and Children." *Liberator* 31, no. 24 (June 14, 1861): 1.

"Out of a Situation." *Vanity Fair* 1, no. 15 (April 7, 1860): 233.

Palmer, Henry W. Contest Entry. 1st series, no. 73. William Oland Bourne Papers.

Penn, August H. "A Story of the War." *Soldier's Friend* 3, no. 9 (August 1867): 1.

Perrine, Thomas A. Contest Entry. 1st series, no. 50. William Oland Bourne Papers.

"A Pleasant Incident." *Colored American* 8, no. 9 (June 2, 1900): 7.

"Premium $500 to the Left-Armed Soldiers of the Union." *Soldier's Friend* 1, no. 7 (August 1865): 2.

"Prepare for the Winter Campaign—Make the Soldier Comfortable." *Daily Nashville Patriot* 22, no. 1751 (August 20, 1861): 2.

"Prepare for the Winter Campaign—Make the Soldier Comfortable." *Memphis Daily Appeal* 12, no. 192 (August 23, 1861): 2.

"Presentation of a Flag to the Thirteenth Connecticut Regiment by Loyal Ladies of New Orleans." *Harper's Weekly* 6, no. 292 (August 2, 1862): 493.

"Printing Press," *Big Blue Union* (Marysville, Kans.) 1, no. 7 (May 10, 1862): 1.
Randall, James Ryder. "My Maryland." *Southern Literary Messenger* 36 (January 1, 1862): 40.
Redkey, Edwin S., ed. *A Grand Army of Black Men: Letter from African-American Soldiers in the Union Army, 1861–1865*. New York: Cambridge University Press, 1992.
Refugitta [Constance Cary Harrison]. "Implora Pace." *Southern Illustrated News* 1, no. 38 (May 30, 1863): 3.
Ringwalt & Brown. *In Commemoration of Emancipation in Maryland, November 1, 1864*. Philadelphia: Ringwalt & Brown, ca. 1864. Gilder Lehrman Collection GLC05701. www.americanhistory.amdigital.co.uk/Documents/Images/GLC05701/0?searchId=e8afca55-9a3b-4792-a488-74491fdf8fe6.
"The Rose and the Ring." *Harper's Weekly* 6, no. 293 (August 9, 1862): 506.
"Salutatory." *Southern Illustrated News* 1, no. 1 (September 6, 1862): 4.
"Scene, Fifth Avenue." *Harper's Weekly* 6, no. 296 (August 30, 1862): 560.
Scott v. Sandford, 60 U.S. 393 (1856).
Seague, R. Watson. Contest Entry, 1st series, no. 4. William Oland Bourne Papers.
Sherman, William Tecumseh. Letter to Caleb Fisher. William Oland Bourne Papers.
Shuften, Sarah E. "Ethiopia's Dead." *Colored American* 1, no. 3 (December 30, 1865): 4.
S.J.A. "Not Dead." *Harper's Weekly* 5, no. 230 (May 25, 1861): 322.
"The Soldier's Grave." *Freedom's Champion* (Atchinson City, Kans.). September 20, 1862, 1.
"Some Uses of a Civil War." *Continental Monthly* 6, no. 4 (October 1864): 361–72.
"A Southern Publishing House." *Southern Illustrated News* 1, no. 3 (September 20, 1862): 4.
"Speech of General Banks." *Soldier's Friend* 2, no. 6 (June 1866): 2.
"Speech of Hon. Henry P. Cheatham, at Raleigh, N.C., on January 1, 1898." *Gazette* (Raleigh, N.C.) 9, no. 48 (January 15, 1898): 2.
Stage, Joseph F. "Company A." *Soldier's Friend* 2, no. 6 (June 1866): 1.
Stanley, Carry. "The Volunteer's Wife." *Peterson's Magazine* 11, no. 4 (October 1861): 256.
Stiles, Burrett. Contest Entry, 1st series, William Oland Bourne Papers.
"Stonewall Jackson's Way." *Southern Literary Messenger* 37, no. 2 (February 1, 1863): 116. Daniel Lucas Bedinger Papers, Virginia Tech Archives.
"A Story of Patriotism." *Douglass' Monthly* 5, no. 10 (August 1863): 856–57.
Taking an Observation from a Dark Point. Philadelphia: Magee, 1861. American

Broadsides and Ephemera, series 1, American Antiquarian Society no. 24742. Archive of Americana, infoweb.newsbank.com.

"Tangled and Raveled." *Harper's Weekly* 6, no. 266 (February 1, 1862): 78.

Taylor, Bayard. "Comments." *Liberator* 34, no. 29 (July 15, 1864): 116.

Taylor, George Lansing. "The Promise Must Be Kept." *Liberator* 34, no. 8 (February 19, 1864): 32.

"To the Left-Armed Corps of the Union." *Soldier's Friend* 3, no. 6 (June 1867): 2.

Townsend, Virginia F. "Wounded and Killed." *Arthur's Home Magazine* 19 (May 1862): 320.

"Trial of the Conspirators." *Harper's Weekly* 9, no. 440 (June 3, 1865): 341–43.

"The Tuberose." *Harper's Weekly* 5, no. 255 (November 16, 1861): 731–32.

"A Typical Negro." *Harper's Weekly* 7, no. 340 (July 4, 1863): 429–30.

"A Typical Negro." *Southern Illustrated News* 2, no. 3 (July 25, 1863): 19.

Underwood, T. Hulbert. "Now." *Liberator* 31, no. 40 (October 4, 1861): 160.

"The Union and Slavery." *New South* 1, no. 6 (September 13, 1862): 1.

Untitled cartoon. *Harper's Weekly* 5, no. 232 (June 8, 1861): 368.

"An Unwelcome Return." *Harper's Weekly* 5, no. 241 (August 10, 1861): 510.

"Wanted Immediately." *Southern Illustrated News* 1, no. 3 (September 20, 1862): 4.

"The War—Making Havelocks for the Volunteers." *Harper's Weekly* 5, no. 235 (June 29, 1861): 401.

Warneford, Lieutenant, ed. *Skedaddle, by "Our Special Correspondent."* London: G. Vickers, 1865.

Waters, William. "Letter from the 26th U.S.C.T." *Christian Recorder* 5, no. 15 (April 15, 1865).

Watson, William H. Letter 94. In *A Grand Army of Black Men*, ed. Redkey, 153–55.

"A Well-Timed Hint." *Semi-Weekly Standard* (Raleigh, N.C.) 11, no. 82 (September 14, 1861): 2.

Wester, Thomas B. Letter 93. In *A Grand Army of Black Men*, ed. Redkey, 216–18.

White, Frederika Macky. Commonplace Book. Frederica Holmes Trapnell Papers. Virginia Historical Society.

Whitehouse, Alfred D. Contest Entry. 1st series, no. 163. William Oland Bourne Papers.

———. Contest Entry. 2nd series, no. 73. William Oland Bourne Papers.

Whitehouse, Phineas P. Contest Entry. 1st series, no. 136. William Oland Bourne Papers.

———. "A True Patriot." *Soldier's Friend* 3, no. 2 (February 1867): 1.

Whitman, Walt. "By the Bivouac's Fitful Flame." In *Drum-Taps*, 16, www.whitmanarchive.org/published/other/DrumTaps.html.

———. "Come Up from the Fields Father." In *Drum-Taps,* 39–40. www.whitmanarchive.org/published/other/DrumTaps.html.

———. *Drum-Taps.* New York, 1865.

———. *Memoranda During the War.* Camden, N.J., 1875. whitmanarchive.org/published/other/memoranda.html.

———. *Sequel to Drum-Taps.* New York, 1865. whitmanarchive.org/published/other/DrumTapsSequel.html.

———. *Specimen Days.* New York: Barnes and Noble, 2007.

———. *Specimen Days.* In *Complete Prose Works,* 7–200. Philadelphia, 1892. New York: Barnes and Noble, 2007. www.whitmanarchive.org/published/other/CompleteProse.html.

Whitney, Mrs. A. D. T. "Peace." *Liberator* 35, no. 33 (August 18, 1865): 132.

Wild, Rosa. "The Parting." *Southern Illustrated News* 2, no. 19 (November 14, 1863): 150.

Willard, C. W. "A Daily Freeman." *Daily Green Mountain Freeman* (Montpelier, Vt.) 1, no. 231 (January 11, 1862): 2.

"Woman in the Ascendant." *Saturday Evening Post,* September 13, 1862, 4.

"The Women of Sparta." *Weekly Register* (Lynchburg, Va.) 1, no. 1 (January 2, 1864): 8.

"The Women of the South." University of North Carolina, Chapel Hill, Wilson Library Special Collections. Confederate Papers. Scrapbook clippings. 172.

Woodbury, Mrs. P. R. "The Statue of Freedom." *Liberator* 34, no. 3 (January 15, 1864): 12.

"Wounded." *Harper's Weekly* 6, no. 289 (July 12, 1862): 442–43.

"Wounded." In *Skedaddle,* ed. Warneford, 26–33.

"Wounded and Killed." *Big Blue Union* (Marysville, Kans.) 1, no. 14 (June 1862): 1.

Secondary Works

Aaron, Daniel. *The Unwritten War: American Writers and the Civil War.* New York: Alfred A. Knopf, 1973.

Adams, Rachel. *Sideshow U.S.A.: Freaks and the American Cultural Imagination.* Chicago: University of Chicago Press, 2001.

Alexander, Jeffrey C. *Trauma: A Social Theory.* Malden, Mass.: Polity Press, 2012.

Algulhon, Maurice. *Marianne into Battle: Republican Imagery and Symbolism in France, 1789–1880.* Trans. Janet Lloyd. Cambridge, U.K.: Cambridge University Press, 1981.

Allibone, Samuel Austin. *A Critical Dictionary of English Literature and British and American Authors, Living and Deceased, from the Earliest Accounts to the Latter Half of the Nineteenth Century: Containing Over Forty-six Thousand Articles.* Vol. 3. Philadelphia: J. B. Lippincott Co., 1871.

Anderson, Benedict. *Imagined Communities: Reflections on the Origin and Spread of Nationalism.* London: Verso, 1983.

Attie, Jeanie. *Patriotic Toil: Northern Women and the American Civil* War. Ithaca, N.Y.: Cornell University Press, 1998.

Banta, Martha. *Imaging American Women: Idea and Ideals in Cultural History.* New York: Columbia University Press, 1987.

Barcousky, Len. "Eyewitness 1862: Life Follows Fiction in Civil War Deaths." *Pittsburgh Post-Gazette,* July 8, 2012.

Barrett, Faith. *To Fight Aloud Is Very Brave: American Poetry and the Civil War.* Amherst: University of Massachusetts Press, 2012.

———, and Cristanne Miller, eds. *"Words for the Hour": A New Anthology of American Civil War Poetry.* Amherst: University of Massachusetts Press, 2005.

Barsley, Michael. *An Investigation into the Sinister History of Left-Handedness.* New York: Hawthorn Books, Inc., 1966.

Bates, Alice L. "The History of the Telegraph in California." *Annual Publication of the Historical Society of Southern California* 9, no. 3 (1914): 181–87.

Baym, Nina. *Woman's Fiction: A Guide to Novels by and about Women in America, 1820–1870.* 2nd ed. Champaign: University of Illinois Press.

Bernat Bennett, Paula. *Poets in the Public Sphere: The Emancipatory Project of American Women's Poetry.* Princeton, N.J.: Princeton University Press, 2003.

Bernstein, Iver. *The New York City Draft Riots: Their Significance for American Society and Politics in the Age of the Civil War.* New York: Oxford University Press, 1990.

Blanton, DeAnne, and Lauren M. Cook. *They Fought Like Demons: Women Soldiers in the American Civil War.* Baton Rouge: Louisiana State University Press, 2002.

Blight, David W. "Decoration Days: The Origins of Memorial Day in North and South." In *The Memory of the Civil War,* ed. Alice Fahs and Joan Waugh, 94–129. Chapel Hill: University of North Carolina Press, 2004.

Bogdan, Robert. *Freak Show: Presenting Human Oddities for Amusement and Profit.* Chicago: University of Chicago Press, 1988.

Boggs, Colleen Glenney. "The Civil War's 'Empty Sleeve' and the Cultural Production of Disabled Americans." *J19: The Journal of Nineteenth-Century Americanists* 3, no. 1 (Spring 2015): 41–65.

Bollet, Alfred J. *Civil War Medicine: Challenges and Triumphs.* Tucson, Ariz.: Galen Press, 2002.

Brockett, Linus Pierpont, and Mary C. Vaughan. *Woman's Work in the Civil War: A Record of Heroism, Patriotism and Patience.* Philadelphia: Zeigler, McCurdy, & Co., 1867.

Burbick, Joan. *Healing the Republic: The Language of Health and the Culture of Nationalism in Nineteenth-Century America.* Cambridge, U.K.: Cambridge University Press, 1994.

Burgett, Bruce. *Sentimental Bodies: Sex, Gender, and Citizenship in the Early Republic.* Princeton, N.J.: Princeton University Press, 1998.

Casey, John A., Jr. *New Men: Reconstructing the Image of the Veteran in Late-Nineteenth-Century American Literature and Culture.* New York: Fordham University Press, 2015.

Castronovo, Russ. *Necro Citizenship: Death, Eroticism, and the Public Sphere in the Nineteenth-Century United States.* Durham, N.C.: Duke University Press, 2001.

Clarke, Frances M. "'Honorable Scars': Northern Amputees and the Meaning of Civil War Injuries." In *Union Soldiers and the Northern Home Front: Wartime Experiences, Postwar Adjustments,* ed. Paul A. Cimbala and Randall M. Miller, 361–94. New York: Fordham University Press, 2002.

———. *War Stories: Suffering and Sacrifice in the Civil War North.* Chicago: University of Chicago Press, 2011.

Coe, Lewis. *The Telegraph: A History of Morse's Invention and Its Predecessors in the United States.* Jefferson, N.C.: McFarland & Co., 2003.

Cohen, Michael. "Contraband Singing: Poems and Songs in Circulation during the Civil War." *American Literature* 82, no. 2 (June 2010): 271–304.

———. "Whittier, Ballad Reading, and the Culture of Nineteenth-Century Poetry." *Arizona Quarterly* 64, no. 3 (Autumn 2008): 1–29.

Cooper, Benjamin. "Franklin H. Durrah, John William De Forest, and the Varieties of Military Experience." *Arizona Quarterly* 67, no. 2 (Summer 2011): 41–72.

Cornish, Dudley Taylor. *The Sable Arm: Negro Troops in the Union Army, 1861–1865.* New York: W. W. Norton, 1966.

Cullen, Jim. "'I's a Man Now': Gender and African American Men." In *Divided Houses: Gender and the Civil War,* ed. Catherine Clinton and Nina Silber, 76–91. New York: Oxford University Press, 1992.

Culpepper, Marilyn Mayer. *Trials and Triumphs: Women of the American Civil War.* East Lansing: Michigan State University Press, 1991.

Cunningham, Roger D. "'A Lot of Fine, Study Black Warriors': Texas's African American 'Immunes' in the Spanish-American War." In *Brothers to the Buf-*

falo Soldiers: Perspectives on the African American Militia and Volunteers, 1865–1917, ed. Bruce A. Glasrud, 186–208. Columbia: University of Missouri Press, 2011.

Daniels, Josephus. "Adolphus Williamson Mangum: Memorial Address Delivered in the Chapel of the University." *North Carolina University Magazine* 10, no. 1 (1891): 1–22.

Dawes, James. *The Language of War: Literature and Culture in the United States From the Civil War Through World War II*. Cambridge, Mass.: Harvard University Press, 2002.

Davidson, Cathy. "No More Separate Spheres!" *American Literature* 70, no. 3 (September 1998): 443–63.

Davis, Lennard. "Constructing Normalcy: The Bell Curve, the Novel, and the Invention of the Disabled Body in the Nineteenth Century." In *The Disability Studies Reader*, ed. Lennard Davis, 9–28. New York: Routledge, 2010.

de Man, Paul. "The Rhetoric of Temporality." In *Blindness and Insight: Essays in the Rhetoric of Contemporary Criticism*, 187–228. Minneapolis: University of Minnesota Press, 1983.

Diffley, Kathleen. *Where My Heart Is Turning Ever: Civil War Stories and Constitutional Reform, 1861–1876*. Athens: University of Georgia Press.

Emberton, Carole. *Beyond Redemption: Race, Violence, and the American South after the Civil War*. Chicago: University of Chicago Press, 2013.

Fahs, Alice. "The Feminized Civil War: Gender, Northern Popular Literature, and the Memory of the War, 1861–1900." *Journal of American History* 85, no. 4 (March 1999): 1461–94.

———. *The Imagined Civil War: Popular Literature of the North and South, 1861–1865*. Chapel Hill: University of North Carolina Press, 2001.

Faust, Drew Gilpin. "Altars of Sacrifice: Confederate Women and Narratives of the War." *Journal of American History* 76, no. 4 (March 1990): 1200–1228.

———. *The Creation of Confederate Nationalism: Ideology and Identity in the Civil War South*. Baton Rouge: Louisiana State University Press, 1988.

———. *Mothers of Invention: Women of the Slaveholding South in the American Civil War*. Chapel Hill: University of North Carolina Press, 1996.

———. *Southern Stories: Slaveholders in Peace and War*. Columbia: University of Missouri Press, 1992.

———. *This Republic of Suffering: Death and the American Civil War*. New York: Alfred A. Knopf, 2008.

Feimster, Crystal Nicole. *Southern Horrors: Women and the Politics of Rape and Lynching*. Cambridge, Mass.: Harvard University Press, 2009.

Figg, Laurann, and Jane Farrell-Beck. "Amputation in the Civil War: Physical and Social Dimensions." *Journal of the History of Medicine and Allied Sciences* 48 (October 1993): 454–75.

Fleming, E. McClung. "The American Image as Indian Princess." *Winterthur Portfolio: A Journal of American Material Culture* 2 (1965): 65–81.

———. "From Indian Princess to Greek Goddess: The American Image, 1783–1815." *Winterthur Portfolio* 3 (1967): 37–66.

Fletcher, Marvin E. "The Black Volunteers in the Spanish-American War." In *Brothers to the Buffalo Soldiers: Perspectives on the African American Militia and Volunteers, 1865–1917*, ed. Bruce A. Glasrud, 191–219. Columbia: University of Missouri Press, 2011.

Flexner, Eleanor, and Ellen Frances Fitzpatrick. *Century of Struggle: The Woman's Rights Movement in the United States.* Cambridge, Mass.: Harvard University Press, 1996.

Forbes, Ella. *African American Women During the Civil War.* New York: Routledge, 1998.

Frank, Lisa Tendrich. *The Civilian War: Confederate Women and Union Soldiers During Sherman's March.* Baton Rouge: Louisiana State University Press, 2015.

Freedman, Estelle B. *Redefining Rape: Sexual Violence in the Era of Suffrage and Segregation.* Cambridge, Mass.: Harvard University Press, 2013.

Freemon, Frank R. *Gangrene and Glory: Medical Care During the American Civil War.* Madison, N.J.: Fairleigh Dickinson University Press, 1998.

Fuchs, Richard L. *Unerring Fire: The Massacre at Fort Pillow.* Mechanicsburg, Pa.: Stackpole Books, 2002.

Garland-Thomson, Rosemarie. *Extraordinary Bodies: Figuring Physical Disability in American Culture and Literature.* New York: Columbia University Press, 1997.

Garner, Stanton. *The Civil War World of Herman Melville.* Lawrence: University Press of Kansas, 1993.

Giesberg, Judith. *Army at Home: Women and the Civil War on the Northern Home Front.* Chapel Hill: University of North Carolina Press, 2009.

Glatthaar, Joseph T. *Forged in Battle: The Civil War Alliance of Black Soldiers and White Officers.* New York: Free Press, 1990.

Hack, Daniel. "The Canon in Front of Them: African American Deployments of the 'The Charge of the Light Brigade.'" In *Early African American Print Culture*, ed. Lara Langer Cohen and Jordan Alexander Stein, 178–91. Philadelphia: University of Pennsylvania Press, 2012.

Hacker, J. David. "A Census-Based Count of the Civil War Dead." *Civil War History* 57, no. 4 (2011): 307–48.

Hager, Christopher. "'if we Ever Expect to be a Pepple': The Epistolary Culture of African American Soldiers." In *Literary Cultures of the Civil War,* ed. Timothy Sweet, 23–38. Athens: University of Georgia Press, 2016.

Hahn, Harlan. "Advertising the Acceptably Employable Image: Disability and Capitalism." In *The Disability Studies Reader,* ed. Lennard Davis, 172–86. New York: Routledge, 2010.

Halkett, Samuel, ed. *Catalogue of the Printed Books in the Library of the Faculty of Advocates.* Vol. 5. Edinburgh: William Blackwood and Sons, 1877.

Halkett, Samuel, and John Laing. *Dictionary of Anonymous and Pseudonymous English Literature.* Vol. 5: *Q–S.* Ed. James Kennedy, W. A. Smith, and A. F. Johnson. Edinburgh: Oliver and Boyd, 1927.

Hankinson, Alan. *Man of War: William Howard Russell of* The Times. London: Heinemann, 1982.

Hargrove, Hondon B. *Black Union Soldiers in Blue.* Jefferson, N.C.: McFarland & Co., 1988.

Harrington, Anne. *Medicine, Mind, and the Double Brain: A Study in Nineteenth-Century Thought.* Princeton, N.J.: Princeton University Press, 1987.

———. "Unfinished Business: Models of Laterality in the Nineteenth Century." In *Brain Asymmetry,* ed. Richard J. Davidson and Kenneth Hugdahl, 3–27. Cambridge, Mass.: MIT Press, 1995.

Harris, Brayton. *Blue & Gray in Black & White.* Washington, D.C.: Brassey's, 1999.

Harris, Lauren Julius. "Cultural Influences on Handedness: Historical and Contemporary Theory and Evidence." In *Left-handedness: Behavioral Implications and Anomalies,* ed. Stanley Coren, 195–258. New York: North-Holland Elsevier Science Publishing Co., 1990.

Hattaway, Herman, and Archer Jones. *How the North Won: A Military History of the Civil War.* Urbana: University of Illinois Press, 1983.

Hemphill, C. Dallett. *Siblings: Brothers and Sisters in American History.* New York: Oxford University Press, 2011.

Herschbach, Lisa Marie. "Prosthetic Reconstructions: Making the Industry, Re-Making the Body, Modelling the Nation." *History Workshop Journal* 44 (Autumn, 1997): 22–57.

Higham, John. "Indian Princess and Roman Goddess: The First Female Symbols of America." *Proceedings of the American Antiquarian Society* 100, no. 1 (1990): 45–79.

Hilde, Libra R. *Worth a Dozen Men: Women and Nursing in the Civil War South.* Charlottesville: University of Virginia Press, 2012.

Holmes, Martha Stoddard. *Fictions of Affliction: Physical Disability in Victorian Culture.* Ann Arbor: University of Michigan Press, 2004.

Hughes, Nathaniel Cheairs, Jr., and S. Kittrell Rushing, eds. *Refugitta of Richmond: The Wartime Recollections, Grave and Gay, of Constance Cary Harrison.* Knoxville: University of Tennessee Press, 2011.

Humphreys, Margaret. *Intensely Human: The Health of the Black Soldier in the American Civil War.* Baltimore: Johns Hopkins University Press, 2008.

Hunton, Addie W., and Kathryn M. Johnson. *Two Colored Women with the American Expeditionary Forces.* Brooklyn, N.Y.: Brooklyn Eagle Press, 1920.

James, Jennifer. *A Freedom Bought with Blood: African American War Literature from the Civil War to World War II.* Chapel Hill: University of North Carolina Press, 2007.

Johnson, Barbara. "Women and Allegory." In *The Wake of Deconstruction*, 52–75. Cambridge, Mass.: Blackwell Publishers, 1994.

Jordan, Brian Matthew, *Marching Home: Union Veterans and their Unending Civil War.* New York: Liveright Publishing Corp., 2014.

Journal of the Congress of the Confederate States of America: 1861–1865. Vols. 1 and 2. Washington, D.C.: Government Printing Office, 1904.

Kaster, Gregory L. "Labour's True Man: Organised Workingmen and the Language of Manliness in the USA, 1827–1877." *Gender and History* 13, no. 1 (April 2001): 24–64.

Ketchum, Alton. "In Search of Uncle Sam." *History Today* 40, no. 4 (1990): 20–26.

Kristeva, Julia. "The Female Body in Western Culture: Semiotic Perspectives." Trans. Arthur Goldhammer. *Poetics Today* 6, no. 1–2 (1985): 133–52.

Kushner, Howard I. "Deficit or Creativity: Cesare Lombardo, Robert Hertz, and the Meanings of Left-Handedness." *Laterality* 18, no. 4 (2013): 416–36.

———. "Retraining Left-handers and the Aetiology of Stuttering: The Rise and Fall of an Intriguing Theory." *Laterality* 17, no. 6 (2012): 673–93.

Jenkins, John Wilber. "The Poems of James Ryder Randall." *South Atlantic Quarterly* 7 (January–October 1908): 242–47.

Johnson, Claudia Durst. "Boker, George Henry." American National Biography Online. www.anb.org/articles/16/16-00142.html (2000).

Jordan, Ervin L., Jr. *Black Confederates and Afro-Yankees in Civil War Virginia.* Charlottesville: University Press of Virginia, 1995.

Lewin, J. G. and P. J. Huff. *Lines of Contention: Political Cartoons of the Civil War.* New York: HarperCollins Publishers, 2007.

Long, Lisa A. *Rehabilitating Bodies: Health, History, and the American Civil War.* Philadelphia: University of Pennsylvania Press, 2004.

Marrs, Cody. *Nineteenth-Century American Literature and the Long Civil War.* New York: Cambridge University Press, 2015.

McDaid, Jennifer Davis. "'How a One-Legged Rebel Lives': Confederate Veterans and Artificial Limbs in Virginia." In *Artificial Parts, Practical Lives: Modern Histories of Prosthetics,* ed. Katherine Ott, David Serlin, and Stephen Mihm, 119–43. New York: New York University Press, 2002.

McGill, Meredith L. *American Literature and the Culture of Reprinting.* Philadelphia: University of Pennsylvania Press, 2003.

McManus, Chris. *Right Hand, Left Hand: The Origins of Asymmetry in Brains, Bodies, Atoms, and Cultures.* London: Weidenfeld & Nicolson, 2002.

McManus, I. C. "The History and Geography of Human Handedness." In *Language Lateralization and Psychosis,* ed. Iris E. C. Sommer and René S. Kahn, 37–57. New York: Cambridge University Press, 2009.

McPherson, James. *Battle Cry of Freedom: The Civil War Era.* New York: Oxford University Press, 1989.

———. *For Cause and Comrades: Why Men Fought in the Civil War.* Oxford, U.K.: Oxford University Press, 1997.

———. *Marching Toward Freedom.* New York: Knopf, 1968.

———. *The Negro's Civil War: How American Negroes Felt and Acted during the War for the Union* (New York: Vintage Books, 1967.

Mezo, Richard E. "Randall, James Ryder." American National Biography Online. www.anb.org/articles/16/16–01342.html (2000).

Mihm, Stephen. "'A Limb Which Shall Be Presentable in Polite Society': Prosthetic Technologies in the Nineteenth Century." In *Artificial Parts, Practical Lives: Modern Histories of Prosthetics,* ed. Katherine Ott, David Serlin, and Stephen Mihm, 282–99. New York: New York University Press, 2002.

Miller, Christanne. "Drum-Taps: Revisions and Reconciliation." *Walt Whitman Quarterly Review* 26, no. 4 (Spring 2009): 171–96.

Millett-Gallant, Ann. *The Disabled Body in Contemporary Art.* New York: Palgrave Macmillan, 2010.

Mitchell, David T., and Sharon L. Snyder. *Narrative Prosthesis: Disability and the Dependencies of Discourse.* Ann Arbor: University of Michigan Press, 2000.

Moore, Frank. *Women of the War: Their Heroism and Self-Sacrifice.* Hartford, Conn.: S. S. Scranton & Co., 1866.

Moretti, Franco. *Distant Reading.* London: Verso, 2013.

Morgan, Winifred. *An American Icon: Brother Jonathan and American Identity.* Cranbury, N.J.: Associated University Presses, 1988.

Neilsen, Kim E. *A Disability History of the United States.* Boston: Beacon Press, 2012.

Nelson, Dana D. "Women in Public." In *The Cambridge Companion to Nineteenth-Century American Women's Writing,* ed. Dale M. Bauer and Philip Gould, 38–68. Cambridge, U.K.: Cambridge University Press, 2001.

Nelson, Megan Kate. *Ruin Nation: Destruction and the American Civil War.* Athens: University of Georgia Press, 2012.

Neuburg, Victor E. *The Popular Press Companion to Popular Literature.* Bowling Green, Ohio: Bowling Green State University Popular Press, 1983.

Nevins, Allan. *The War for the Union: The Improvised War.* New York: Charles Scribner's Sons, 1959.

Noble, Marianne. "The Ecstasies of Sentimental Wounding in *Uncle Tom's Cabin.*" *Yale Journal of Criticism* 10, no. 2 (1997): 295–320.

Norton, Anne. *Alternative Americas: A Reading of Antebellum Political Culture.* Chicago: University of Chicago Press, 1986.

Nudelman, Franny. *John Brown's Body: Slavery, Violence, and the Culture of War.* Chapel Hill: University of North Carolina Press, 2004.

O'Connor, Erin. *Raw Material: Producing Pathology in Victorian Culture.* Durham, N.C.: Duke University Press, 2000.

OED Online. Oxford University Press.

Padilla, Jalynn Olsen. "Army of 'Cripples': Northern Civil War Amputees, Disability, and Manhood in Victorian America." PhD diss., University of Delaware, 2007. ProQuest (3277826).

Perry, James M. *A Bohemian Brigade: The Civil War Correspondents—Mostly Rough, Sometimes Ready.* New York: John Wiley & Sons, 2000.

Plum, William R. *The Military Telegraph During the Civil War in the United States.* Chicago: Jansen, McClurg & Co., 1882.

Putzi, Jennifer. *Identifying Marks: Race, Gender, and the Marked Body in Nineteenth-Century America.* Athens: University of Georgia Press, 2006.

Quarles, Benjamin, ed. *The Negro in the Civil War.* New York: Russell & Russell, 1968.

Randall, J. G., and David Donald. *The Civil War and Reconstruction.* Boston: D. C. Heath and Co., 1961.

Richards, Eliza. "Correspondent Lines." *ESQ: A Journal of the American Renaissance* 54, no. 1–4 (2008): 145–70.

Rosenburg, R. B. "'Empty Sleeves and Wooden Pegs': Disabled Confederate Veterans in Image and Reality." In *Disabled Veterans in History,* ed. David A. Gerber, 204–28. Ann Arbor: University of Michigan Press, 2000.

Ryan, Mary P. *Women in Public: Between Banners and Ballots, 1825–1880.* Baltimore: Johns Hopkins University Press, 1990.

Samuels, Shirley. *Facing America: Iconography and the Civil War.* New York: Oxford University Press, 2004.

———. "Introduction." In *The Culture of Sentiment: Race, Gender, and Sentimentality in Nineteenth-Century America,* ed. Shirley Samuels, 3–8. New York: Oxford University Press, 1992.

———. *Romances of the Republic: Women, the Family, and Violence in the Literature of the Early American Nation.* New York: Oxford University Press, 1996.

———. "Women at War." In *The Cambridge Companion to Nineteenth-Century American Women's Writing,* ed. Dale M. Bauer and Philip Gould, 143–156. Cambridge, U.K.: Cambridge University Press, 2001.

Sánchez-Eppler, Karen. "Bodily Bonds: The Intersecting Rhetorics of Feminism and Abolition." *Representations* 24 (Fall 1988): 28–59.

———. *Touching Liberty: Abolition, Feminism, and the Politics of the Body.* Berkeley: University of California Press, 1997.

Scarry, Elaine. *The Body in Pain: The Making and Unmaking of the World.* New York: Oxford University Press, 1985.

———. *Resisting Representation.* New York: Oxford University Press, 1994.

Schantz, Mark. *Awaiting the Heavenly Country: The Civil War and America's Culture of Death.* Ithaca, N.Y.: Cornell University Press, 2008.

Schultz, Jane E. *Women at the Front: Hospital Workers in Civil War America.* Chapel Hill: University of Chapel Hill Press, 2004.

Serlin, David. "Crippling Masculinity: Queerness and Disability in U.S. Military Culture, 1800–1945." *Gay and Lesbian Quarterly* 9, no. 1–2 (2003): 149–79.

———. *Replaceable You: Engineering the Body in Postwar America.* Chicago: University of Chicago Press, 2004.

Shyrock, Richard H. "A Medical Perspective on the Civil War." *American Quarterly* 14, no. 2 (Summer 1962): 161–73.

Silkenat, David. "'A Typical Negro': Gordon, Peter, Vincent Colyer, and the Story behind Slavery's Most Famous Photograph." *American Nineteenth Century History* 15, no. 2 (2014): 169–86.

Silverman, Gillian. *Bodies and Books: Reading and the Fantasy of Communion in Nineteenth-Century America.* Philadelphia: University of Pennsylvania Press, 2012.

Simkins, Francis Butler, and James Welch Patton. *The Women of the Confederacy.* Richmond, Va.: Garrett and Massie, 1936.

Simpson, Brooks D. "Nast, Thomas." *American National Biography Online.* www.anb.org/articles/17/17-00616.html (2000).

Smith, J. Mark. "Apostrophe, or the Lyric Art of Turning Away." *Texas Studies in Literature and Language* 49, no. 4 (Winter 2007): 411–37.

Smith, John David. "Introduction." In *Black Soldiers in Blue: African American Troops in the Civil War Era,* ed. John David Smith, xiii–xxiii. Chapel Hill: University of North Carolina Press, 2002.

———. "Let Us All Be Grateful That We Have Colored Troops That Will Fight." In *Black Soldiers in Blue: African American Troops in the Civil War Era,* ed. John David Smith, 1–77. Chapel Hill: University of North Carolina Press, 2002.

Smith, Kristen M. *The Lines Are Drawn: Political Cartoons of the Civil War.* Athens, Ga.: Hill Street Press, 1999.

Sorisio, Carolyn. *Fleshing Out America: Race, Gender, and the Politics of the Body in American Literature, 1833–1879.* Athens: University of Georgia Press, 2002.

———. "The Spectacle of the Body: Torture in the Antislavery Writing of Lydia Maria Child and Frances E. W. Harper." *Modern Language Studies* 30, no. 1 (Spring 2000): 45–66.

"The Statue of Freedom." Architect of the Capitol. www.aoc.gov/cc/art.

Statue of Liberty. National Park Service, 2014. www.nps.gov/stli/historyculture/people.htm.

Steward, T. G. *Buffalo Soldiers: The Colored Regulars in the United States Army.* 1904. Rpt. Mineola, N.Y:. Dover Publications, 2014.

Straubing, Harold E. *In Hospital and Camp: The Civil War Through the Eyes of Its Doctors and Nurses.* Harrisburg, Pa.: Stackpole Books, 1993.

Sullivan, George. *In the Wake of Battle: The Civil War Images of Mathew Brady.* New York: Prestel, 2004.

Sweet, Timothy. "Introduction." In *Literary Cultures of the Civil War,* ed. Timothy Sweet, 1–20. Athens: University of Georgia Press, 2016.

———. *Traces of War: Poetry, Photography, and the Crisis of the Union.* Baltimore: Johns Hopkins University Press, 1990. ProQuest (3444704).

Taylor, Amy Murrell. *The Divided Family in Civil War America.* Chapel Hill: University of North Carolina Press, 2005.

Taylor, Joshua C., with a contribution by John G. Cawelti. *America as Art.* Washington, D.C.: Smithsonian Institution Press, 1976.

Tompkins, Jane. *Sensational Designs: The Cultural Work of American Fiction, 1790–1860.* New York: Oxford University Press, 1986.

Trudeau, Noah Andre. *Like Men of War: Black Troops in the Civil War, 1862–1865.* Boston: Little, Brown, 1998.

U.S. Census Bureau. *U.S. Census, 1880: Douglas, Colorado,* roll 90. Ancestry.com.

———. *U.S. Census, 1880: Elyria, Lorain, Ohio,* roll 1042. Ancestry.com

———. *U.S. Census, 1900: Boston Ward 12, Suffolk, Massachusetts,* roll 681. Ancestry.com.

Venet, Wendy Hamand. *Neither Ballots Nor Bullets: Women Abolitionists and the Civil War.* Charlottesville: University Press of Virginia, 1991.

Vettel-Becker, Patricia. "Sacagawea and Son: The Visual Construction of America's Maternal Feminine." *American Studies* 50, no. 1–2 (Spring–Summer 2009): 27–50.

Volo, Dorothy Denneen, and James M. Volo. *Daily Life in Civil War America.* Westport, Conn.: Greenwood Press, 1998.

Wachtell, Cynthia. *War No More: The Antiwar Impulse in American Literature, 1861–1914.* Baton Rogue: Louisiana State University Press, 2010.

Walton, Eugene. "Philip Reed: Slave Caster of Freedom." *Examiner* (Washington, D.C.), March 1, 2005. Rpt. in *Chicken Bones: A Journal for Literary and Artistic African-American Themes.* www.nathanielturner.com.

Warner, Marina. *Monuments and Maidens: The Allegory of the Female Form.* Berkeley: University of California Press, 1985.

Weaver, John D. *The Brownsville Raid.* College Station: Texas A&M University Press, 1992.

Weller, Emil. *Lexicon Pseudonymorum.* Hildesheim, Germany: Georg Olms Verlagsbuchhandlung, 1963.

Whites, Leeann. "The Civil War as a Crisis in Gender." In *Divided Houses: Gender and the Civil War,* ed. Catherine Clinton and Nina Silber, 3–21. New York: Oxford University Press, 1992.

Williams, Heather Andrea. "'Commenced to Think Like a Man': Literacy and Manhood in African American Civil War Regiments." In *Southern Manhood: Perspectives on Masculinity in the Old South,* ed. Craig Thompson Friend and Lorri Glover, 196–219. Athens: University of Georgia Press, 2004.

Wilson, Edmund. *Patriotic Gore: Studies in the Literature of the American Civil War.* New York: Oxford University Press, 1966.

Wood, Marcus. *Black Milk: Imagining Slavery in the Visual Cultures of Brazil and America.* Oxford, U.K.: Oxford University Press, 2013.

———. *Blind Memory: Visual Representations of Slavery in England and America: 1780–1865.* New York: Routledge, 2000.

Yee, Shirley J. *Black Women Abolitionists: A Study in Activism, 1828–1860.* Knoxville: University of Tennessee Press, 1992.

Young, Elizabeth. *Disarming the Nation: Women's Writing and the American Civil War.* Chicago: University of Chicago Press, 1999.

INDEX

Page numbers in italics refer to figures